Small Gro
Communic

A Customized Version of
Small Group Work in the Real World:
A Practical Approach, Third Edition
by Mark L. Staller, Andrea D. Thorson-Hevle,
and Bryan R. Hirayama

Redesigned and Edited by the
Glendale Community College of Arizona
Department of Communication

Cover images © Shutterstock, Inc. Used under license.

www.kendallhunt.com
Send all inquiries to:
4050 Westmark Drive
Dubuque, IA 52004-1840

ISBN 978-1-5249-3923-6

Published in the United States of America

Table of Contents

Chapter 1:

Introduction to Small Group Communication

© Andresr, 2013. Used under license from Shutterstock, Inc.

Chapter Objectives

- Understand the definition of small group communication.
- Identify the different types of small groups which exist.
- Appreciate the prevalence and importance of small groups.
- Learn how to decrease "grouphate."
- Understand the many disadvantages and advantages of small group work.

Small groups work. When human beings join forces in small groups, they can get remarkable things done. That is why you are taking a course in small group communication, and that is why you are reading a textbook about small group communication. You are being trained in small group communication so that you can work effectively with others in small groups.

In this introductory chapter, you will learn just what small group communication is, and you will learn about the many different types of small groups that exist. You will see the important role that small groups play in both the popular imagination and in the real world, and you will discover that almost every important human endeavor is carried out by people working together in small groups.

You will also learn that small group work in the real world is very different from the small group interactions portrayed on so-called "reality" shows. Although there are some drawbacks to small group work, you will learn that there are many more benefits to working with others in small groups. By the end of this introductory chapter, you should be motivated to fully engage in small group interactions in your small group communication course and in all the areas of your private and public life.

Definition of Small Group Communication

Definition of a small group: *For purposes of our class, small group communication is defined as: three or more people in a face-to-face interaction working interdependently to achieve a common goal. If a group is successful, it will achieve synergy. In other words, your group achieved something better than you could do by yourself.*

You may be assigned to small groups in your college classes, but merely being assigned to a small group by an instructor does not automatically make you a small group member. First, you must accept your membership in a small group: you must be willing to be part of the group, and you must identify yourself as a small group member. Second, the other members of the small group must accept you as a group member. If you do not help the group to reach its goals, you may be considered an "outsider." If, however, you work together with your small group members to accomplish group tasks, others will acknowledge and accept that you are a part of the group.

Some synonyms for the term "group" are the terms "band," "cadre," "cell," "cohort," "committee," "crew," "gang," "squad," and "team." What is the difference between a group and a team? The term "group" is fairly general, whereas the term "team" is more specific and refers to a specific kind of small group. Most teams are small groups, but not all small groups are teams.

FIGURE 1.1

Most teams are small groups, but not all small groups are teams

Teams differ from general small groups. Teams have very specific, very clear goals and roles. For example, the obvious goal of a sports team is to win sports competitions, and each member of a sports team has a very specific designated role to fill or position to play. Many other types of small groups do not have such obvious goals, and small group members may have to work together to clarify group goals and determine the appropriate role(s) for each person in the group. The following sections break down our definition by analyzing size, interaction, interdependence and common goal.

Size of Group

In order to recognize the important role that small groups play in the real world, you need to consider exactly what constitutes a small group. What is the minimum size of a small group? What is the maximum size of a small group? And what exactly makes a small group a group?

FIGURE 1.2
Two people are a dyad

FIGURE 1.3
The minimum size for a small group is three people.

The minimum size of a small group is at least three people. Two interacting people are considered to be a couple, a pair, or a dyad. A couple of people become a "group" when a third person is introduced. Athos, Porthos, and Aramis, the "Three Musketeers" brought to life by French novelist Alexander Dumas, could be considered a small group. Their motto, "All for one, and one for all," indicates that the three united their efforts together in order to become more than just an aggregate of people.

An "aggregate" of people consists of several human beings that may have no substantial connection to each other except for the fact that they are being lumped and counted together by an observer. For example, a random group of people standing at a bus stop may be talking to each other, but they do not necessarily constitute a small group.

The maximum number of people in a small group depends on the task or goal of the group. The group needs enough people to accomplish the goal of the group, and the skills and expertise among group members to get the job done. Of course, a very large group may make it difficult to conduct business due to the number of people in the group. Thus, groups of 5–7 are desirable.

*While small groups increase in size arithmetically, the intragroup relationships that have to be managed increase exponentially. In 1950, William M. Kephart calculated the number of potential intragroup relationships as group size increased. A standard chart that appears in many small group textbooks is based on his work.

As the Figure reveals, adding just one or two people to a small group can greatly increase the relational complexity of that group. Consequently, small groups are like amoebas: once they reach a certain size, they divide and form subgroups.

Size of Group	Number of Relationships
2	1
3	6
4	25
5	90
6	301
7	966

FIGURE 1.4
Small group relationships quickly grow in complexity as group size increases.

INTERACTION

Much of the time in our course will be spent discussing how group members can communicate effectively in your group. We will study how verbal and nonverbal communication affects interaction along with how various cultural elements influence our interaction with others.

INTERDEPENDENCE

In order for groups to be successful, groups must develop a level of group cohesion. Members must realize that their actions affect other group members. Group members must be able to "count on" each other to do their part to achieve the goal. If one member does not do their part, the group may not be able to proceed. Interdependent group members share the blame for group failure and share the credit when successful.

COMMON GOAL

All group members must understand the goal of the group in order for them to be effective. Some groups need to work together to define a goal while others are given a problem to solve, a policy to be developed, or to interpret a policy in existence. Needless to say, it's essential for group members to comprehend the goal of the group.

The Complexity of Small Group Communication

In addition to relational complexity, small groups also offer a unique, complex communication setting. **Small group communication** is not the same as **interpersonal communication**, the one-on-one communication that occurs between two communicators.

If you have ever experienced some form of psychological **triangulation**, then you have experienced first-hand the difference between one-on-one interpersonal communication and small group communication. You may have good interpersonal interactions with two different friends, but when the three of you must interact together at the same time and "triangulation" kicks in, friendships can be strained. You discover the truth of the old proverb, "Two is company, but three is a crowd."

Small group communication is also different from public speaking. The distinguishing feature of public speaking is that one person (the speaker) speaks, while other people (the audience) listen. In a small group, there are many different possible communication patterns.

© zulufoto, 2013. Used under license from Shutterstock, Inc.

FIGURE 1.5

*In a small group, any group member can give or receive nonverbal and verbal messages at almost any time. Although one small group member can dominate a group discussion, a good small group discussion often involves a give-and-take between multiple communicators, and small group members rapidly transition back and forth between being small group communicators and observers of the communication interactions of the other members.

Thus, small groups create both relational and communication complexities. As you communicate and interact with other small group members, you are taking part in a very intricate, very complicated group activity. Your small group communication class and this textbook will help you better understand this complex process.

Types of Small Groups

You will find it easier to identify and appreciate the small groups around you when you understand the different types of small groups that exist. There are at least ten different types of small groups: primary groups, work groups, study groups, play groups, therapy groups/support groups, decision-making and problem-solving groups, focus groups, quality circles, and virtual groups. A brief description of each type of group follows.

Primary groups: Groups of people, often related by blood, who live together in social units. These primary groups work to fulfill basic physical and social needs, providing food, clothing, shelter, and companionship. All other small groups are classified as "secondary" small groups.

© Andy Dean Photography, 2013. Used under license from Shutterstock, Inc.

FIGURE 1.6

Work groups: Groups formed to complete specific tasks. A work group may be formed to complete a specific project with a deadline and then be disbanded when the project is completed, or people may be assigned to work groups that perform routine, on-going production, service, or maintenance tasks.

Play groups: Groups of people who come together for recreational purposes. These groups may be formed spontaneously and meet sporadically, or they may be formally organized and meet on a regular basis. Children are sometimes enrolled in play groups as part of their socialization process. They learn to function outside of their primary group by participating in various informal and formal play groups. However, even after being fully integrated into society, teenagers and adults may still elect to participate in play groups to fulfill on-going social and recreational needs.

Study groups: Groups that are formed to enhance learning. The process of studying together in small groups enhances the learning of both weak and strong intellects: when the more adept group members explain concepts and principles to the less adept members, both subgroups benefit.

Therapy/Support groups: Groups formed and supervised by psychiatrists and psycho-therapists to aid their patients in the therapeutic process. Several different therapeutic approaches can be accelerated and enhanced through group therapy. Support groups are sometimes formed to help people deal with difficult life situations such as illness, trauma, family dysfunction, and addiction. People may participate in support groups for a short period of time in order to make it through a crisis situation, or they may commit to regular, extended participation to maintain health, or sobriety, or to help and support others. They may be facilitated by professionals or lay group members.

Decision-making/Problem-solving groups: Groups charged with the responsibility of making important decisions or solving difficult problems. Organizations often rely on numerous ad-hoc and standing committees to make important or controversial policy recommendations and to respond to problems that arise inside and outside of the organization.

Focus groups: Groups formed and queried by companies or political parties in order to gather opinions about products, services, or issues. Focus groups are usually assembled for a brief time. Once the opinions and reactions of the focus group members are recorded, the focus group is disbanded and the focus group results are analyzed and shared.

Quality circles: Small groups of people used in business and industry to analyze, evaluate, and improve the quality of a product. The members of a quality circle are usually drawn from every employee group involved in the production process.

FIGURE 1.7

Virtual small groups meet online.

Virtual groups: Small groups of people distinguished not by their group goal or function, but by their method of meeting and communicating. With the advent of communication technologies, some small groups now use computer-mediated communication to work together even while separated by time or distance.

As you review the nine types of small groups in the list which follows, consider how many small groups you have participated in, or are now participating in. When I did this exercise about five years ago, I was able to identify over forty different small groups of which I was a member. I challenge you to identify at least twelve small groups in which you currently participate or have participated in in the past.

SIX TYPES OF SMALL GROUPS

1. Primary groups
2. Work groups
3. Study groups
4. Play groups
5. Therapy/Support groups
6. Decision-making/Problem-solving groups
    a. Focus groups
    b. Quality circles
    c. Virtual groups

To stimulate your thought process, a random list of various groups follows. Try to classify these groups according to the nine types mentioned above, and then identify any small groups you currently belong to that are of the same type.

Various Small Groups or Small Group Settings

_____ Neighborhood watch group
_____ "Wolf pack" of close friends
_____ Sports team
_____ Meeting for cancer survivors
_____ Assigned college class group
_____ Classmates doing homework
_____ Smoke-free campus committee
_____ Bible Study group
_____ College roommates
_____ Choir performance
_____ Pick-up basketball game
_____ Habitat for Humanity project
_____ Meeting for battered women
_____ Thursday game night with friends
_____ Terrorist cell
_____ Political fundraising dinner
_____ Quality control meeting
_____ Jury deciding a verdict
_____ Family council meeting
_____ A commune
_____ Board meeting
_____ S.W.A.T. team intervention
_____ Prayer group
_____ Cleaning crew at work
_____ A.A. meeting
_____ Sales team
_____ Student government meeting
_____ Street gang
_____ Garage band
_____ Chicano/Chicana club
_____ Homecoming committee
_____ Intimate dance party at home
_____ Meditation group
_____ College department meeting
_____ Doctors making rounds
_____ Green party meeting
_____ Landscaping crew
_____ Student disciplinary committee
_____ Bulletin board discussion
_____ Theater troupe performing
_____ Weekly lunch date
_____ Supreme Court decision
_____ Quilting club
_____ Veteran's organization meeting

As you classify the various small groups listed above, not only should you be able to identify many small groups of which you have been a part, but you should also begin to appreciate how prevalent small groups are in the world around you. The following section of this introductory chapter emphasizes both the prevalence and importance of small groups.

The Prevalence of Small Groups in the Real World

Sometimes the film-making art memorializes real life: the fictional Hickory High basketball team that won the state championship in the 1986 sports drama *Hoosiers* is based upon the actual Milan High School team that won the 1954 Indiana state championship tournament. With an enrollment of only 161 students, Milan High was the smallest school to ever win a single-class state basketball title. Through incredible dedication and teamwork, the small Milan basketball team amassed a 28–2 overall record and beat Muncie Central High, a school ten times its size, in the final round of the championship tournament.

The 2009 sports drama *The Perfect Game* is based upon the experiences of the Little League team of Monterrey, Mexico. In July 1957, *Los Pequenos Gigantes* ("The Little Giants") were issued three-day passes by the US consulate in Monterrey so they could compete in a tournament in McAllen, Texas. They were supposed to play for one day, and then, after being eliminated, have two days for sightseeing.

When The Little Giants won the Texas tournament, the US consulate in Washington extended their stay in the United States indefinitely until they were eliminated in the Little League playoff system. Two months later, the scrappy Mexican Little League team was still in the United States after winning six tournaments in a row, including the 1957 Little League World Series. Their pitcher, Angel Martinez, pitched the first (and, so far, only) perfect game in a championship Little League World Series game. *Los Pequenos Gigantes* demonstrated that their accomplishment was not a fluke by winning the Little League World Series again the following year (1958).

The 2004 biographical sports film *Miracle* commemorates an upset win of the US men's hockey team at the 1980 Winter Olympics. Dubbed the "Miracle on Ice" in popular culture, the young, inexperienced US hockey players shocked the heavily favored Soviet hockey team when they won their play-off game by a 4–3 score.

The December 3, 1999 *Sports Illustrated* magazine named the "Miracle on Ice" as the top sports moment of the 20th century. Coach Herb Brooks prepared a team of amateur and collegiate players to take on a seemingly unconquerable Soviet hockey team. The Soviets had won the previous four ice hockey Olympic gold medals and were heavy favorites to win again. However, coach Brooks trained and drilled his team hard and built up their stamina so they could go head-to-head with the world-class Soviets for all three periods. The US team upset the Soviets and went on to win the Olympic gold medal.

The 1954 performances of the Milan High School basketball team, the 1957 (and 1958) Monterrey, Mexico Little League baseball team, and the 1980 US men's Olympic hockey team demonstrate that human beings really can accomplish amazing things when they work together in small groups and teams. By focusing on their group goal and pulling together, the members of these sports teams overcame incredible odds and accomplished very difficult tasks.

If you think that sports are not part of "real" life, consider the major part that small groups play in almost every human endeavor. Whenever there is a very difficult or important task to accomplish, human beings almost always form small groups to get the job done.

If you have a life-threatening illness or injury, your operation will be carried out by a surgical team. If there is a serious criminal threat in your neighborhood, a S.W.A.T. team may be called in to defuse the situation. If your house catches on fire, hopefully a firehouse crew will work together to extinguish the blaze. If you serve on the front lines in the military, you will rely upon your squad members to help you stay alive.

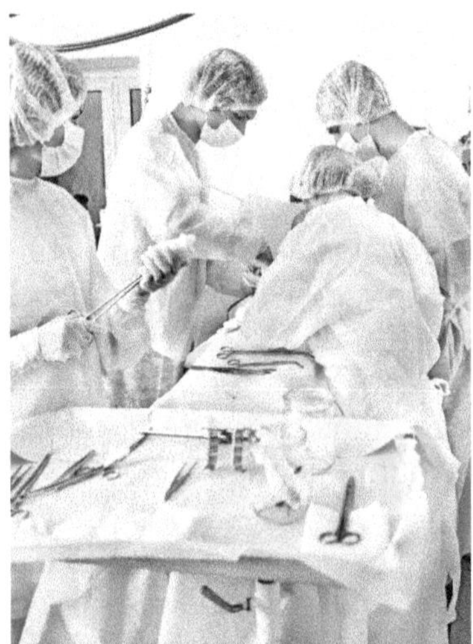

FIGURE 1.8
A Surgical Team

FIGURE 1.9
A Fire Crew

FIGURE 1.10
A SWAT Team

Small Groups in Business

American industry learned the importance of small groups in the 1950s and 1960s when Japanese automakers began to make automobiles that were superior to the American vehicles that had dominated the market for decades. American social scientists determined that a major factor in the Japanese success was the use of "Quality Circles." The Japanese automotive companies formed small groups composed of every type of employee group involved in the production process and asked them to evaluate their vehicles and make suggestions on ways to improve both the quality of the vehicles and the effectiveness of the production process.

American businesses responded to the Japanese challenge by introducing Quality Circles and other small group configurations into the American workplace. Americans learned that individual genius and effort can be enhanced and magnified by small group work. Small groups are now used throughout American business and industry because bottom-line profits increase, and products and services improve when people work together in small groups. If you enter the American work force, you will very likely be part of a work crew or project team.

FIGURE 1.11
A Project Team

FIGURE 1.12
A Quality Circle

FIGURE 1.13
A Cleaning Crew

Small Groups in Law

In crucial matters of the law, such as determining crimes and punishments, human beings rely on small groups. If you have been accused of a major crime, you are going to rely on a legal team to prove your innocence or to argue for a reduced penalty. For serious crimes, the state will convene a small group of people—a jury—to determine your guilt or innocence and to determine the appropriate punishment. If there is a crucial decision to be made about how to interpret a federal law, the nine justices of the US Supreme Court will be consulted.

© Konstantin Chagin, 2013. Used under license from Shutterstock, Inc.

FIGURE 1.14
A Legal Team

© bikeriderlondon, 2013. Used under license from Shutterstock, Inc.

FIGURE 1.15
A Jury

© Everett Historical, 2013. Used under license from Shutterstock, Inc.

FIGURE 1.16
The United States Supreme Court (Taft Court)

Small Groups in Education

The American education system is permeated by small group work at every level. Students are encouraged to form study groups because they learn and retain their course materials more effectively when they study together in small groups. Instructors use small group configurations and activities in class because student motivation and learning increases. Educational personnel serve on committees and work together in small groups to design and monitor educational courses and programs. Schools and universities are run by administrative teams, and they are overseen by supervisory boards.

© Monkey Business Images, 2013. Used under license from Shutterstock, Inc.

FIGURE 1.17
A Study Group

© Robert Kneschke, 2013. Used under license from Shutterstock, Inc.

FIGURE 1.18
A Small Group Activity

© iofoto, 2013. Used under license from Shutterstock, Inc.

FIGURE 1.19
A Department Meeting

Small Groups in Musical Entertainment

Much of the music we love to listen to was produced by human beings playing their instruments and singing together in small group ensembles or bands. When human beings combine their creative musical efforts together, amazing music can be created. We owe some of the greatest aesthetic experiences of our lives to small groups who play music together, and to the production crews and road crews which make their concerts possible.

FIGURE 1.20
A Musical Group

FIGURE 1.21
A Lighting Crew

FIGURE 1.22
A Sound Crew

Small Groups in Government

In the United States of America, government of the people, by the people, and for the people often occurs through the use of small groups. On the local and county levels, most day-to-day political decisions are made by city councils and supervisory boards. At the state and national levels, politicians rely on election committees to design and run their campaigns. Once elected, politicians rely on administrative teams to run their capitol offices and set up meetings with their constituents. Their staffs consult small focus groups to determine the needs and attitudes of various constituent groups.

In politics, what sometimes looks like the effort of a single individual is actually the result of small group work. For example, although laws and bills will sometimes have the name of a single politician attached to them, the details of these laws and bills are actually hashed out in legislative committees. Also, when the supreme leader of our country, the president, has to make difficult and important decisions, he or she almost always consults the president's cabinet, a small group of expert advisors who pool their wisdom to give the president different perspectives on important issues he or she must address.

FIGURE 1.23
A City Council Meeting

FIGURE 1.24
A Political Focus Group

FIGURE 1.25
A Presidential Cabinet

Small group work is at the heart of every important human endeavor. When you examine the fields of sports, medicine, law enforcement, military defense, business, law, education, entertainment, and politics you find that small groups are prevalent and that their influence is pervasive.

"Reality" Television and Misconceptions about Small Groups

We have now firmly established the prevalence and importance of small group work in the real world: human beings can accomplish incredible things when they work together in small groups, and the most important life tasks and the most difficult life decisions are usually placed in the hands of a small group of people. Thus, the centrality and effectiveness of small groups portrayed in many television shows and movies is a reflection of reality. Art is imitating life.

Unfortunately, the "reality" genre developed on television in the last two decades has created some misconceptions and negative attitudes about small group work that we must address. The small groups and small group interactions presented on many reality shows are not authentic, and the general reality game show format does not mirror real life.

One of the first and still one of the most popular "reality" game shows airing in the United States is CBS's *Survivor.* The format used on *Survivor* was created by British television producer Charlie Parsons in 1992, and there are now over 45 different international versions of this show produced around the world. Season one of the US version aired in the year 2000, and over 32 seasons have been aired since then (with two seasons often produced in one year).

The producers of *Survivor* drop 16 to 20 competitors off in a remote location for approximately 40 days. The competitors are placed in small group "tribes," and these tribes compete in a series of challenges to win products and cash prizes. As the competition advances, "tribal councils" are held and people are "voted off the island." When the number of competitors has been cut sufficiently, the survivors compete against each other until there is one "sole survivor" who is declared the winner and receives (in the US version) a million dollar prize.

The format of *Survivor* has proven to be very popular with the viewing audience. The intrigue and dramatic interactions between the tribe members makes for compelling television viewing, and the gradual elimination of contestants leads to a satisfying climax each television season.

In 2004, Mark Burnett, the producer of the American version of *Survivor*, introduced a new reality game show called *The Apprentice.* Following the same *Survivor* format, 16 or so business people or celebrities are divided into teams and pitted against one another to see who will come out on top in order to win a one-year apprenticeship running one of Donald Trump's companies. As the teams compete against each other in various challenges, individuals are systematically "fired" from the competition. Each week, competitors are asked to reveal who should be fired, and why.

That same year, 2004, the reality game show *The Biggest Loser* was launched using the same basic format. People are divided into teams, made to compete against each other, and slowly eliminated. The winner of the show is the person who loses the largest percentage of body weight without being eliminated by the other competitors.

These reality game shows present a very warped view of small groups and small group interactions. The producers edit the footage and then air the most "dramatic" moments of the competition. The viewers often see the competitors at their worst, and they can get the impression that

CBS/Photofest © CBS

FIGURE 1.26
Survivor

NBC/Photofest © NBC

FIGURE 1.27
The Apprentice

NBC/Photofest © NBC

FIGURE 1.28
The Biggest Loser

small group work involves endless bickering, posturing, psychological manipulation, and unpleasant confrontation.

It is important to realize that "reality" game shows are not realistic. They are produced primarily for entertainment purposes, and they do not accurately portray how human beings routinely work together in small groups in the real world.

It is even more important to realize that the goal of most small group work in the real world is not to be the last person standing. In the real world, small group members are rarely "eliminated" or asked to leave a group. In fact, the goal of many small groups in the real world is to maintain good working relationships among small group members and to sustain group membership as long as possible.

Contrary to the "process of elimination" formula adhered to in "reality" game shows, human beings in the real world very often strive to help and support other small group members. A goal in many real-world small groups is to provide an atmosphere that will allow small group members to work productively together for years and even decades.

The Phenomenon of "Grouphate"

How do you currently view small group work? Are you energized and excited about working together with others in small groups, or do you detest and despise the thought of being a member of a small group?

If you would rather avoid working with others in small groups, you are not alone. In fact, enough of the general population has very strong negative emotions related to small group work (some estimate as high as 25%) that a term has been coined to describe this phenomenon: **grouphate**.

"Grouphate" is the official academic term for the disdain that some people feel for small group work. This disdain is revealed in the following famous quotations about committees and committee meetings:

"A Committee is a body that keeps minutes and wastes hours."
(Anonymous)

"A committee is a group of the unwilling, chosen from the unfit, to do the unnecessary."
(Anonymous)

"A committee is a group of people who individually can do nothing, but as a group decide nothing can be done."
(Fred Allen)

"To kill time, a committee meeting is the perfect weapon."
(Milton Berle)

"A committee is a cul-de-sac down which ideas are lured and then quietly strangled."
(Sir Barnett Cocks)

"To get something done, a committee should consist of no more than three people, two of whom are absent."
(Robert Copeland)

"A committee is a thing which takes a week to do what one good man can do in an hour."
(Elbert Hubbard)

"If you want to kill any idea in the world, get a committee working on it."
(Charles F. Kettering)

The distaste and disdain for committees and committee meetings exhibited in these famous quotations is applied by some people to small group work in general, no matter what type of small group is being considered. There are at least five causes for grouphate: 1) inaccurate, warped views of small group work; 2) dysfunctional family backgrounds; 3) bad past experiences in other small groups; 4) fear of loss of control; and 5) the desire to avoid conflict and people problems. Let us consider each of these causes of grouphate at greater length.

Inaccurate, warped views of small group work: Although the famous quotations shared above are funny, and although there may be some truth to some of these quotations, the cynical slant of these "committee" quotations helps to create a very negative perception of small group work. We have shared these quotations to establish the reality of grouphate, but small group work in the real world is not as hapless, helpless, and hopeless as these quotations imply.

Dysfunctional family backgrounds: The primary small group experience for most human beings is the family unit. Most people spend thousands of hours interacting with family members in this primary small group before reaching adulthood. If you grew up in a functional, healthy family unit you are probably comfortable working in small groups. However, if you grew up in a dysfunctional, unhealthy family environment you may be quite uncomfortable in a small group setting.

Bad past experiences in small groups: Even if people have been raised in healthy primary small groups (family units), they may have had unpleasant, and even traumatic, experiences in other secondary small groups. Memories of unproductive group meetings, difficult small group members, or unpleasant confrontations in the past can cause some people to avoid working in small groups in the present.

FIGURE 1.29

Fear of loss of control: Since small group work requires several individuals to work together, no one individual can control what happens in a small group. Consequently, people who need or want a high level of control in their lives may find small group work disconcerting. Small group members can influence one another, but no one member, not even a strong group leader, has total control over what happens in a small group.

The desire to avoid conflict and people problems: Conflict is inevitable in small group work. When people work together in small groups, differences of opinion are bound to arise. Furthermore, where there are people, there will be "people problems." In addition to dealing with small group tasks, small group members must deal with each other. Some people would rather not deal with conflict or other people, so they try to avoid situations where they have to work in small groups altogether.

If you self-identify as a person with some degree (or a great degree) of grouphate, consider the causes listed above to determine from where your negative feelings about small group work originate. Fortunately, it is possible to reduce these negative feelings, especially if you use the following tips.

Tips for Reducing or Eliminating Grouphate

First, realize that every small group is not your family. If your grouphate is primarily a result of past family dysfunction, this is a very important psychological step to take. As an adult, you need to consciously recognize when you are letting past family patterns and behaviors inhibit your ability to work effectively with others. Your family upbringing, for better or worse, has a powerful influence on your perceptions, attitudes, and behaviors.

If you grew up in a dysfunctional family, you may have inaccurate perceptions of, and poor attitudes about, small groups. You may also have ineffective behaviors that you bring to small group settings and situations. This textbook and your small group communication instructor can help you form accurate perceptions and develop good attitudes about small groups. You can also use this textbook and your experiences in your small group communication class to develop effective behaviors that will make you a productive, valuable small group member.

Second, realize that each small group is unique and has the potential to work well. If you have had bad experiences with small groups in the past, do not let the memories of these past experiences unduly influence your present small group experiences. Since the present small groups you are in are composed of new, different group members, there is no reason to think that your past bad experiences will necessarily be replicated. If you bring a positive attitude and hopeful expectation to each of the small groups in which you currently participate, you increase the odds that you will have much more positive, much more successful, small group experiences.

© Lilia, 2013. Used under license from Shutterstock, Inc.

FIGURE 1.30
Like seashells, every small group experience is unique.

If you have had wonderful experiences with small groups in the past, remember that each small group is unique. The small groups you are currently in may not be as cohesive or effective as a past small group in which you were involved. Allow each small group experience you have to be what it is. Each small group you are in has the potential to work well, but this potential may or may not be fully realized. Expecting past small group experiences—whether bad or good—to be necessarily repeated in your current small groups will lead to disappointment and dissatisfaction.

Third, be willing to give up some control. If you expect or demand total control in a small group setting, you will make yourself and everyone else miserable. The give-and-take of small group work requires small group members to share power and to give up control to some extent. If you want people to respect your opinions and rights, then you must also respect their opinions and rights.

© Minerva Studio, 2013. Used under license from Shutterstock, Inc.

FIGURE 1.31

Giving up some control does not mean you have to become a doormat and let everyone walk all over you. It does not mean that you must give up your autonomy and that you must go along with whatever other group members suggest. It does mean, however, that you are willing to enter into a cooperative relationship with your group and its members. In order to work well and play well with others, you must cooperate.

Fourth, correct and revise your inaccurate, negative perceptions of small groups. Develop positive thoughts and positive self-talk about small group work. Although there are some disadvantages related to working in small groups, there are many more benefits and advantages. Use the list of benefits at the end of this chapter to "retrain your brain" if you tend to focus on the problems connected with small groups.

Focusing on the positive aspects of small group work is not naïve or unrealistic. A realistic view of small group work should recognize both the benefits and drawbacks. Let us first consider the drawbacks and negative aspects of small group work, and then we will end this first chapter by considering the benefits and positive aspects of small group work.

Disadvantages of Small Group Work

1. Small group work takes time. It takes time to solicit and receive input from all small group members. It takes time to clarify differences of opinion and to manage intra-group conflict. When time is of the essence, sometimes small group work is not the best choice.
2. Small groups sometimes contain difficult group members. (Chapter three lists ten different types of difficult people.) Human beings have personality defects. When the personality defects of small group members are significant, they can interfere with the small group process.
3. Small group relationships are complex. It takes time, energy, and skill to manage and maintain small group relationships. A person who joins a small group primarily to accomplish a task or to fulfill a duty or obligation may be intimidated by the relational complexity and relational focus of small group work.
4. It is difficult to schedule group meetings. Due to the many different schedules, life goals, and obligations of small group members, finding a time when all small group members can meet is often a challenge and a source of conflict.
5. Small group meetings can be unproductive. After struggling to find a time and a place to meet, it is disappointing and even demoralizing when a small group meeting is unproductive. When small groups lack a well-thought-out meeting agenda and an effective meeting chair, small group meetings can seem like a waste of time.
6. Unpleasant conflicts and arguments are possible. When human beings work together, differences of opinion will arise that can lead to major conflicts and arguments. A minor disagreement, if handled poorly, can lead to a major altercation. A badly managed conflict can leave group members with frayed nerves and negative emotions.

FIGURE 1.32
A realistic view of small groups must acknowledge the drawbacks of small group work.

Advantages of Small Group Work

1. Human beings often make better decisions and solve problems more effectively when they work together in small groups. It may take more time for small groups to work together, but this time investment usually pays off in better results.
2. Small groups can exploit the special skills and abilities of their individual members. Human beings may have personality defects, but they also have unique skills and abilities that can be used to benefit the larger group.
3. Small group membership fulfills basic human social needs. Small group membership gives you the opportunity to "network" and to make friends, but even basic work relationships with several different human beings can improve your overall

physical and mental health. Although small group work involves relational complexity, human beings are social creatures who thrive when they have meaningful relationships with others.

© Brian A. Jackson, 2013. Used under license from Shutterstock, Inc.

FIGURE 1.33

4. Small group discussion results in a variety of different perspectives. Although it is difficult to schedule meetings because of the various life goals and obligations of small group members, the variation and diversity present in small groups creates multiple perspectives. Consequently, a small group can develop a rich, robust view of an issue or problem, a view which incorporates the different perceptions and perspectives of the individual group members.

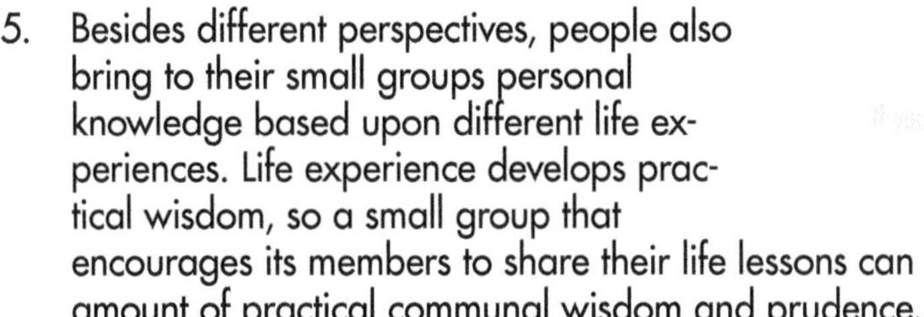

5. Besides different perspectives, people also bring to their small groups personal knowledge based upon different life experiences. Life experience develops practical wisdom, so a small group that encourages its members to share their life lessons can generate a substantial amount of practical communal wisdom and prudence.

6. Small group members can share the work load. When individual members come prepared to a small group meeting, and when a thoughtful meeting agenda is developed and followed, a substantial amount of work can be accomplished. Working effectively together, a small group of people can get much more work accomplished than even the most productive individual. The old adage is true: "Many hands make light work."

© emran, 2013. Used under license from Shutterstock, Inc.

FIGURE 1.34

7. Small group work can help you learn to manage conflict effectively. Although in small groups there is the potential for unpleasant, unproductive conflict, there is also the potential for productive, healthy conflict. Small groups are most productive and fruitful when they promote and manage a substantial amount of healthy conflict. As a small group member, you can practice and perfect effective conflict management skills that you can use in many different life situations.

FIGURE 1.35

8. Small group work can help you improve your communication skills. As you work with your small group members, you can improve your interpersonal and small group communication skills. As you report the results of your work to others outside your small group, you can improve your public speaking skills.
9. Small group work can provide increased responsibility, accountability, and motivation. Small group communication classes (and other college classes) that require students to work together in small groups usually have high student success rates and low student attrition rates because the individual students feel a sense of responsibility to their small groups. Because they feel responsible for their groups, and because their small groups hold them accountable for their work, small group members often discover they are highly motivated to participate regularly and to produce high quality work.

FIGURE 1.36

FIGURE 1.37

FIGURE 1.38

10. Small group work lets you learn about yourself and others. When you work closely with others, you are exposed to, and can gain insight into, different types of people. Your small group members can also give you feedback which will help you gain insight into your own personality and your own communication strengths and weaknesses.
11. Small group work allows you to receive help and support from others. Your small group members can encourage you when you run into difficulties, and they may even be able to help you get through these difficulties directly or indirectly. When you are a valued member of a small group, there are people who "have your back."
12. Small group work gives you a chance to practice **interdependence**. Human beings begin life totally dependent on their caregivers, and then pass several milestones of independence as they mature. However, independence is not the height of human development: mature human beings realize that they depend on others, and that others depend on them (interdependence). Working in a small group gives you opportunities to receive help and support from others, and it also gives you opportunities to give help and support to others in return.

We have purposely made the list of benefits of small group work twice as long as the list of drawbacks in order to encourage you in your small group participation. It was not difficult to generate the list of benefits because there really are many more positive aspects of small group work than there are negative aspects. Keep your mind focused on these positive aspects and you should be able to remain committed to small group work even when problems and difficulties arise.

Drawbacks of Small Groups	Benefits of Small Groups
1. Small groups take time.	1. Small groups get better results.
2. Small groups can contain difficult people.	2. Small groups can exploit special skills and abilities of group members.
3. Small group relationships are complex.	3. Small groups fill basic social needs.
4. It is difficult to schedule meetings.	4. Small groups provide multiple perspectives.
5. Meetings can be unproductive.	5. Small groups can draw upon different life experiences.
6. Conflicts and arguments are possible.	6. Small groups can share the workload.
	7. You can learn effective conflict management strategies.
	8. You can improve your communication skills.
	9. Small groups provide increased responsibility, accountability, and motivation.
	10. Small groups let you learn about yourself and others.
	11. You can receive help and support from others.
	12. You can give help and support to others.

FIGURE 1.39
The benefits of small group work outweigh the drawbacks

Summary

If you have read through this first chapter of your small group textbook, you have a solid foundation for engaging in small group work. You now know what constitutes a small group, and you can list and describe different types of small groups which exist. You understand that small group communication and small group relationships are complex, and you can distinguish small group communication from both interpersonal communication and public speaking.

You now have a better appreciation for the prevalence and importance of small group work both in the popular imagination and in the real world. You know that small group work is essential and crucial in the fields of business, sports, medicine, law, education, entertainment, and politics.

You now realize that the small groups portrayed on television "reality" shows are unrealistic, and that small groups in the real world are not as dysfunctional or cutthroat as the small groups depicted for entertainment purposes. You also now know some of the causes of "grouphate," and you have some practical methods for reducing or eliminating grouphate.

After learning the drawbacks and disadvantages *and* the many benefits and advantages of small group work, you have the knowledge you need to remain committed to your small group involvements, and you are able to look forward to a rewarding learning experience in your small group communication course.

Glossary

Aggregate: An aggregate of people is a group of human beings that have no substantial connection to each other except the fact that they are being lumped and counted together by an observer.

Dyad: Two interacting human beings; also called a "couple" or "pair."

Focus group: Groups formed and queried by companies or political parties in order to gather opinions about products, services, or issues.

Grouphate: The disgust and disdain that some people feel for small group work.

Interdependence: The principle that human beings need one another. In the arc of human development, people pass from an initial stage of almost total dependence to various milestones of independence. However, mature human beings realize that they are interdependent; they depend on others, and others depend on them.

Interpersonal communication: The one-on-one communication that occurs between two communicators.

Public speaking: A form of mono-logical communication in which one person (the speaker) transmits a sustained verbal message to several people (the audience).

Primary groups: Groups of people, often related by blood, who live together in social units to fulfill basic physical and social needs; often called "families."

Quality circle: A group of people which analyzes, evaluates, and improves the quality of a product. These people are often drawn from all the employee groups involved in the production process.

Secondary groups: Any small group of people not designated as a "primary group." These people come together for secondary reasons beyond providing for their basic physical and social needs. Secondary groups include work groups, play groups, study groups, therapy groups, support groups, decision-making and problem-solving groups, focus groups, and quality circles.

Small group: Three to twelve people united together around common goals and feeling a sense of belonging to their social unit.

Small group communication: A complex form of human communication that involves the sending and receiving of verbal and nonverbal messages among several people at once. People involved in small group communication are simultaneously acting as the communicators of messages and the observers of communication messages.

Team: A small group with a great degree of cohesiveness. Group members have designated, specialized roles.

Triangulation: Psychological triangulation can occur when three people are involved in a communication transaction or three-way relationship. The positive interpersonal relationships and communication that occurs when the people interact as dyads is strained when all three must interact together at the same time.

Virtual groups: Groups which use computer-mediated communication to work or play together even while separated by time or distance.

Works Cited or Consulted

Bales, F., Robert. (1950). *Interaction Process Analysis: A Method for the Study of Small Groups.* Cambridge, MA: Addison-Wesley. (*Book-length work by an early pioneer of the study of small group communication.*)

Ekeh, P., Peter. (1974). *Social Exchange Theory: the two Traditions.* Cambridge, MA: Harvard University Press. (*A book-length treatment of the Social Exchange Theory.*)

Homans, George C. (1958). Social behavior as exchange. *American Journal of Sociology*, 63 (6), 597–606. (*Probably the first scholarly article proposing the Social Exchange Theory.*)

Kephart, M., William. (1950). A quantitative analysis of intragroup relationships. *American Journal of Sociology*, 55, 544–549. (*William Kephart's analysis of possible intragroup relationships that established these possible relationships increase exponentially even while group membership increases arithmetically.*)

Murray, S., & Ouellette, L. (2008). *Reality TV: Remaking television culture.* New York, New York University Press. (*Collection of essays examining and discussing reality television in America.*)

Myers, A., Scott., & Goodboy, K.A. (2005). A study of grouphate in a course on small group communication. *Psychological Reports* 97 (2),381–386. (*Grouphate theory applied to actual small groups in Communication classes.*)

Sorensen, S.M. (1981). Group-hate: A negative reaction to group work. A paper presented at the annual meeting of the International Communication Association, Minneapolis, MN. (*Primary source for the origin and development of the theory of grouphate.*)

Chapter 2:

Why Do People Join Groups? How Do Groups Develop?

Chapter Objectives

- Identify why people join groups.
- Explain theories of why people join groups.
- Explain theories of how groups develop.

Why We Join Groups

Let's discuss why humans tend to join groups in the first place. Let's start with you. Think about the last time you joined a group. Perhaps the group you recently joined was an educational group, a book club, a remote control car group, a scrapbooking or sewing group, study group, or recovery group of some kind. You likely joined your group because you had something in common with the group you joined. We tend to join groups because they have things in common with our own interests, ideals, and motives. Most small group scholars have come to the consensus that the reasons humans join groups is primarily because of needs, attraction, goals, and occasionally out of simple obligation.

Reasons We Join Groups

1. Physical attraction to group members
2. Attraction to group goals or ideals
3. To satisfy our needs
4. To feel in control
5. To be controlled
6. To have affection
7. To feel included
8. To fulfill our individual goals
9. To fulfill our group goals
10. To gain the benefits of synergy
11. To gain or provide support

ATTRACTION

Interpersonal attraction is the degree of force between two people that results in them coming close together or creating separation. Just as some magnets pull together or repel, so do humans. In the last group you were in, you may have felt a degree of interpersonal attraction. **Physical attraction** is a common reason why people join groups as well. For whatever reason, research shows that the more physically attractive someone is, the more likely others will want to be around that person. Yet, it seems that as time goes on, people are less and less concerned with the degree of physical attraction in others. **Group attraction** refers to the degree of force between one person and the goals and ideals of a given group. Some people are simply attracted to the group goals, which can vary greatly from group to group. For instance, one author of this book belongs to a scrapbooking group. One of the reasons I was attracted to the group was because I was able to accomplish tasks and still have socialization with my friends. However, I equally enjoy shooting my compound bow and various types of guns with my family because I like the shared goals of getting better at a skill.

FIGURE 2.1

Interpersonal attraction in small groups occurs between two people. Inspires people to come together or keep apart.

The last area of attraction we will discuss is called proximity. You might be raising your eyebrows at this point. What does proximity have to do with attraction? Well, it seems actually quite a lot. Basically, the more you are around someone the more likely you are to become attracted to them. **Proximity** is advantageous—it can increase effectiveness and efficiency in groups and make interactions less time consuming. The more you get to know others, the more you realize they are different or similar to yourself, and that will also then lead to attraction or repellent outcomes.

A **complementary need** is a need driven by a desire to be with people who complement our own characteristics, but are not similar to us. For instance, if someone is highly organized and ready to help, but reluctant to or scared to lead a group, they may like working with people who are inherently leaders. Additionally, you may seek out members of a group who are a good fit your personality—this doesn't mean similar to your personality, but rather complementary. For instance, sometimes a very passive personality works well with a more assertive personality in small group settings.

Some people, on the other hand, are attracted to others because they are alike in personality, values, or beliefs. This is an attraction based on **similarity**. Most people tend to search for others who are similar to them. These people make us feel safe, we know what to expect (or at least we think we do), and we know how to communicate with them (we know the rules and norms). Some common characteristics used as criteria to determine the degree of likeness are: attitudes, beliefs, behaviors, hobbies, interests, occupation, race, ethnicity, language, dialect, and communication style. This is, however, not an exhaustive list.

Attraction to groups can be due to:

Physical attractiveness
Group attractiveness
Proximity attractiveness
Degree of Complimentary
Degree of Similarity

FIGURE 2.2
Many people are able to accomplish more in a group than they could have alone. Often times these individuals find they complement others well and because of that productivity and satisfaction in the group increases.

FIGURE 2.3
[illegible] tend to join groups that have similar belief systems as themselves.

Schutz's Theory of Interpersonal Behavior

In order to understand human beings desire to be a part of a group, communication scholars utilize theories. Theories explain why something occurs. We are constantly improving theories or sometimes we discover that our theory is completely wrong.

The following theories explain why people join groups.

FIGURE 2.4

In our everyday lives, we tend to surround ourselves with people who value the same things we do.

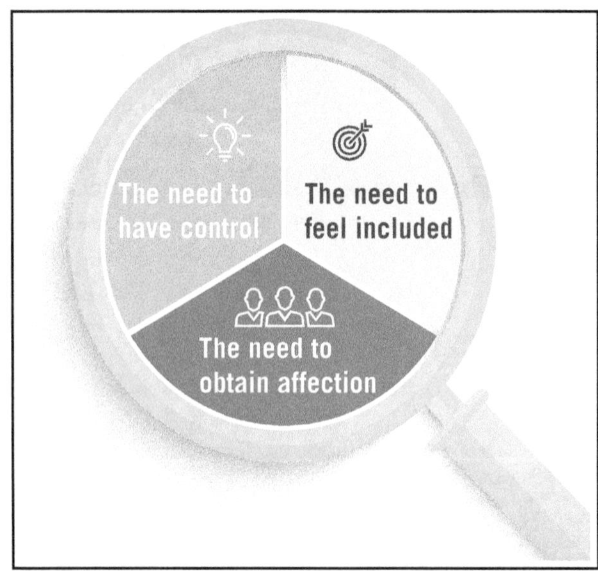

FIGURE 2.5

Schutz's Need Theory

NEEDS

Every human has needs. Some of us need to exercise to get out our frustrations. Other people may need to partake in some artistic outlet, like ceramics, painting, or acting. Some people need to feel like they belong to something; that they are a part of something. And still others need to feel they are accomplishing a task as a smaller part of a greater whole.

William Schutz crafted a theory about needs, influence, and interaction based on his studies of how people interact and influence one another. Schutz proposes that humans have three basic needs: to be included, to be in control, and to be affectionate. Schutz created the **Fundamental Interpersonal Relations Orientation (FIRO)** in an attempt to measure group members perceptions or feelings related to inclusivity, control, and affection or openness. The FIRO measure is composed of six scales of nine-item questions. Schutz's theory is useful in small groups just as it is in interpersonal relationships because it captures a persons' desires to have closeness to others, to exhibit control over others, or even how much socialization one may want.

In Schutz's theory you will find some similarities to other theories discussed previously in this book, as well in the basic discussion of why we join groups. You might see yourself in some of these descriptions. The first need Schutz discussed is the basic need of *inclusion*. This need is pretty simple: humans like to be included; we can see this from an early age. For whatever reason, humans need to feel like they are contributing to something, that they are needed, and that they are understood. Inclusion also may help people feel good about themselves. If you were granted entrance into a prestigious group that would likely increase your self-esteem or your self-worth. The inclusion need is a really basic need, but a very important one.

Another need Schutz identified is also one you might find to be quite elementary; the need for *affection*. Humans tend to like affection. In fact, affection is a very critical need, and the lack of affection can result in very real side effects, both emotional and physical. According to research conducted by Kory Floyd, an associate professor at Arizona State University's[1] Hugh Downs School

[1] Research on affection at ASU is supported by the American Psychological Foundation. For more information about specific studies, contact Kory Floyd, Ph.D., Hugh Downs School of Human Communication, 480.965.3568. Send e-mail to: kfloyd@asu.edu Visit the Communication Sciences Laboratory at: http://www.asu.edu/clas/communication

of Human Communication, "Highly affectionate people tend to have better mental health and less stress. They also react to stress better." (as qutd. In Reseachmatters.asu.edu, 2010).[2] Other research has found that serotonin is significantly decreased as our level of affection is decreased, and our overall health is improved with the presence of affection. In the group setting, affection can include instances of supporting others emotionally or the process of becoming close to others through the sharing of similar experiences.

A third need Schutz's theory discusses is called the *control* need. This need varies from person to person. The need to have control is a strong need in some people and really not strong at all in others. This need can be understood as a desire to have power and authority over others. It can also be brought about by trust issues and past negative experiences. Others, however, have a need to have others hold power over them. This might be seen in instances where someone is new and needs help and training, or a matter of low self-esteem leading them to believe they cannot do something on their own and thus they feel more secure letting someone else have the power.

Related to the group environment, Schutz's theory proves useful because it explains why people may join groups. People may join groups because they like feeling like they are a part of something, that they are included. They also might join groups because they receive some form of support from others or they may join because they need to exert some form of control over others or feel controlled.

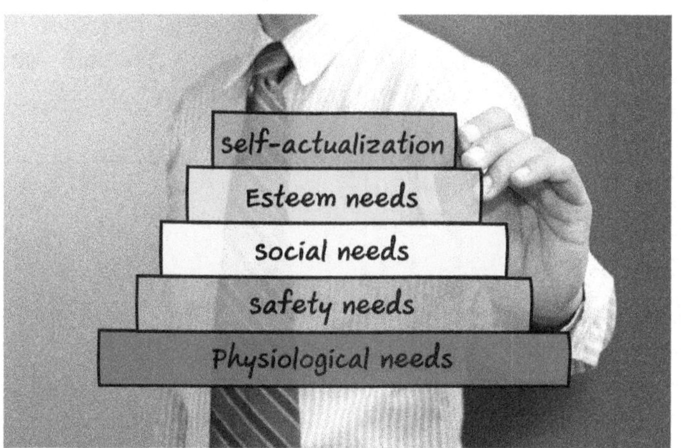

FIGURE 2.6
Maslow's Hierarchy of Needs

MASLOW'S HIERARCHY OF NEEDS

One of the most commonly used needs-based theories is Abraham Maslow's Hierarchy of Interpersonal Needs, which was discussed briefly in the Theory chapter. The Hierarchy of Interpersonal Needs theory depicts the claim that humans have needs and that there are various categories of needs. It also suggests that in order for humans to be concerned with certain needs, they first have to obtain the lower-ordered needs.

The first order of needs is called the *physiological* needs which refers to the idea that people must first obtain the needs they have for air, water, and food—the basics. The second order of needs is referred to as *safety* needs, which refers to the need for humans to feel safe and secure. After the first two sets of needs have been met, a human can become concerned with the need to obtain love and have a sense of belonging (third-order needs). This need is met with the love and affection of the family unit until one gets a bit older and starts looking outside the family unit to have these needs fully met. Relationships, friendships, intimacy, and basic affection from others become a strong need for most humans. Maslow refers to these kinds of needs as *social* needs.

Maslow's Hierarchy of Needs asserts that people do not care to know about higher-ordered needs when lower-level needs have not yet been satisfied. The **Hierarchy of Interpersonal Needs Theory** illustrates that humans have needs and there are various categories of needs. It also suggests that

[2] http://researchmatters.asu.edu/stories/effects-affection-960

in order for humans to be concerned with certain needs they first have to obtain the lower-ordered needs. Consider the five categories of needs:

1. Physiological Needs: refers to the idea that people must first obtain the needs they have for air, water, and food—the basics.
2. Safety Needs: refers to the need for humans to feel safe and secure.
3. Love and Belonging Needs: refers to the idea that humans need to have a sense of belonging, be shown affection, and give affection. One finds these needs in romantic relationships with others and friendship relationships.
4. Esteem Needs: refers to the desire people have to belong to something; to share a sense of community. This need is often fulfilled through recognition, prestige and status, or power.
5. Self Actualization: refers to the plateau; the point at which we are all striving to reach. Self actualization is reached when all the needs are fulfilled and one can lead a truly autonomous and full life.

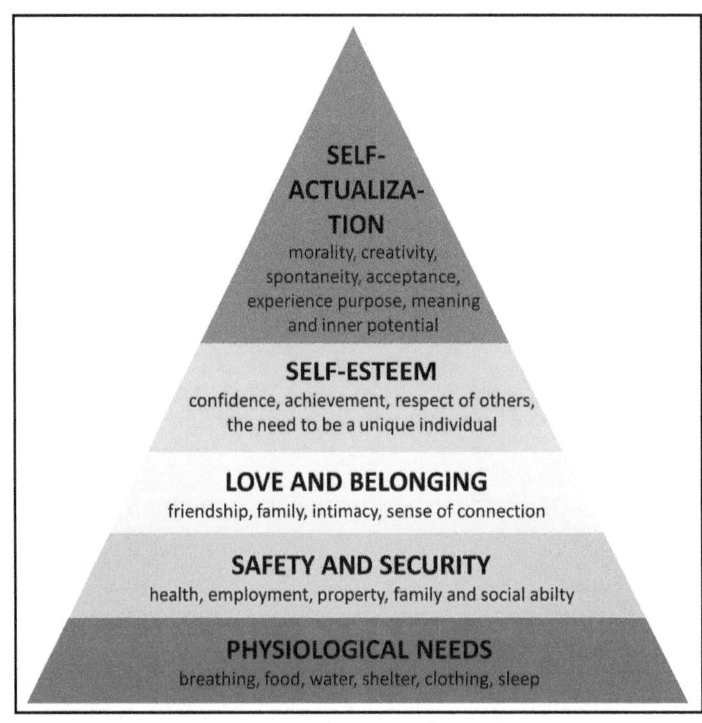

FIGURE 2.7

Maslow's pyramid of needs helps us understand how humans prioritize their needs.

Think how many groups exist in our society that people join to meet their interpersonal needs. Think how many groups you could join to help people.

Systems Theory

One of the most dominant and most widely accepted small group communication theories is called Systems Theory. Systems Theory is the interrelationship between elements. Theorists assert that small group communication work is systematic and thus groups are interdependent, adaptable, open, flexible, and affected by their environments. According to Systems Theory, small groups are systems that are constantly altered by variables. In 1950, theorist Ludwig Von Bertalanffy created the Systems Theory as a way to explain the process of input, output, and other variables that exist in small groups.

Systems Theory examines and evaluates how groups are influenced by their environments and how they function as a result. In the end, Von Bertalanffy's theory suggests that small groups do not exist in a fixed state, but rather they are constantly changing and are highly dependent. What are they dependent on? There are three types of variables present in any small group:

1) process variables,
2) input variables, and
3) output variables.

There are also a few key components to Systems Theory:

1) interdependence,
2) synergy,
3) entropy,
4) openness to environment,
5) equifinality, and
6) multifinality.

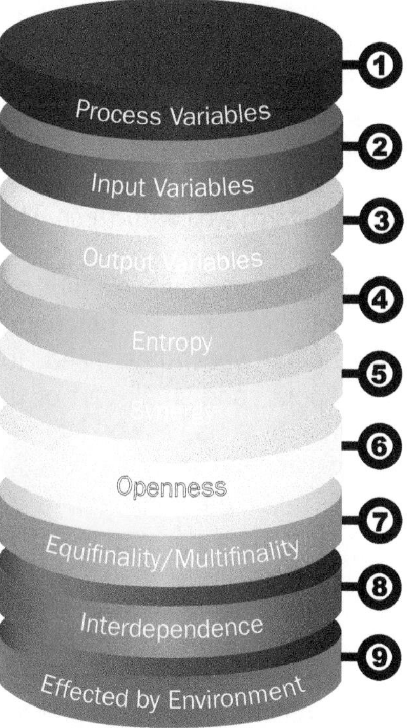

FIGURE 2.8 Systems Theory

Arguably one of the most useful contributions of Systems Theory is that it allows us to easily see, in the case of small groups, a degree of multi-level causation. Multi-level causation means that each and every simple or big change in the system (group) is caused by not just one factor, but several factors. For instance, imagine a small group of people ages 18–36 years of age working together on a group project for a class. Let's start at the end, a student approaches the teacher and demands to be placed in another group because they simply cannot continue working with the assigned group. The student's decision to leave the group is not likely because of one simple moment, or one simple reason. It is far more likely that there were a series of events, variables, and principles that led to this final decision. Systems Theory's primary premise is that the whole won't function without all of its parts and that one of the parts not working will in turn affect the output. Perhaps this is more easily un-

FIGURE 2.9

derstood in car world. Picture a car in your mind. Go ahead; pick the Ferrari, the Porsche, the lifted truck or the 1967 Ford.

Now, imagine you're behind the wheel of this vehicle. You are coasting down a beautiful winding road; the ocean to right, the slope of a giant mountain to your left. The air is fine, nice even; you can smell trees and salt in the breeze. You look to your passenger seat, and you see your partner or best friend, you smile at each other as if to say, "yeah, this is great." And then all of a sudden, the vehicle pulls you to the right (remember the side with that beautiful ocean—yeah that side). You pull your steering wheel left and press down on the brake pedal. You pull off to the side of the road and see that you have a flat tire. You also have a bent rim. So you go to the trunk and pull out the spare tire, some tools, and the jack. You begin using the jack to elevate the car, then you remove the lug nuts with the wrench, you replace the tire and when you go to reach for the wrench, you hear a strange sound . . . . a "pop!" followed by a "ting, ting . . . ting . . . ting" as something shoots off bouncing as it plunges further and further away down the steep hill down toward the ocean. Your wrench is gone. Now you have a car with three functioning wheels. Is the car going to perform well with three wheels instead of four?

In one moment, everything is working; all the parts are functioning correctly doing what they need to and then "pop!" one small part of this great big machine isn't working as it should. Systems Theory would say that a car, much like a small group of people, is a structure that functions based on many interdependent variables and thus one simple variable will affect the entire system. One part of the car not functioning properly affects the outcome. Similarly, had someone not put coolant in the car, the car may have overheated, the air conditioner may have stopped working, and thus the entire car shut down. One part affects the whole. This example may have seemed all too close to home for some of you. What happened in this situation is very similar to what happens in groups.

FIGURE 2.10

[illegible]

In order to understand Systems Theory, we must understand its "parts." First, let's discuss **interdependence**. Interdependence was discussed in the vehicle example earlier. Fundamentally, the group as a system is made up of several parts. If there is a change in any one part, it will undoubtedly affect the rest of the system or group. Consider if you will, adding a new group member to an already functioning and established group. When a new member is added to a group, the level of "uncertainty" changes. The way the group communicates might change; the process of discussions, and even distribution of work, will change. Thus, one change (the addition of a new member), affected the entire system (the entire group). The group is made up of parts that are interdependent.

Openness to the environment is the second component in Systems Theory, and it is quite similar to the concept of interdependence. However, instead of asserting that the parts are all linked and can alter the whole, openness to the environment asserts that the group is constantly affected by the environment from which it resides. This means that not only do the actions or lack of actions by group members create a change in the group, but also the various factors of the surrounding environment can affect the group. For instance, the structure of the group may change, the rules and norms, attitudes and behaviors, climate and needs may be altered, and these will all have an effect on the group in some way. If a group is "open" to these environmental changes, then it will adjust and accommodate, those who are inflexible will be "closed" to the environment and often find themselves in more troublesome positions.

FIGURE 2.11

Boundaries and rules are directly related to open and closed systems. In an open system, you are willing to absorb and consider different perspectives and ideas. In a closed system, you are shutting off the outside influences and possibilities. Rules and boundaries help your group establish how open or closed it will be and should be. For instance, there may be times that the group must decide to close themselves slightly or tightly based on some external conflict that is having a negative consequence on the group's output. For instance, when a woman becomes pregnant, her entire group of people is pregnant. People outside the group (strangers, in-laws, co-workers) will often feel the need to expound their wise and tried advice on the woman, partner, or other children. This advice, while potentially good intentioned, can cause a great amount of stress, anxiety, fear, or even anger. If this happens, the group may decide it's best to become more closed and make specific rules about soliciting or participating in the advice giving of others.

CONSIDER DECREASING THE DEGREE OF OPENNESS WHEN:

1. members are experiencing excessive anxiety or stress as a result of outside input.
2. members are becoming apathetic and disengaged in the group due to outside input.
3. the success of the group is being hindered.
4. excessive conflicts are generated and escalated with the presence of outside environments.

Next, we need to understand the concept of **synergy** which asserts that a system is much more than just the sum of its parts. Just as you like to think you are more than just a human—a system of blood, muscle, fat, bones, tendons, water and organs—groups are more than a simple structure made up of its members. Groups are said to have synergy when the total unit is better than the individuals.

Think about your local school board. These are small groups of people that get quite a lot accomplished, arguably more than they would be able to do alone. This group would then have positive synergy. It is also possible for a group to have negative synergy. Negative synergy refers to a group being less than the sum of its parts. You might see negative synergy in a group that has too many leaders. It is not uncommon to end up with less efficiency and less effectiveness in groups where there are multiple leaders or people fighting for that position. You may have seen this occur in sports teams, your fantasy football league, a group of friends, a work group, or a child's sporting event. Somehow these groups actually underperform as opposed to doing better. There is no guarantee for any one group; we all have the same opportunity, but because everything in a group is so interdependent, predictability of synergy is impossible and unique to every group.

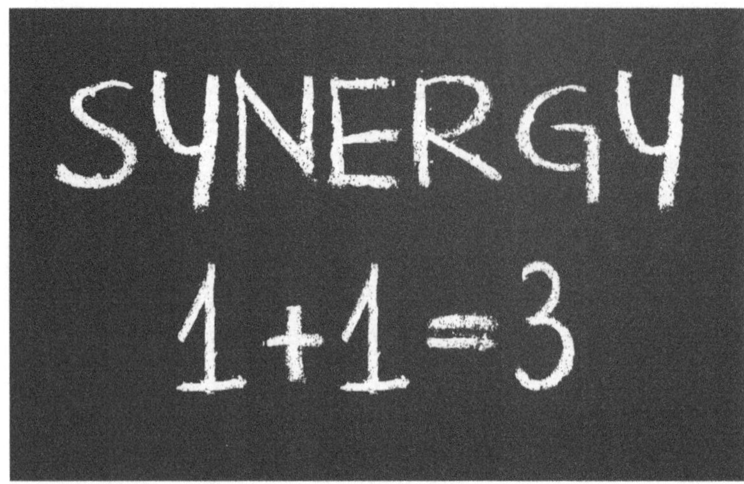

FIGURE 2.12

Synergy suggests that the group is more than the simple total of its parts. One plus one is not two, it is much more.

The third component in Systems Theory is **entropy**, which is a general measurement of disorder or chaos in a group. Why are we measuring chaos? Well, research has shown us that groups thrive in balanced, harmonious, trusted, and reliable environments. Groups do not do as well when they are chaotic. For instance, groups that have weekly meetings at the same time and place every day and for the same time period have a sense of consistency, a lesser degree of chaos, and thus a higher degree of predictability and reliability. A group that consistently changes their meeting times and days, and whose members are infrequent in their attendance, will tend to have higher degrees of chaos. Which group ends up having the best Product? Statistically speaking, the group with the lesser degree of chaos will end up in a better position.

Recognize, however, that disorder and chaos are not the only distinguishing factors; it is one of the many we are discussing. In fact, the near opposite of entropy is called equifinality which is the next component. **Equifinality** is the idea that people can take on diverse roles in a group and yet

FIGURE 2.13

The three variables in small groups: input, process, and output variables.

end up in the same place. Conversely, several different systems may reach the same outcome even if they did not start out in the same place. The concept of **multifinality**, the last component in Systems Theory, states that systems or groups that start out at the same place may reach different ends. A simple example of these two concepts is traffic routes. Let's say you want to get to Bigfork, Montana, so you look at the map and find a lovely route that stays on major highways and interstates. Someone else also wants to go to Bigfork and picks a route that uses several off-the-highway roads. You both reach Bigfork even though you took different ways to get there (this is equifinality). You would reach multifinality if two groups were given the exact same assignment "using 1,000 cubes of sugar, one stick of glue, and 100 straws to make a structure that is at least three feet high and can hold a 16 oz. soda" and come up with a product that is very different even though they started with the exact same parameters (multifinality).

After examining how Schutz, Maslow, and Systems Theory explain why people join groups, it is now critical that we examine the process by which groups develop.

Small Group Formation and Development

When we enter groups we sometimes have a set of expectations or preconceived notions, and we may have decided what our role in that group will be. All of these things can contribute towards a disastrous experience in a small group. When we join a small group, it is important that we stop, breathe, and recognize that this is a NEW group. This new group doesn't likely have the same people, goals, motivations, agenda, or rules of our previous groups, so our approach, roles, and expectations should be different. All of these components will come together beginning with the first meeting of the new group. As we have learned, there are many different types of groups and thus many different reasons why people join groups. With the large variety of groups that exist, are there situations and/or stages that we can expect to encounter in just about every group? According to several theorists, the answer is a big "yes."

There have been several theories about how small groups develop and many of them have similarities. We will discuss various approaches, but we will pay the most attention to the most commonly accepted development theories. Bruce W. Tuckman crafted one of the more widely used and applied theories of group development. Tuckman conducted research at Princeton University and was a small-group Research Psychologist at the Naval Medical Research Institute. While researching various group encounters from beginning to end, he found that groups all tend to go through four primary stages of development. He also determined that group members were widely unaware of the stages they were progressing through; it seemed instead to be a semi-natural process that each group entered into one stage at a time. According to Tuckman, there are four stages in group development: forming, storming, norming, and performing.

FIGURE 2.14
Tuckman's Group Development Stages

FORMING

When groups "form," members are entering into the group for the first time. This is a stage where members meet, greet, and start to set up their group expectations, goals, and even rules. This is also the point that everyone is getting to know one another. Members will often self-disclose in this phase, sharing personal information about themselves with others. However, this information will be fairly shallow, like divulging an interest in ice-skating, water sports, or crafts. Members often self-disclose in order to find similarities with one another. It is important to note, however, that a very small portion of groups get directly to the task at hand without entering into any personal discussions whatsoever. You may find this amongst highly experienced and structured businesses.

Ways to Decrease the Awkwardness of the First Meeting

1. Remind yourself that everyone feels a little awkward, so your awkwardness is actually normal.
2. Ask yourself why you feel awkward. Are you feeling this way because of a past experience or fear of the unknown? A sense of pressure, or fear of judgment? If you can identify why you feel this way, you can address the problem with the appropriate self-talk and other possible solutions.
3. Remind yourself that being afraid of what others will think of you is a waste of your time. You can't control what others think about you, so you might as well just relax, be yourself, and know that even if you don't make a perfect impression you will have more opportunities.
4. Know that shyness is a choice and you can choose to exhibit less shyness if you set your mind to it.
5. Pretend to be a little more confident than you actually are. Successful people do this all the time. You don't have to wear your insecurities on your sleeve and putting forward a bit of confidence despite your insecurities can go far.
6. Focus on what you have in common with others as opposed to what you don't have in common.
7. Reduce your anxiety or fears beforehand. Using positive self-talk and power poses before you interact with others is beneficial.
8. Suspend your tendency to assume things about other people. Just as you want people to get to know you before they make snap judgments and assumptions about who you are, give this same respect to your group members. People are not always what they seem.
9. Use positive or "prosocial" body language. This means uncrossing your arms and allowing yourself to use your hands naturally as you speak. Prosocial body language shows others that you are open to them, interested and willing to communicate. Your posture, eye contact, and facial expressions are the key indicators of your willingness to be social with others.
10. Don't say things that focus on your insecurities. For instance, avoid saying things like, "I'm so nervous," "I feel really awkward right now," or "I'm an idiot."

The forming stage is primarily composed of members getting oriented with each other and the group task. A large part of this orientation is members figuring out the various boundaries and expectations that others have for them and that they have for others. Most interpersonal communication between members will be to "get along" and be perceived as nice; being liked is valued at this stage. Members are trying to determine the degree to which other members are safe, so they soak up all information they can about others. Members will pay attention to the way people talk, what they talk about, and how they talk about it; all these bits of information are collected in order to make a summative judgment about similarities, differences, and safeness.

While collecting interpersonal information to form judgments about and approaches towards one another, the group members will likely be discussing the tasks and goals of the group. The group will attempt to define its primary purpose and how it will function. The degree to which specific tasks and roles are decided on varies from group to group. Visit our chapter on Leadership and Roles to gather more information about the various tasks, roles, and leadership styles that may be addressed in the forming and storming stages of group development.

STORMING

The **storming** stage of group development refers to the conflict and uncomfortability that comes after group members have met and gotten to know each other. Specifically, stage two—storming—is when members experience conflict, competition, and organization. It is not uncommon for people to experience friction. Some personalities, as they say, just don't mix well. However, when we are in a group, it is our job to set aside personal differences and get the job done. Regardless of our desire to get this accomplished, there is inevitably going to be a stage that is characterized by competition, chaos, and conflict between members. During this stage you will see some polarization between some, but hopefully not all group members. This is also the stage that tasks and roles have been assigned and thus where emotional responses to these assignments may be seen. You may see cliques, alliances, and power struggles between members wanting more powerful positions.

For instance, perhaps a group voted on who should be the leader of the group. Let's say Brian was voted to be the leader and Mitch was upset, as he felt his experience and age made him more qualified to be in a leadership position. Given these feelings, Mitch becomes distant from the group process, refusing to give his opinion when asked and overall decreasing his impact, input, and presence in the group. This would be an example of storming. The storming stage of group development is the stage where initial conflicts with personalities, tasks, roles, and rules occur.

The storming stage, although seemingly chaotic and even scary, is actually quite productive. This stage is where the members will hash out their responsibilities, argue, and discuss various rules. This is also the time when attitudes, beliefs, and values start to clash. Unlike the forming when members were willing to be passive, get along, and play nice, the storming stage is characterized as a time where people are done with the niceties and move on towards getting things accomplished. The problem is, everyone tends to have their own idea for how things should get accomplished and who should be leading.

Weather the Storm: Ways to Keep the Storm from becoming a Tsunami

1. Focus on similarities, not differences.
2. Remember that first impressions will last a long time.
3. Refrain from any potentially insensitive jokes about any group (this is a good rule in general, but you may not know someone is a member of a certain culture group until it is too late.)
4. Create hyper focus on the goal at hand.
5. Be inclusive; ask for opinions.
6. Establish trust through positive talk and reinforcing your positive traits as a leader or member.
7. Show a willingness to help and be flexible.
8. Reduce your anxiety beforehand with positive self-talk, preparation, and confidence.
9. Be willing to compromise.
10. Suspend your judgment and stereotypes and see people as individuals.
11. Try to listen to others before making comments, judgments or interrupting.
12. Focus on the group goals and set aside your individual goals.
13. Recognize when you are arguing out of ego rather than what is best for the team.
14. Allow everyone to participate and be an active listener.
15. Create a list of rules and expectations for the group as a whole.
16. When establishing yourself in groups, do not put others down as a means of raising yourself up.
17. If you "click" with someone, don't make that connection a source of hurt for others.
18. If you find yourself not "clicking" with others, try to establish a similarity of some kind. Shared experience is a strong bonding device.
19. Don't take things personally.
20. Remember you should not be competing with others to the point that it hinders the group output and climate.

Organization or disorganization becomes an area of focus at this stage because groups are becoming more concerned with accomplishing their goals and are often feeling the pressures of the task. It is not uncommon during this stage to see members argue about the rules and expectations of the group and the members. Some members may want punishments for members coming to meetings unprepared, while others want to reward the prepared people. Some may want to have the ability to kick people out if they underperform, and others may want strict rules and deadlines, still others may prefer a more supportive approach. No single approach is right for all occasions; thus, this storming stage is actually beneficial because it allows the members to come to a consensus on the structure of the group and generate some group norms. In order to get through the storming phase, you need to give your group some organization and expectations.

NORMING

Group researchers Wood, Phillips, and Pedersen (1986) define norms as "standardized patterns of belief, attitude, communication and behavior within groups." Daniel Feldman (1984) asserts, the development and enforcement of group norms . . .

"Norms are the informal rules that groups adopt to regulate and regularize group members' behavior. Although these norms are infrequently written down or openly discussed, they often have a powerful, and consistent, influence on group members' behavior. Once norms are present they serve to systematically influence future integration and structure in the group."

FIGURE 2.15
The third stage in group development is the norming phase, which is when the group begins to click. The norming phase is characterized by cohesion, productivity, compliance, and roles.

Norming is that wonderful phase in your group development when everything comes together. Everyone knows the rules, the structure, their roles, and expectations. The competitiveness and conflict of the storming stage is gone and there is group cohesion, a sense of community, shared values, and a problem solving climate. Preconceived judgments crafted in the forming and storming phases dissipate.

During this stage the group will finally work together instead of in parts. Personal opinions can be expressed and controversial opinions are welcomed and met with open mindedness and consideration. According to Fisher (1974), the norming phase is where members finally "express fewer unfavorable opinions toward decision proposals." Norms can be decided-upon structures, but they can also be unconscious efforts towards a more cohesive group. What this means is that some norms are consciously and deliberately discussed and followed while others are integrated more naturally and members often participate in these norms without even knowing it.

PERFORMING

Performing is the final stage in group development where legitimate work is being completed for the group as a whole. The tensions are gone, the norms are set, and the work is being accomplished. This stage is characterized by tasks and ongoing communication. If there is a problem, this is the stage that groups will analyze the problem, generate solutions, pick the best solution,

© Monkey Business Images, 2016. Used under license from Shutterstock, Inc.

Adjourning marks the end of the group task and/or project and is the true final stage of group development.

and carry it out. If there is a presentation to be done by the group, this presentation would take place in the performing stage as well.

In Tuckman's original theory, there was an additional step known as **adjourning**. Although it lost support over the years and has been widely ignored as part of this stage process, we find it worthy of discussion. Adjourning or Termination occurs when the group has a clear ending point. Not all groups have a clear ending point, but many do. For instance, if you are doing a group project in one of your classes, there is a clear ending point. As soon as you are done with your presentation for class, as a group, you are done—there is no need for the group to remain intact because it no longer has a goal to accomplish. For some groups, the coming end is welcomed, and for others it is sad and bittersweet. Consider how you will adjourn your group.

Once all three types of needs have been met, humans will strive for the *esteem* need. The esteem need is the desire people have to belong to something, to share a sense of community. This need is associated with power and status; a general need to be recognized. The final and highest-level of the Hierarchy of Needs is called *self-actualization*. Self-actualization is unlike the other needs, in that it cannot be satisfied through your outer world, your peers, your family, or your friends. Rather, self-actualization is a need you must fulfill yourself. It is in this stage that people become fully and completely autonomous and fulfilled people.

Summary

Finally, this chapter walked you through the various stages of group development and introduced you to a few theories. We also discussed practical ways you can overcome the obstacles you may face. We discussed the reasons people join groups in the first place. We hope this chapter gave you a foundation of understanding that will allow you to function better in your real world small groups.

Author of Group Development Theory	Stages and Phases They Address
Tuckman	Forming, storming, norming, performing
Fisher	Orientation, conflict, emergence, reinforcement

Glossary

Adjourning or Termination: Occurs when the group has a clear ending point.

Complementary need: A need driven by a desire to be with people who complement our own characteristics but are not similar to us.

Forming: A stage where members meet, greet, and start to set up the perimeters of their group expectations, goals, and even rules. The forming stage is primarily composed of members getting oriented with each other and the task.

Fundamental Interpersonal Relations Orientation (FIRO): Is an interpersonal instrument designed to measure perceptions or feelings related to inclusivity, control, and affection or openness in groups.

Group attraction: Refers to the degree of force between one person and the goals and ideals of a given group.

Group goals: Goals that supersede individual goals and are accomplishments for the group as a whole.

Hierarchy of Interpersonal Needs: A theory that depicts the claim that humans have needs and that there are various categories of needs. It also suggests that in order for humans to be concerned with certain needs they first have to obtain the lower-ordered needs.

Individual goals: Personal aspirations a person has for joining a group that is separate from group goals.

Interpersonal attraction: The degree of force between two people that results in them coming close together or creating separation.

Norming Stage: A phase in your group development when everything comes together. Everyone knows the rules, the structure, their roles and expectations. The competitiveness and conflict of the storming stage is gone and group cohesion, a sense of community, shared value, problem-solving climate, and preconceived judgments crafted in the forming and storming phases dissipate.

Performing: The final stage in group development where legitimate work is being completed for the group as a whole.

Physical attraction: The degree to which you are physically attracted to someone's outer appearance.

Storming: A stage of group development referring to the conflict and uncomfortability that comes after the group has met and got to know each other.

Works Cited or Consulted

Feldman, C.D. (1984). The development and enforcement of group norms. *Academy of Management Review,* 9 (1), 47–53. (*A journal article which explores the development of group norms and why they are enforced.*)

Fisher, B.A. (1974). *Small group decision making: Communication and the group process.* New York: McGrawHill. (*Fisher's early book exploring small group decision making and how it is effected by the group development process.*)

Maslow, A. H. (1943). A theory of human motivation *Psychological Review,* 50, 370–396.

Research on affection at ASU is supported by the American Psychological Foundation. Retrieved October 2013 from http://researchmatters.asu.edu/stories/effects-affection-960.

Schutz, W.C. (1958). FIRO: *A three dimensional theory of interpersonal behavior.* New York, NY: Holt, Rinehart, & Winston.

Tannenbaum, R. & Schmidt, W. (1958). How to choose a leadership pattern. *Harvard Business Review* 36(2), 95–101.

Wood, R.J., M.G., Phillips., & J.D. Pederson. 1986. *Group discussion: A practical guide to participation and leadership.* New York: Harper and Row. (*A practical guide for small group decision making that has been updated and published in new editions for at least three decades.*)

Chapter 3:

Group Norms and Roles

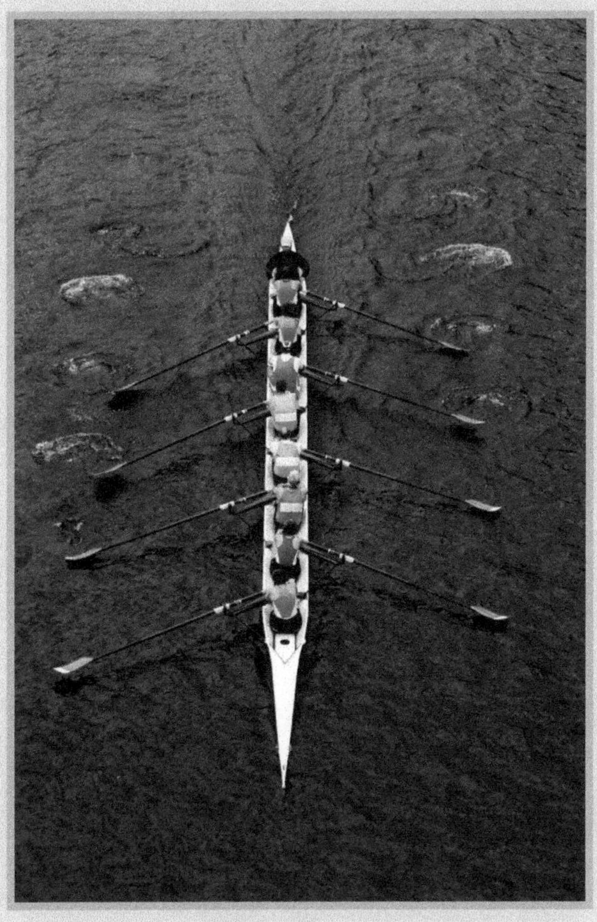

Chapter Objectives

- Understand the development of group norms.
- Identify task, maintenance, and self-centered roles in groups.

We now understand why people join groups and how they develop. It is also important to understand how groups develop their culture or the norms by which they operate. This chapter investigates the development of group norms in addition to identifying the types of roles we play in groups.

Norms

In groups, norms may be implicit or explicit. Implicit norms are rarely discussed or written down. Members of one group know how to act and behave. For example, as a college student you know that you should come into class, take a seat, and prepare to take notes. No one has to tell you how to act or behave. It's implicit.

Explicit norms, on the other hand, are frequently discussed. Often they are written down for everyone to see. So when you walk into the classroom and see a sign that says "No eating, drinking, or smoking," these norms are explicit, everyone in the group is reminded how to act and behave.

In addition to norms being implicit or explicit, there are for types of norms that may be implicit or explicit. These are: interaction, procedural, achievement, and status norms.

Interactive norms suggest how group members will communicate with each other. Will they take turns speaking? Is it appropriate to interrupt? Will you call each other by their first name or by titles?

Procedural norms determine how the group will get the job done. Formal groups use parliamentary procedure to set the procedural norms. Courts utilize a judge to determine if procedure is violated. Informal groups often develop implicit procedures that determine the process of the group.

Achievement norms set the quality and quantity of the group's output. In your project, your group may want to earn an "A." Thus, your group will need to determine how much work to put in at a certain level of quality to achieve an "A" on your project. Some groups set goals based on quantity. If you have ever worked a job that pays a commission or requires a certain amount of sales, your achievement goal is based on quantity.

Status norms are related to the influence that a group member has over the group. Some group members have status or influence because they possess a title such as president or chair person. As such, they may have more influence over the group's decisions. On an implicit level, a group member may influence the group simply because they are an excellent communicator.

*GET YOUR NORMS STARTED

1. In order to create conscious group norms, try collecting a long list of possible rules and expectations. Give every member a different colored marker. Print the lists off for all members. Have everyone mark their top five rules/expectations that they would like to see implemented in the group. Below you will find some potential options for rules in your group.
2. Members who are more than five minutes late are considered "late" to the meeting.
3. Members who are more than 20 minutes late are considered "non-attendees."
4. The first person who speaks remains the speaker—no interruptions until the speaker is finished.
5. Before votes are taken, every member must contribute an opinion.
6. All ideas will be respected and given consideration.
7. All meetings over two hours will have a 10 minute break after an hour.
8. Each member is expected to finish their assigned part by the deadlines or another member may pick up the task.
9. Group members must notify all group members if they will miss a meeting with at least a 24-hour notice unless it is an emergency.

You participate in norms everyday. Your main culture has norms, your sub-cultures have norms, and your groups and teams have norms. In the United States it is a norm to ask someone how their day is when you see them, even if you have no legitimate interest in the answer. It is simply asked for etiquette "norm" reasons. Most people respond to the question, "How are you doing today?" with, "Fine, thanks." Regardless of how that person's day has actually been, they will most often reply with "fine" because that is our cultural expectation and we understand people are asking out of etiquette not true inquiry. In your generation, there was likely a fashion item that was the "norm." If you grew up in the 70s you might have worn bell-bottom pants and long straight hair. In the 80s you might have worn acid washed jeans and neon socks. In the 90s you might have worn M.C. Hammer pants and a side pony. These were the norms then, and today we have norms too. What norms can you think of?

So what is the benefit of norming? Well, in small groups, norms serve to create predictability, which means humans will tend to feel safe. When we know what to expect, when we feel we know the rules and how to operate within a system, we are more confident and feel more secure. For instance, there are certain groups you might belong to now or in the future that require you to dress a certain way, eat a certain way, and even hold yourself a certain way; if you didn't know the rules for that group, you wouldn't feel secure. Knowing the norms of a group makes it easier to fit in, feel accepted, and function. It also reduces anxiety.

Consider this example,

"When I was dating in my 20's, I dated a man who was very wealthy. His family members were wealthy millionaires, and the people he spent his time with tended to come from privileged backgrounds. I was not born into a rich family. While I had some rich friends and certainly had good

FIGURE 3.1

[illegible]

manners, I had not been brought up in an environment of economic privilege and "old money" traditions. When I was invited to a group dinner with my partner, I didn't have much anxiety. All the people at this dinner were interested in having a discussion about a current court case—most members of the group had some legal background. My partner thought given my education in constitutional law I would be interested in helping the group discuss the case. I welcomed the opportunity. I hadn't really given the fact that they were all from highly privileged backgrounds much thought, but I knew my etiquette class from high school might come in handy. I really didn't have anxiety about the dinner at all, that is, until I arrived. The reservations were for a "members only" restaurant; the dress was business formal, which I didn't know in advance. My dress was nice, but it obviously was not nice enough for this particular restaurant or group of people. I became anxious and nervous. My heart raced and I felt clammy.

Everyone sat and began to discuss the wine list. One by one they provided their opinion followed by a display of competence with regard to wine. My turn came and I felt ill equipped to participate in the discussion, so I didn't. The dish for cleaning your fingers arrived—I remembered this from etiquette class and was proud of myself for doing it correctly. Some people think its warm water to drink, thank goodness I did not. Then the main meal was served followed by a palette cleansing ice cream before the next dish would come out. I had no idea what a "palette cleansing" ice cream was. Well, it was clear I was unfamiliar, and because I felt like I didn't know the rules I was quieter than usual and even awkward at times. My date was befuddled by my newfound quietness and at moments even embarrassed. Had I known the group norms, I could have participated in the group discussions and functioned more normally. Not knowing the norms of the group and the setting lead to a negative experience."

Understanding how group norms function in groups is important. According to Feldman (1984), "group norms can play a large role in determining whether the group will be productive or not."

A lesser known, but very useful theory, is one proposed by Tannenbaum and Schmidt. The Tannenbaum and Schmidt Continuum measures the degree of autonomy, self-direction, self-sufficiency, and maturity. Because this model is a continuum and not an actual process, it has the ability to be flexible and ever changing. According to the Tannenbaum and Schmidt Continuum, as groups are together longer, they manifest an environment of freedom and autonomy. The groups that are mature are self-directing and self-sustaining and the leadership role is more delegating and encouraging than telling and directing. In short, in the beginning of a group, the leader, or "manager" as the theory terms it, has a great deal of power and is highly directive. At the other end of the spectrum is where the leader should strive to take their team—towards the point where the team needs the leader or "manager" only for some minimal delegating and mostly for encouragement.

Roles within Groups

Every member within a group plays many roles that will determine the success or failure of the group. Each individual group member should perform tasks and play roles to help the group achieve its goals. It is important that people understand what they are responsible for when they join a group and how their roles and responsibilities will impact the work of the group.

A **role** is the part a group member plays within a group or the primary responsibilities a member has within a group. Based on a group member's skill sets, experience, expertise, personality, and appointed position or title, each individual member is expected to play their part as the group works towards accomplishing its goals. If you have ever watched a t-ball game where players are unaware of their roles on the field, you have likely witnessed the chaos that is created by this lack of understanding. As players progress, there is a clear distinction in the roles players have on the field. A phrase often discussed in the context of sports, and other contexts as well, is "know your role." This saying can be especially helpful for people new to small group work as they try to figure out how to make the greatest impact in their group.

TYPES OF ROLES

There are two specific categories of roles within small group work. Some of these roles are clearly defined and transparent while the other types of roles are more implicit or taken-for-granted within small group work. **Formal roles** are the duties and responsibilities that are assigned to an individual in a group. Formal roles can be assigned prior to a member entering into a group or can be assigned or volunteered for once a small group has formed. In small group communication courses, students often volunteer or are assigned formal roles once the group has taken shape. These formal roles may or may not be set in writing, but it is clear as these roles are taken on what is expected of the people who step into them.

The second category of roles within small group work is informal roles. **Informal roles** are the duties, responsibilities, and other jobs that emerge through the interaction of the group as they work towards their goals. Informal roles often work in concert with formal roles but the relationship between them is not necessarily stated explicitly or directly. The duties and responsibilities of

FIGURE 3.2

People may have to play very different roles in their small group.

informal roles are often not clearly stated, and it is assumed that group members will also complete certain tasks given their formal roles within a group in conjunction with these informal roles. If a group member is formally assigned to be the group's Assistant (see the Group Task Roles description below), it may be assumed that they will email out the minutes and supporting documents for upcoming meetings prior to the scheduled meeting time. It is taken for granted that group members will possess the transferrable skills of sending emails and attaching documents as well as be aware that this is an expectation of the formal role they have been appointed to or signed up for. Informal roles aren't as fixed or rigid as formal roles and can be exchanged between group members without the shifting of titles. These roles may often emerge from group work as a need is recognized. For example, one of the members in a small group who has a good working relationship with all the group members may take on the role of mediator as their peers vent their frustrations. Although it is not a formal role assigned to one member in the group, a member who has clearly established these type of relationships with group members may take on this type of informal role. Most of the roles taken on by group members start off as informal roles, but these informal roles may later become formal roles within the group. This can be especially true in a small group communication course. Regardless of the category a role falls into, formal and informal roles can help group members understand the broader set of task and maintenance roles they will encounter in small group work.

Member Roles

The specific roles, formal or informal, individual group members are held accountable for can be categorized into three separate sets: 1) group task roles, 2) group building and maintenance roles, and 3) individual or self-centered roles. Benne's and Sheats's (1948) seminal work on the roles of group members still informs the study of the small group process today. Formal and informal roles can be understood through these three sets of roles.

- **Group Task Roles** are specific task-oriented responsibilities that help a group work towards accomplishing their goals or fulfilling their charge. Task roles are specifically geared towards the work that is required to generate effective plans and implement those plans or solve a specific problem. For example, the group task role of every sport team is to win games. That is the actual task that they set out to accomplish each game, match, or contest. Sometimes task roles are composed of smaller tasks that are a necessary precursor to the overarching or ultimate goal/task. Football teams don't start on their own one-yard line and then magically appear in their opponent's end zone. Each yard the ball is carried or thrown in the air, down after down, contributes to their short-term goal or task of scoring a touchdown. First-downs are benchmarks that must be met during their march down the field. This example mirrors small group task roles that contribute to the ultimate group task or goal.
- **Group Building and Maintenance Roles** are specific relationship-oriented behaviors that help the group initiate and maintain the interpersonal relationships among members within small groups. Without constant relational maintenance work being done within the group to make sure strong relationships are created and maintained, small groups can get off track. Winning teams are likely to have a sense of commitment towards each other and the bonds between players are sometimes as important as the skill levels in certain positions. Without a sense of loyalty and commitment towards each other, small groups can let their tasks take a back seat to interpersonal conflicts. Group solidarity is a fragile product of the communication between members, and it is through the group building and maintenance roles that group cohesion is possible. When people think of small group work, their primary focus is often the task roles addressing what the group is trying to accomplish. However, it is the group building and maintenance roles that facilitate the accomplishing of most of these task roles.

- **Individual Roles** are self-oriented or self-centered behaviors when an individual within the group puts their needs, wants, and desires before that of the group. It would be misleading to assume individuals within a group are solely focused on what the group is able to accomplish (task roles) and how they are able to get along (group building and maintenance roles). People also have a vested personal interest in the work of the group. In Small Group Communication courses, the individual drive to perform well is often the desire to earn a passing grade in the course. In small group work within larger organizations, maybe it is a pending promotion which is driving individual performance within the group. This type of self-oriented interest is expected and healthy on some level for small group work, but when group members are consistently more fixated on their individual goals, it can be unhealthy for the group.

It should be understood that these roles do not happen in groups in a sequential order and that one role is not active in a group while the other roles are dormant. Task, maintenance, and individual roles are constantly ebbing and flowing throughout the group process, requiring both individuals and leaders to be aware of role-dominated moments and to work to balance the group so the group can function effectively. Role-dominated moments are times when the group is focused more on one role versus another. Sometimes group members deviate from the agenda because group members are catching up and working on building and maintaining their relationships with each other. Although this can be unnerving at times, especially for group members who are more task-oriented, it can be a necessary and helpful way for groups to balance other role-dominated moments that are likely to occur (e.g., looming deadlines and submission dates). It is very healthy for members and groups to oscillate between different member roles, but when more and more meetings are being dominated by a social agenda versus a task agenda, it might be beneficial for the group to recalibrate and get refocused. Balance is a key to successful small group work.

> TIP: There are a number of important things to keep in mind when dealing with people who display self-centered behaviors. Groups have to make a concerted effort to deal with these potentially destructive behaviors so the relationships within the group and the group goals are not jeopardized. Do not validate these self-centered roles by giving self-centered group members the time to distract the group from accomplishing their tasks.

Groups will naturally go through role-dominated moments and should try to rework or realign themselves to find a healthy balance between group task roles and group building and maintenance roles. It may be healthy for a group to be dominated by one type of role over another. It is natural for a newly formed group to socialize more (group building and maintenance roles) in the beginning, but as due dates approach it is also natural for a group to be more focused on getting the work done (group task roles). Just as groups can be dominated by certain types of roles, individuals can also get hung up on specific task, maintenance, and individual roles. In the table below, there is role-specific vocabulary that group members should be aware of and take into account when interacting with others within small groups.

Other Role-Specific Vocabulary	Definitions
Role Status	The formal or informal ranking, level of importance, or social or political position roles are given inside and outside of groups. Certain positions within small groups, and large groups for that matter, traditionally have more power, importance, and/or a status based on their position within the hierarchy of the group. (E.g., The military is known for its vertical ranking system and the roles that individual members serve carry with them a level of status or importance).
Role Reversal	When members within a group take on an alternative or contradictory role than they are usually in or expected to fulfill. (E.g., The group slacker stepping into the recognized leadership role. Or the person who is usually the biggest cheerleader or source of positive energy suddenly becomes a pessimist or the downer of the group).
Role Conflict	When members take on different roles within a group or within two groups and those roles contradict each other. (E.g., A group member who is a part of a movement on campus to prohibit alcohol consumption on school grounds, but is also a part of a fraternity responsible for organizing a big fundraiser and party that has always revolved around alcohol).
Role Specification	When an individual within a group is assigned, formally or informally, their primary role within a group. Often times, group members are assigned to specific tasks because of their expertise or skill set, or training or technical skills in a certain area. It is fitting that these members would be assigned to a specific role. However, sometimes very specific roles that require certain skills and abilities are assigned or taken on by people who do not have previous skills, training, or experience in an area. Also, some group members may gravitate towards certain roles because of their skill set or their level of comfort with the task. (E.g., As a soon as the rest of the small group finds out that you are a Communication major and that you communicate with ease and confidence, you are likely going to be elected to do the reporting out. Your skill set and experience will shine through in this case and it will be almost a common-sense decision).
Role Fixation	When a group member takes on a specific role within the group, or in other groups as well, and will continue to perform this role no matter what the circumstances are. There is a level of comfort and confidence that may provoke them to not want to take on new roles within groups. (E.g., Despite the qualifications or skill set of another group member for group secretary, a group member will not step out of the position).

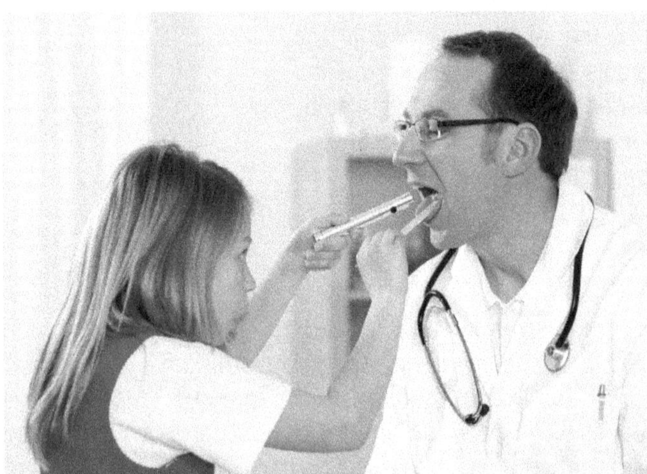

FIGURE 3.3

Role reversal can help you better understand another person's role.

There are many different group task roles, group building and maintenance roles, and self-centered individual roles that have been identified and labeled. The following lists provide you with many of these labels and descriptions of the roles these labels are meant to identify.

LABELS FOR GROUP TASK ROLES

Group Assistant: The group assistant is sometimes solely responsible for documenting and keeping the minutes of the meetings and other gatherings, and acts as the group's memory. The group assistant often helps the group get focused in new meetings by providing an accurate account of what was discussed and accomplished in previous meetings and events. Students who are tech savy, personally need good notes to keep track of their life, and those that really like to be involved and engaged often take on this role. It isn't always necessary to have a group assistant in small groups, but they are often a great asset to a group.

Acclimatizer: This group member helps orient the group in meetings and other discussions by summarizing what has taken place in the past. The acclimatizer differs from the recorder in the sense that they may or may not be responsible for documenting and keeping the minutes from previous meetings. Acclimatizers often have fond memories of their group work experiences and are invested in the work of their groups. Their insights and reflections are shared to help the group reach group goals. Acclimatizers are likely to pose poignant questions and interject pieces in group conversation that get the group really feeling comfortable and motivated.

Coordinator: These group members look for opportunities to collaborate and maximize individual's skills and abilities. Through their efforts to bring people together, coordinators want to see the group succeed and see that people are put in roles that will further the group in reaching their goals. A member in the group who may be very creative but lacks abilities using technology to bring ideas to life might be asked by the coordinator to work with another team member with more technological expertise.

Procedural Technician: Within any group it is important to have someone who has a specific skill set to handle the technical issues related to group work. Procedural Technicians may have experience with contractual language, scheduling, networking, material and equipment requisitions, and other necessary elements to help group meetings run effectively. They also help make group decision-making as painless as possible. However, sometimes their attention to detail may be viewed as group sabotaging behavior. A procedural technician is likely to forsee future holidays, library shutdowns, and other types of obstacles that will impact the group and will make mental note of it until they can share these ideas with group members.

Fire Starter: A fire starter is a member of the group who is an active member of the group through idea sharing and other constructive efforts. These group members are often the first to speak and to get their ideas in the minds of the fellow group members. These members want to get the ball rolling and might be the first member to move the group from socializing to a task focus. These individuals are passionate about the work that is being done, and they can contribute a great deal to the group.

Researcher: A researcher is a member of the group who seeks specific information in the form of facts, figures, and statistics to clarify ideas in the group decision-making process. Many students lack this quality in their student life, so finding a researcher who enjoys information and the hunt for information can serve the group well. Researchers often need clear instructions and a direction to head.

Opinion Seeker: An opinion seeker is someone who is constantly looking for the thoughts and opinions of other group members. Opinion seekers also often hope to achieve consensus within the group during group decision-making.

Information Sharer: An information sharer is a group member who provides invaluable information to the group in the form of relevant facts, recent research, and other informational resources necessary for the group to be informed about a given topic. How the information is presented to the group and how the group feels about the information sharer will shape how others view this member. If their attempts to share information with the group are done with arrogance or cockiness, the person can go from the information sharer to the know-it-all.

Opinion Giver: An opinion giver is someone in the group who isn't afraid to share their personal thoughts, beliefs, or reservations. Other group members might describe this member as always willing to offer their "two cents" for any given topic or discussion. The opinion giver, when paired with other task role motivations, can help the group a great deal, especially if people are shy or timid in sharing their thoughts. However, when driven by pessimism or when they lack a good work ethic, the opinion giver can complicate the group process as they get closer to their goals.

Elaborator: Elaborators are group members who break ideas down through hypothetical and real examples. Elaborators use a combination of critical and creative thinking skills to help the group understand ideas holistically. "Forward thinking" is a phrase used to describe these group members. They often help the group to understand the consequences of their decisions or specific courses of action.

FIGURE 3.4

[illegible]

Evaluator-Critic: Although this description may be negatively charged initially, the critic plays an intricate role in helping the group see ideas from a variety of perspectives. Through their assessment of ideas, this member's critical thinking skills helps the group identify the strengths and weaknesses of their thoughts and plans. This individual helps with both procedural and task-oriented issues. What gives this role a potential negative function is the communication style of the evaluator-critic. When an evaluator-critic communicates their ideas with the intention of pushing the group forward, the group process can be improved. When there are signs of insincerity, sarcasm, or what could be perceived to be negative motivations for sharing their criticisms, these individuals are not well received.

Energizer: The Energizer, who may also be thought of as the hype-person in the group, empowers others to do their best and actively contribute to the group. The energizer has a genuine desire to see others contribute, do well, and help the group succeed. Energizers often have an infectious quality about them, and their positive attitude and charisma can rub off on their fellow group members. Energizers are especially helpful when groups are down to the wire for deadlines or are working through obstacles in their group process.

LABELS FOR GROUP MAINTENANCE ROLES

Follower: The follower role is what most people traditionally think of when they think of a group member. Followers participate in the group by doing what is asked of them, doing what they are capable of, and above all showing their involvement in group work through their desire to contribute. In most cases, followers don't want or do not take the initiative to take on leadership roles. However, the follower role is very important: without followers, small group leaders would have no one to lead.

Encourager-supporter: This group member is constantly praising others for their contributions and is willing to lend an open ear to group members. Because of their positive nature, groups often like having these encouraging and supportive members around. These group members are often known for their empathetic or people-centered listening approach. Small groups need someone to stay positive and encourage others when they will undoubtedly start to question their work and the work of the group. Encourager-supporters can be invaluable to a group when they are also honest about what the group is doing and the quality of work that is being created.

Peacekeepers: Like this label suggests, the peacekeeper is someone who looks to help solve problems that plague the group or bring group members back to focus on the issues at hand. Their skills in mediation help the group resolve conflicts and function effectively as the group pursues group goals. Peacekeepers often act as liaisons between disgruntled or conflicting parties, interjecting comments when necessary but overall trying to facilitate peace within the group. Peacekeepers are often effective empathetic listeners who can sooth group members.

FIGURE 3.5

Compromiser: Finding a middle ground is the character of a compromiser. Compromisers help group members find a feasible solution by aligning ideas and minimizing differences between ideas and people. The ultimate goal of compromisers is successful outcomes, so they promote agreement and group decision-making. Compromisers understand the give-and-take relationship when working in groups, and they look to bridge the gap between disparate ideas to find a workable solution to group problems. Often times in small group work, the entire group will not agree on the course of action to take. It is about give and take with small group work. A compromiser understands this relationship of give and take and tries hard to help people to be more flexible.

Tension releaser: Known for his or her comedic timing and fun-spirited nature, the tension releaser gives groups mental time off from their daunting tasks and sometimes strained relationships. Tension releasers help to manage stress among and between group members by making friendly jokes, breaking up tension with their humor, and recalibrating the tension and stress levels within the group. An effective tension releaser understands the delicate balance between task related work and maintenance related work, and they know that too much work without a moment of downtime may be counterproductive. However, tension releasers who solely focus on the downtime, having fun, and being relaxed can cause a distraction to the group.

Translator: Not everyone is a great communicator. The translator may be better versed than others and help socially inept or introverted people get their ideas on the table for group discussion. Often effective at reading verbal and non-verbal communication, translators take what they understand from other group members and help to clarify potentially unclear or unvoiced ideas. In some ways they act as an advocate for the less vocal and less expressive group members.

LABELS FOR INDIVIDUAL ROLES

The following list of negative, self-centered, individual roles that people sometimes play in small groups should sound familiar. At the end of Chapter 3 of this textbook, you were introduced to a list of "Top Ten" people you would not want to have in a small group. Many of the individual roles described below have already appeared on the "not wanted" list in Chapter 3. As you read through this list of self-centered, individual roles that should be avoided in a small group, see how many you can identify as "repeats" from Chapter 3.

Aggressor: Often believing that their ideas are superior to others, aggressors want to get their ideas heard and clearly mark the ideas of others as trivial, misguided, uninformed, and/or ridiculous. Aggressors have the tendency to put other group members down through direct and indirect comments. Sarcasm, exaggeration, and other strategies used by aggressors are often hurtful and create tension within the group. Much like opinion givers, aggressors want to be heard. However, unlike the many constructive group maintenance behaviors group members can take on, the aggressor lacks the social finesse to be heard without hurting others. Their communication practices are marked with egocentrism.

Blocker: Unlike the optimist in the group who is always seeing the positive in ideas and in people, the blocker is constantly stopping ideas in their tracks. It is often their pessimism or discontent for group work that fuels their agenda of stopping progress by being negative, disagreeable, stubborn, overly competitive, and/or full of contempt. Sometimes, this devil's advocate disagrees for the sake of argument or exercise and could on some level really agree with the group and their decisions. Some people get pleasure and gratification from shooting down the ideas of others.

Monopolizer: Much like the name suggests, this group member's authoritative style leads them to try to dominate group discussions by interrupting others and asserting their opinions and thoughts without concern for other voices within the group. Monopolizers constantly want the speaking floor and to keep their ideas in the ears of group members.

Recognition seeker: The recognition seeker, who shares characteristics with the monopolizer, is constantly looking for the attention of other group members. These group members often boast and brag about their previous accomplishments and can be disruptive by trying to constantly become the center of attention.

Group clown: There is a fine line between helping the group to stay loose and release tension and a group member doing things to distract people from achieving their group goals. A group clown, who at times can be entertaining, causes more of a disruption or hindrance to the group process than amusement. Group clowns are often quite impressed with themselves and their ability to become the center of attention due to their comedic antics.

Dissenter: These group members disengage from the group process by acting disinterested, above the work or trivial pursuits of the group, annoyed by the work or by individual group members, and/or they just stop contributing productively to the group in any meaningful way. Dissenters are often obvious in their efforts to communicate their discontentment with the group and/or group tasks.

Self-Discloser: Sharing personal information is an important part of becoming closer interpersonally within a group. However, the self-discloser takes these disclosures to the next level by disclosing too much information and/or too personal information. Disclosers are often seeking emotional support from other members. By excessively disclosing they might receive some of this support, but in the process disclosers often get groups off their path in reaching group goals. Disclosers can often emotionally drain group members, impacting the productivity of individual members and the group.

Insecure: Insecures may or may not possess the skills to help the group accomplish their goals, but because they are constantly seeking sympathy and help from others, it is hard to determine which of the two cases they fall into. Insecures often use self-deprecating comments and self-putdowns to draw attention to their perceived inferiority and lack of skills. This can become a drain to the emotional stability of other group members and causes other group members to also take on more task responsibilities to compensate for the lack of productivity of the needy insecure.

Hidden agenda member: In some cases, group members enter groups and stay in groups for the wrong reasons. The hidden agenda member is someone who has a vested interest in the group that is heavily influenced by an outside factor. The selfish motives that influenced them to join the group can cloud their vision and behavior within the group, leading to conflict on a variety of levels. Although all group members have personal interests outside group interests that drive their work, most group members who join the group eventually adopt accomplishing group goals as a top priority. A member with a hidden agenda, however, can undermine and disrupt the achievement of group goals and objectives.

The list of labels above identifying group members based on their behavior is by no means exhaustive. There is just not enough room in this text to lay them all out here. There are a number of things to keep in mind when reading this list. First, it is important that group members don't look to label others. Most people are aware that although some labels are openly accepted by others, in many cases they can be taken as a sign of disrespect. Someone on a basketball team may be referred to as the team ball-hog, for example. In some cases, labels are owned and celebrated. In other cases, they are hurtful and mean. Word to the wise—use these labels to understand the behaviors of others and not to mark someone and the way they are in small groups. People do not always welcome labels. Also, use these labels to help make the most of what people naturally bring to the table as small group members. With the right leadership, even some of the harmful roles someone can play can be turned into something positive for the group.

Second, it is far more important to be observant of group participation and be concerned with the group's dynamics instead of labeling people. It is important that people monitor the behaviors of group members and balance their task and maintenance roles. Third, group members are likely to have a number of roles within a group that could be labeled, and these roles could change over time. In some cases, group members could exhibit contradictory behaviors. For example, someone could be the aggressor in a series of meetings, then have a change of heart and act as an opinion seeker. Lastly, people aren't the labels used to describe them. Group members are more than the simple labels sometimes used to recognize behaviors.

TIPS TO BEING EFFECTIVE WITH GROUP ROLES

Being an effective group member requires a lot from each individual. At the heart of this is communication. Without effective communication skills, small group work can become a burden and downright frustrating. When channels of communication are open, when the expectations for group members are clear, and when everyone clearly communicates their commitment to the work not just by words alone but by following through with their roles and responsibilities, small group work can be very rewarding. Understanding one's roles and the roles of others may be the first step to working through the process and producing the desired results of the group. Knowing your roles, performing to the expectations of those roles, and holding people accountable to do the same is the right way to make the small group process a successful positive experience. Below are a number of helpful tips to making the most of your roles in small groups:

- Step into roles that you have experience or that you believe you can be successful in for the group. People often "stay in their own lane" when it comes to small group work in that they continue to perform the roles that they have experience with. The group assistant has likely played that role before and had some success with it. When thinking about what they can do and are willing to do to best help the group, they will often fall back on these comfortable personas. Absolutely it is important to do what you are comfortable with in small groups, but do not limit yourself. In a small group communication class in college, you should be pushing yourself to try on different hats and take on different roles to see where you can thrive. You won't know unless you try. Although it can be scary, if you believe there is a role that you are suited for but are afraid for whatever reason to step into, you have to take a chance. Do not cheat yourself of this self-discovery.
- Realize that people are capable of changing. People are dynamic and forever changing creatures, and their roles in the group should not feel like prisons they cannot escape. Small group work is complicated, and one thing all small group members should understand is that the only thing that is constant is change. People are likely to bail on roles they do not feel comfortable with, do not have time for, or lack the skills to fill. The group clown is capable of becoming the emergent leader of the group. The assigned leader may feel that change is necessary because of other commitments they have made. Individuals and groups must remain flexible with roles to be successful, but above all, they must accept change and recognize change is possible.
- Realize that people can play a variety of roles. Each group member has task roles, group building and maintenance roles, and sometimes even self-centered individual roles that they play. However, they can also play multiple roles, both formally and informally, within each of these role types. Is it possible for someone to be both a follower and a tension-releaser? When it comes to group building and maintenance roles, absolutely. People can play multiple roles which are complimentary within a category of roles but also have contradictory roles within one of the three sets of roles. Is it possible for someone to be a harsh evaluator-critic but in other instances be an energizer? Absolutely. The goal at the end of the day is to play roles that are constructive for the group and the group process. A group clown can be so much more than just a clown if they allow themselves to be and if the group doesn't pigeonhole them to be just that.
- Since people play numerous roles in small groups, it is important that they begin to recognize when it is appropriate and conducive to the group to allow those different roles to be communicated out. There is nothing wrong with being the group clown until it starts to impede the group in reaching task goals and it becomes a distraction, disruption, and point of contention. Again, it is about creating a healthy balance in small group work between task and relationship maintenance roles. There is a time and place to really push each other to reach task goals, but also a time to draw back and lighten things up. It takes time, knowledge, and skills to know when and when not to bring those different roles into the group.

ROLES AND COMMUNICATION: CLOSING THOUGHTS

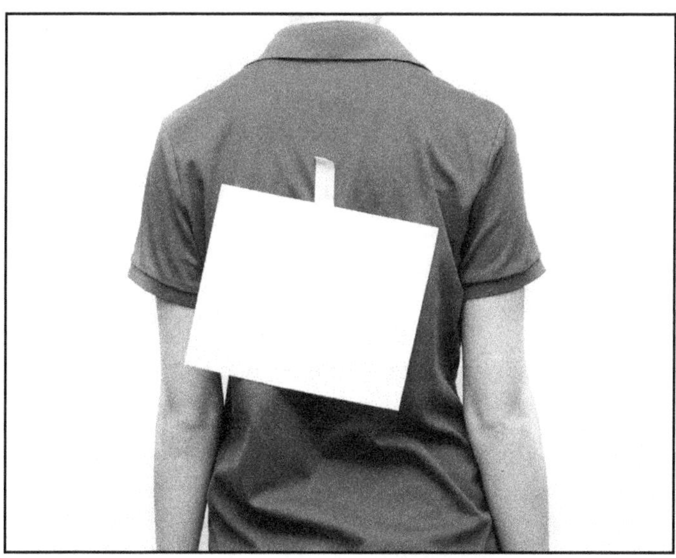

FIGURE 3.6

Regardless of how the roles for small group work emerge, communication is at the center of all group work. What people say and when and how they share those ideas with others potentially has meaning. While working in small groups, individuals should be mindful of their language and the ways in which language is used. Communication scholars unequivocally agree that nonverbal communication plays a huge role in how others interpret verbal messages. As important as it is for leaders to be mindful, empathetic, and emotionally intelligent, it is also equally important that all group members follow suit. Demonstrating communication competency through being both appropriate and effective while communicating within small groups can create a safe and conducive atmosphere for productivity. Treating each other with respect and civility and taking on a perspective of agreeing-to-disagree while working together can save individual group members, as well as the group as a whole, heartache and unnecessary distractions. Developing the skills discussed in this textbook and looking for opportunities to gain new communication proficiencies will inevitably help people in their personal and professional lives. Small group members should constantly be taking mental notes from all of their small group experiences in order to make better decisions in future small group work.*

Glossary

Empathy: The act of perspective taking where an individual tries to understand a specific event or series of events through another person's point-of-view while considering their current position and life circumstances.

Formal roles: The duties and responsibilities that are assigned to an individual or a position within a group.

Group Maintenance Roles: The responsibilities group members take on that center around the relationships within the group.

Group Task Roles: The roles that group members step into that are more centered or focused on task responsibilities.

Individual roles: Self-oriented or self-centered behaviors where an individual within the group puts their needs, wants, and desires before that of the groups.

Informal roles: The duties, responsibilities, and other jobs that emerge through the interaction of the group as they work towards their goals.

Role: The part or primary responsibilities a member has within a group.

Role conflict: When members take on different roles within a group or within two groups and those roles contradict each other.

Role fixation: When a group member takes on a specific role within the group, or in other groups as well, and will continue to perform this role no matter what the circumstances are.

Role reversal: When members within a group take on an alternative or contradictory role than they are usually in or expected to fulfill.

Role specification: When an individual within a group is assigned, formally or informally, his or her primary role within a group.

Role status: The perceived level of importance, power, prestige, or authority of a given role within a group.

Self-Centered Roles: Behaviors taken on by individuals that communicate a concern for self over a concern for others.

Technical Skills: Often referred to as "hard skills" involves specified abilities in a particular field that have been developed through a combination of education, training, and hands on experience.

Transferrable Skills: Often referred to as "soft skills" are skills that are essential to performing job tasks but may not have required specific training or education and are not unique to any one particular field of study or work.

Works Cited or Consulted

Benne, K., & Sheats, P. (1948). Functional Roles of Group Members. *Journal of Social Issues,* 4(2), 41–49. (*One of the first research articles pointing out the importance of small group roles.*)

Feldman, C.D. (1984). The development and enforcement of group norms. *Academy of Management Review,* 9 (1), 47–53. (*A journal article which explores the development of group norms and why they are enforced.*)

Tannenbaum, R. & Schmidt, W. (1958). How to choose a leadership pattern. *Harvard Business Review* 36(2), 95–101.

Chapter 4:

Leadership in Groups

Chapter Objectives

- Identify the relationship of power to leadership.
- Understand various approaches and theories of leadership.

Theories Previewing: Leadership and Roles

Chapter Four focuses on leadership and members. More specifically, chapter four investigates the relationship of leadership to the concept of power, approaches to leadership, and identifies several theories of leadership.

Five Power Resources

Human beings have been harnessing different power resources—fossil fuels, solar energy, nuclear energy, hydro power, thermal energy, wind power—to drive the engines of civilization. There are different power resources that you can harness for small group work.

FIGURE 4.1

In 1959, social psychologists John R. P. French and Bertram Raven published a groundbreaking study of power bases that identified five basic power resources used in groups and organizations. Their original article, "The Bases of Social Power," can be found in *Studies in Social Power,* edited by D. Cartwright (Ann Arbor Michigan, Institute for Social Research, 1959). The section that follows, with some modification, is based on their work. The five power resources you can use to influence the members of your small group are 1) legitimate power, 2) expert power, 3) punishment power, 4) reward power, and 5) personal power. When changes need to occur in your small group, you can draw upon these five different power resources.

Legitimate power: Legitimate power comes by being appointed or elected to a leadership position. For example, you might be designated as a "squad leader" by an authority outside your small group or you might be elected "team captain" by your team members. Your official title gives you a certain amount of power and authority as soon as it is bestowed upon you. If your small group officially appoints you to play a particular role in your group, you have been given the "legitimate power" that comes with that role's title.

Expert power: Expert power comes with specialized training or knowledge. For example, if your small group is tasked with building a structure and they learn that you are a structural engineer, your words will carry great weight as you give advice about how to proceed. Specialized knowledge gives "expert power" to those who possess it.

FIGURE 4.2

Punishment power: Punishment power comes with the ability to impose penalties. It is the main power resource used by despots, but even democratic societies use punishment power in their legal systems. Human beings generally seek pleasure and avoid pain. Penalties are designed to create painful consequences for unwanted behaviors. For example, a small group may develop a group guideline that motivates members to complete their work by specifying a penalty to be meted out if deadlines are missed.

Reward power: Reward power is the opposite of punishment power. Reward power comes with the ability to grant a reward or favor when behavioral expectations are met. If you are trying to get a horse to move forward, you can whack it from behind with a big stick (punishment power), or you can coax it forward with a tasty carrot (reward power). Unless you are in a group of vegetarians, carrots will probably not work as motivators in your small group, but you can draw upon reward power by offering appropriate privileges and incentives to group members when they accomplish assigned tasks or reach agreed upon goals.

FIGURE 4.3

Personal power: Personal power comes from possessing certain personality traits, like charisma. Charismatic people can persuade and influence others through the force of their personalities. Other character traits that produce personal power are practical wisdom and moral goodness. Practical wisdom gives a person the ability to make good decisions. Moral goodness gives a person the ability to aim for what is right and good and true. Practical wisdom and moral goodness are two of the main character traits that most people want in their leaders. Very few people want to follow either a good-hearted fool or an evil genius.

FIVE POWER RESOURCES
1. Legitimate Power: Being appointed or elected as a leader.
2. Expert Power: Having specialized knowledge or training.
3. Punishment Power: Having the ability to impose penalties.
4. Reward Power: Having the ability to grant favors or incentives.
5. Personal Power: Possessing certain positive personality traits.

Here are some practical tips for using the five different power resources:

- If you have been assigned or elected to a leadership position in a small group, do not over-rely on this legitimate power. Do not continuously assert that people must do your bidding because you are "squad captain" or "team leader." If you do not also use some other power resources, you may become "leader" in name only.
- To gain expert power, you must share your knowledge and expertise with your small group. Share your expert knowledge humbly, and your expertise will be acknowledged and welcomed. To maintain expert power, keep up with developments in your field of expertise.
- If you use punishment power, make sure the punishment fits the crime: impose penalties that are appropriate for the observed behavioral infractions. If the penalty is perceived to be out of proportion, people will focus on your "unfair" penalty rather than on the improper behavior you are trying to correct.
- Do not overuse reward power. Do not give incentives or rewards to group members for accomplishing basic tasks that everyone should be willing to perform. Otherwise, group members may lose their intrinsic motivation to do good work because they always expect an extrinsic reward.
- Develop personal power by increasing your confidence and your adherence to sound ethical principles. You can increase your confidence by increasing your competence and by believing in yourself and your abilities. You can increase your adherence to sound ethical principles by consciously choosing a moral code to live by and by periodically evaluating if you are living up to these moral ideals.

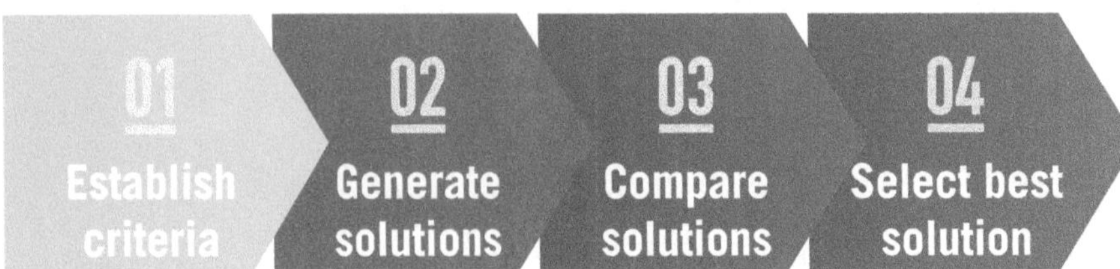

Steps Towards Achieving Goals with the Functional Perspective

Approaches to Leadership

LEADERSHIP STYLES

Behavioral Theory by Lewin, Lippitt, and White identifies three different leadership styles: authoritarian, democratic, and laissez-faire. The categories are distinguished by the degree of power and influence exerted by leaders onto their groups. Authoritarian has the most display of power and influence, democratic is mid-level, and laissez-faire is very laid back to the point that the leaders display no more power and influence than any other member of the group. Through the years Behavioral Communication Theory has led to distinguishing several leadership categories.

For instance, in 1978, Burns discussed the Transactional versus Transformational leader. The Transactional Leader is characterized as having power to discipline and reward the group for their work. The leader is evaluative, assertive, trains others, and inflicts punishments or rewards. The Transformational Leader, on the other hand, motivates the group to be as effective and productive as it can possibly be. Unlike the Transactional Leader the Transformational Leader will focus on positive communication and reaching group goals more than displays of power and influence.

More recently, in 2005, Carmazzzi coined the term "environment leader," which refers to someone who nurtures their group in an effort to impact the emotional and psychological situation of the group as a whole. This type of leader uses positive communication to influence the group and move it towards its goals.

As you may have noticed there are some similarities among some of these leadership categories. Scholars and theorists are constantly extracting new ideas from what they observe in the real world and trying to place those findings in various categories so that we can discern where we would fit and what kinds of adjustments we should consider making. In small group settings, research supports the idea that less authoritative and controlling leaders are usually more effective leaders. Consider the list and determine which type of leader you might be according to the information provided.

FIGURE 4.4

Transformational Leaders motivate the group to be as effective and productive as possible.

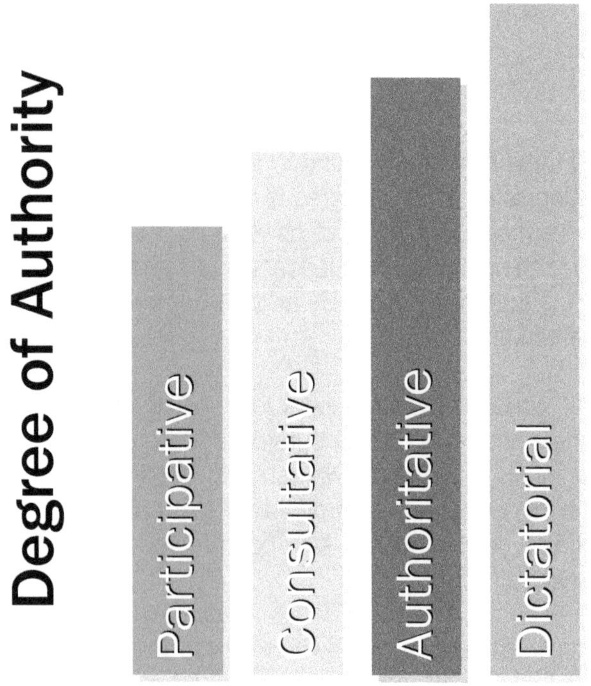

Degree of Authority

Participative

Consultative

Authoritative

Dictatorial

FIGURE 4.5

Not every leader leads the same, approaches tasks the same, has the same expectations or even experiences, but they also tend to vary with regard to their leadership styles. Over the years, researchers and scholars have come to accept four primary leadership communication styles. While others exist, the four discussed herein are used most often and determined to be the most common categories. The four categories of leadership style are: dictatorial, authoritative, participative, and consultative. According to **Leadership Style Theory**, the higher the degree of authority the more likely they will be dictatorial or authoritative in their leadership style.

Although the categories of leadership style seem self-explanatory, let's examine them. The *Dictatorial Leader* displays constant and total power of decision making and overseeing. A dictator-style leader tells others what to do and how to do it. The leader will hold them totally accountable for any outcomes. A leader who has a Dictatorial Leadership style will regularly use extreme means of discipline and be hypercritical, and often micro-manage. This style of leader will not solicit input from their team regardless of the skill and experience of that team. The leader believes they have the best ideas; they hold the power to make the decisions; and have little to no regard for the opinion, perspectives, desires or needs of others. This leadership style is not ideal for small groups because the nature of small groups is to work together, and the dictatorial style leader has no interest in that pursuit.

The second type of leader is called the *Authoritative Leader*. The Authoritative Leader does have a high degree of authority and power, but they do not exert that power as forcefully as the dictatorial leadership style. Authoritative Leaders are also called autocratic leaders by some researchers and theorists. Similarly to the dictatorial style, the authoritative style does not rely on the input of others; instead, they tend to make independent decisions. Unfortunately, this style of leadership is also not the most effective. Group members define these leaders as being bossy, rude, and controlling. This style is most appropriate and effective in small groups when the group is running short on time, and thus decisions must be made and carried out quickly. Authoritative Leaders are critical of opinions that differ from their own, believe they are the most qualified, are competitive to a fault, action-oriented, and rarely provide motivation or encouragement to their team.

The third type of leader is *Consultative*, which means they are highly task oriented, and considers and values the opinions of others. One of the primary concerns of Consultative Leaders is to create an environment that fosters group effectiveness. Consultative leaders are concerned with mentoring and facilitating the team by encouraging creativity, uniqueness, and discussion. The Consultative style is a great style to have in small groups. This style takes advantage of the members' unique skill sets and because this style consistently asks for the opinions of others, the effectiveness of the team is high.

The *Participative Leadership Style* is characterized by pure group efforts and a lack of authority. You will not see a Participative Leader assigning jobs and making decisions without consulting the group. Unlike the Authoritative and Dictatorial styles, this style allows the leader to consistently seek the opinions of others and thus have a high degree of satisfaction amongst its members and more desirable outcome.

THE NATURALISTIC PARADIGM

The theories discussed thus far have been widely produced from scholars and studies in research-type environments. The research from various studies leads theorists and scholars to come to some basic conclusions, assumptions, visions, and structures that help guide or evaluate small group communication. There is, however, another school of thought. This school of thought is called the Naturalistic Paradigm.

Fundamentally, the Naturalistic Paradigm seeks to discover ideas based on real world groups. In the majority of other theories we commonly use in small group communication, groups are formed for the purpose of examination, or in some cases, college classrooms are used as a means of gathering data. This data and group experience is limited in that the participants have a significantly limited amount of time to get to know each other, have little in common, are bound by external pressures (school), and may not have the drive, loyalty, or even interest in the group that real world groups would experience. As small group communication scholar Lawrence R. Frey (1994, p. 554) points out, "The ability to generalize from student, zero-history laboratory classroom groups to real-life, bona fide groups are limited, primarily because students unlike their real-world counterparts, have little investment in these groups and the tasks they are asked to solve, and because the laboratory/classroom setting hardly mirrors the significant contextual factors that impinge on groups in the real world."

FIGURE 4.6

Given these obvious limitations, some scholars have concentrated their efforts more directly on natural means of collecting data and deriving theory. For example, a study conducted in 1994 by Barge and Kenton found that the relational history within groups had a substantial impact on the communication patterns in the group, specifically during discussions. In the end, small group theories, although diverse, and some seemingly incongruent; are actually here to help us understand the world and predict the world.

Leaders and Leadership

In many small group communication textbooks, students almost always find a section on leadership that outlines the communicative behaviors of effective leaders. It has been my experience, however, that students read these chapters and wonder, "When are the authors going to explicitly discuss communication?" It is important to understand that everything a person does can be understood as communication. Hopefully after reading the previous chapters of this textbook you understand that both the verbal and nonverbal behaviors of people constitute communication.

During this discussion of leadership and communication, please begin to take on a holistic view of leadership that recognizes the totality of a person's behavior instead of focusing merely on what effective leaders say. Communication is much more complex and multifaceted than the mere list of words people use and the statements they make.

"Leaders" and "leadership" are not exactly the same thing. First, let's explore who a leader is in the context of small groups. A **leader** is a designated or emergent person who is held responsible for a group's task or charge. **Designated leaders** are appointed or assigned by either the group members themselves or by outside entities such as upper management or people in greater positions of power. **Emergent leaders** are people who, for a variety of reasons, achieve or earn their place as a leader within a small group. Through this definitional lens, leaders are either appointed or step into leadership positions, and they are held responsible for the actions of the group. Before discussing the different types of responsibilities held by leaders within a small group, let's further discuss designated leaders and emergent leaders.

FIGURE 4.7

Leaders lead with more than just their words.

DESIGNATED LEADERS

Designated leaders have also been referred to as Appointed Leaders or Traditional Leaders. There are countless examples in everyday small group work where a leader was designated for the group.

- Work teams within an organization may have a leader that was designated because of a variety of factors such as his or her competency level, expertise, experience in leadership roles, or plain out favoritism of the initiator of the small group.
- Coaches designate team captains. Hopefully this selection process is based on the communication skills of the players, their ability in and their position, and their capacity to encourage and motivate others. In some cases it is their popularity among the players on the team that catches a coaches eye and prompts the coach to appoint them to this role.
- Camp directors may assign certain counselors the responsibility of supervising certain tasks at the camp. One counselor may be put in charge of supervising the daily camp clean up. Another counselor may be chosen to coordinate the end-of-summer variety show.
- In some Small Group Communication classrooms, instructors designate small group leaders to handle communication between the instructor and the groups. Group members may also select a person, designating them to take on certain leadership roles in the group.

There are many other examples of designated leaders in companies, organizations, and even in families. The roles and responsibilities of the designated leaders have many unique dimensions created in part by the process through which they were selected and by the expectations put on them by their assigning parties.

The process of selecting a designated leader should at its best be strategic and deliberative. The people responsible for choosing leaders should have a formal or informal process that carefully considers all qualified candidates. That process may include testing for certain proficiencies and reviewing performance evaluations, but it can also be based on more subjective measures such as likability and reputation.

FIGURE 4.8

Designated leaders are appointed or chosen to their leadership positions.

However, there are times when the selection of a leader is not strategic and deliberate, but instead the decision is made haphazardly, out of convenience, or through obligation or tradition. That is not to say that a leader selected in a more casual way might not be a good leader, but the process of designating that leader might be a point of contention for group members. Whether strategic and deliberate, or done without any real planning or precaution, effective and ineffective leaders can come from either selection process. The most qualified can't always rally their troops to accomplish the assigned tasks, and sometimes the person who was just thrown into the position for no good reason proves to be a great leader for their group.

Designated leaders often retain the "leader" role or label until those who appointed them as leaders remove them from their leadership position or until the group becomes very dissatisfied with their leadership. If a group is very dissatisfied with a designated leader, the leader may be demoted, or they may choose to step down voluntarily.

Designated leaders sometimes face adversity when they are assigned to a group. When a small group is formed and a leader is assigned, it might stir up feelings of resentment which can cause dissent among group members who might question why this person was selected. If a designated leader enters into a well-established group that views the group culture as healthy and functional, the new "blood" of the leader being introduced into the group may be perceived as a threat to maintaining homeostasis or stability. Entering an established group as a newly designated leader can be especially complicated if the position the new leader is filling was held by someone who was revered by the group members.

Furthermore, when a member of a group is newly appointed to a leadership role in the group, the dynamics of his or her relationships with group members will inevitably change. This change may create new opportunities for the group to work more effectively together to accomplish their task or goal, but sometimes this leadership change creates interpersonal conflicts that can do damage to the group process. In an ideal world, whether a designated leader is assigned to a new group or an already existing group, the group would accept this person and their role and follow their lead and their vision in accomplishing the small group's objective.

Lastly, there is often an expectation that designated leaders will act and communicate like leaders. Designated leaders have been stereotypically known to take on the behaviors associated with their leadership position. This can translate into dressing the part, being more assertive, not fraternizing with subordinates, and avoiding other behaviors unbecoming to a person in their position. The relationships designated leaders have with their group members are often impacted by their appointed position. When put into a leadership position, it is often assumed that leaders will do everything they can to maximize the success of the group as they work towards their goals, regardless of the effect their actions may have on their small group relationships. Some of the negative stereotypes and connotations about new leaders may have been derived from this pressure to produce desired results and to focus on task goals over interpersonal relationships in groups.

Although it seems like designated leaders are likely to experience stress in their interpersonal relationships with their fellow group members, this doesn't have to be the case. It depends on a combination of two factors: 1) the directive leaders have from those who designated them leaders, and 2) the expectations of the type of relationships they want the designated leader to have with group members. However, just because a person is a designated leader doesn't mean the relationships they have with their group will be negative. It is really is up to the leader to make the most of their assigned role.

EMERGENT LEADERS

In other cases, another type of leader can emerge. Emergent leaders exhibit certain behaviors that may put them in a place to become a leader or to take on group roles associated with leadership. Some of the factors that may propel an individual group member to become an emergent leader are:

- The level of expertise or experience they have with a given topic or task.
- The efficiency and quality of their work.
- Their communicative practices and behaviors.
- Their passion and enthusiasm for the task.
- The inability of the current leader to effectively lead the group.
- Their relationships with other group members.
- The level of respect others have for them or their reputation that might serve the group well when sharing the product of their small group work.
- Other skills and abilities.

Rising to be a leader this way is organic and is often better received than having a designated leader put into a group. That is not to say that interpersonal and group conflicts might not arise and complicate the leadership of this person, but when someone emerges as a leader from within an existing group, their leadership is often perceived more positively and accepted more readily. For example, after working on a number of projects together with a student organization focused on campus life at her college, Kehlani stepped in as the new leader to help tackle the smoking policy. Her work, the respect she earned from her fellow club members, and how well she was able to communicate with college administrators on other issues put her among the leaders in the club. Although this responsibility would normally fall to the Student Organization's president, this emergent leader was supported by those within the organization and it became a natural fit for her to take this policy change on.

FIGURE 4.9

Some leaders are appointed, and some leaders emerge over time.

In the late 1960s and early 1970s Ernest Bormann and researchers at the University of Minnesota observed how leaders emerged in informal discussion groups. The Minnesota Studies established that informal small group leaders emerge over time through a "method of residuals." The small group unconsciously eliminates obviously unfit members as group leaders, and eventually the most appropriate small group leader is recognized and validated. Emergent leaders might find their fair share of obstacles dealing with group dynamics. In addition to the types of conflict described in Chapter 3 of this textbook, resentment by designated leaders or other group members who desired a leadership position may surface and create role conflict (see below for a definition of role conflict). Also, emergent leaders who step into a leadership role with the best intentions may take on the communicative practices or behaviors of typical designated leaders and alienate themselves from the cohesive group they were once partially responsible for creating.

Regardless of how leaders enter a group, by being designated or by emerging as leaders, it is through their communication behaviors that the group will succeed or fail at the tasks they have been charged with. Thinking through a systems approach to leadership, leaders will help shape the culture of the group (input), and depending on their skills and abilities to communicate effectively in any given situation a group might find itself in (throughput), will change what a group produces as a finished product (output). Now that it is clear what a leader is, the ways in which a leader may enter into a group, and the impact this type of leader might have on group dynamics, let's explore the definition of leadership and the major theories used to study leadership.

LEADERSHIP

Defining a word sets boundaries around how it will be understood. However, any word can have multiple meanings that increase its complexity, depth, and richness as a verbal symbol. The definitions offered here will hopefully start to shape your understanding of leadership, but please keep in mind that other definitions offer critical insight into leadership that is necessary for a well-rounded understanding of leadership. For our purposes (in the context of small group communication), **Leadership** is the ability of individuals working with others to think and behave (through communication) in intentional and unintentional ways to influence the thoughts and behaviors of others to accomplish a shared goal or goals. To better understand this definition of leadership, let us break it down further and tease out some of the important facets.

Leadership is the ability to communicate effectively to motivate others to produce at their highest level while also working together with the small group members to be productive and successful in reaching group goals. Leadership, unlike leaders, is not appointed. It is something people create through their communication with others. For example, it isn't enough for a leader to bark orders at the small group members. Leadership is about promoting understanding and empowering individuals to do their work and understand the larger group goal and feel like they are contributing to the success of the group.

Leadership is working with others to accomplish shared goals. Leadership by definition doesn't occur in a vacuum or in a textbook. It happens between members within a group through their communication practices. Communication competency accompanied by the technical skills necessary for the group tasks is a healthy combination of the essential elements of effective leadership.

Leadership is thinking and behaving in intentional and unintentional ways to make a positive impact on the group during the process of accomplishing shared goals. Thinking like a leader doesn't automatically mean leadership is taking place, and acting like a leader doesn't ensure that others will follow. Leadership is thinking and behaving in ways that group members recognize, acknowledge, respect, and respond to so that group members move toward accomplishing the group's goals.

Leadership is thinking and behaving in an *intentional* manner through language practices (verbal communication/oral communication) and behaviors (nonverbal communication). Leaders who are intentionally or unintentionally insensitive with their language or who fail to monitor their behaviors may not be living up to their full potential in their leadership position.

Leadership also embodies the *unintentional* because what is not said and done can speak just as loudly as the words or actions themselves. When leaders contradict themselves, it can call their leadership into question. For example, a leader who assures the group that their ideas will be heard at an upcoming organizational meeting but never mentions these ideas during his or her speaking time in that meeting might betray the trust of group members who worked hard on the development of the ideas. Leaders must constantly keep in mind that everything they do can have meaning to others. Leadership requires a command over verbal and nonverbal communication so the desired meaning is shared between group members.

FIGURE 4.10
Effective leaders help their teams reach their goals.

Leadership is influencing the way others think and behave through communicative behaviors and practices. Leadership is often thought of as an individual running ahead of the pack, helping the group find their way or get to their desired destination. Although this may be true in some cases, most small group work requires a different approach to helping the group find the finish line. Some of the most effective leaders are thought of as ready and willing to do whatever it takes to help their group reach their goals. That can mean running ahead of the group, identifying dangers, or digging into the trenches to do the work alongside fellow group members. It could also mean leading from the middle to keep the group's spirits up as they endure the trek ahead of them. Similarly, it could also mean leading from the back of the pack and pushing the group from behind while also getting them to push themselves. Lastly, if you follow this analogy, it could simply mean leading from the side lines and letting the group members who have the training and expertise run their race while providing the support they need to do their job. It is through their verbal and nonverbal communication that leaders seek to influence group members to complete their tasks. A leader's actions inevitably, on some level, influence the group members, and it is the intent of any good leader to be conscious of his or her communication in order to shape the way others think and behave so they can be more effective as a cohesive group.

Leadership is about reaching shared goals. When individuals step into a leadership position, they must be aware that something is at stake after all the work is done. In small group communication courses, it is expected that after all of the group collaboration and work, a final product in the form of a report or project will be presented. Leadership requires people to be cognizant of group goals and to help the group to work towards achieving these goals. It is often very simple: if groups don't reach their goals, the leader has failed to lead effectively and their leadership will be judged accordingly.

Leadership is as complicated as it sounds, but at the same time it can seem to novice and veteran leaders as the "easy lifting" in group work. Now that we have a working definition of leadership and its many components, let us turn our attention to theories of leadership. These theories of leadership have shaped how scholars and the everyday person have come to understand leadership over time. These theories are fundamental in building a robust understanding of leadership and the different lenses we can use to look at leadership and leaders.

LEADERSHIP THEORIES: MAKING SENSE OF LEADERSHIP

Over the years, scholars have attempted to identify and explain the phenomenon of leadership. It is important to understand the theories that have dominated leadership research and the insights each theory offers people who are studying leadership in the small group context. In Chapter 4, you learned about the Functional Theory of leadership because it is so important for leadership in small groups. You also were introduced to the Style Theory of leadership. In this chapter, you will learn about three other leadership theories: Trait Theory, Transformational Theory, and Situational Theory. Let's turn our attention to these five leadership theories.

Trait Theory

Trait theory, which is often referred to as the "Great Man" theory, was originally couched in the idea that leaders are born with characteristics that position them for leadership. This theory later adopted a more progressive stance that simply identified and demarcated the characteristics, behaviors, and traits necessary for leadership. Although most theorists and scholars in the field of leadership have abandoned the idea that people are born as leaders or that certain traits make people destined for leadership, this theory dominated leadership research for decades. In some ways popular culture, personal and family narratives, as well as the accounts of people close to famous leaders perpetuate this theory's popularity. When people say things like, "I always knew they were special and destined for greatness", and "there was just always something special about them," these comments imply that these special people were just born as leaders.

It is easy to see how the Trait Theory arose out of actual cultural practices. Generations of leaders from the Roman Empire to the Ming Dynasty were given their leadership roles by birthright. One

FIGURE 4.11
Statue of Gaius Julius Caesar

FIGURE 4.12
Statue of Emperor Sun Quan

line of reasoning behind passing leadership from one generation to the next was that these leadership qualities were in their bloodline and were a part of their noble right.

The idea of leadership through lineage has been rejected in modern times, so Trait Theory is one of the least useful leadership theories for understanding how people become leaders in small groups. You are not born with traits that will make you a good or bad small group leader. In order to understand leadership in small groups, you will need to move beyond the Trait Theory of leadership.

> Remnants of the Trait Theory still find their way into speeches and comments about leaders. People often comment on a person being a "born leader," or "always being the head of the pack." At face value it is easy for people who know leaders best to agree with these types of statements, but these assertions are more complimentary than literal. Most people do not accept that leadership is a trait people are born with.

Transformational Leadership Theory

Although less relevant within the context of small group work, Transformational Leadership Theory describes the rare and novel phenomena of leadership that has an unforgettable and at times revolutionary ability to create change. Transformational leaders exhibit qualities that help empower their societies or organizations to accomplish great and important tasks. According to this theory, transformational leaders display a combination of attributes that allows them to motivate people to go beyond merely accomplishing simple tasks. Transformational leaders transform their followers into agents of change. Through their communicative practices and behaviors, transformational leaders often have an infectious quality about them that has been described as charismatic, inspirational, passionate, and innovative. People like Martin Luther King Jr., John F. Kennedy, Walt Disney, and Steve Jobs might be labeled transformational leaders. Transformational leaders can empower people to reach their fullest potential.

FIGURE 4.13

Since Transformational leaders are most commonly political leaders or leaders of organizations or companies, Transformational Leadership Theory has limited applications to small groups. Like Trait Theory, it is mentioned as a leadership theory that you should know about, but it is not recommended as the leadership theory that will best help you to understand leadership in small groups. The last three leadership theories we will discuss, Styles Theory, Situational Theory, and Functional Theory, are more relevant theories for small group work.

Styles Theory

According to Styles Theory (introduced in Chapter Four) there are three different leadership styles: Autocratic, Democratic, and Laissez-faire. Autocratic leaders are people who have the resources of power and authority to control group interaction and decision-making. This leadership style is very authoritative and is often described as dictatorial. Communication from autocratic leaders often follows a strict downward pattern where orders are given from the leader under the directive that members will follow orders. Opportunities for input and/or feedback from followers or group members is limited or non-existent with autocratic leaders. Autocratic leaders might also be thought of as very task-oriented leaders who in many cases are worried about individuals fulfilling their tasks within the group. They are also traditionally less concerned about the interpersonal, or relational maintenance, roles within the group. It could be argued that this leadership style has its time and place in group work. For groups that are sidelined by interpersonal interference, an autocratic leader with a strong sense of task responsibilities might provide the focus a disorganized group needs to accomplish their tasks. This is in stark contrast to the other styles of leadership described by this theory.

Democratic leaders promote a culture of equality and participation within a group. This style of leadership is very much like it sounds: it promotes shared governance where participation is welcomed and there are open channels for ideas to flow between the democratic leader and the group members. Democratic leaders are often thought of as having a healthy balance between the task responsibilities and the interpersonal relationships of the group members. The communication practices of democratic leaders are often described as mindful, empathetic, and inclusive. Although this leadership style seems to provide a healthy balance between both task and interpersonal responsibilities, it could be argued that this middle-of-the-road leadership style doesn't help to produce the highest quality work and errs on the side of leaders wanting to be liked versus getting the work done. As with most things, there are costs and benefits to one approach versus the other.

Laissez-faire leaders are more observers in the frame of the traditional understanding of leadership. *Laissez-faire* is a French phrase that roughly translates into "let it be," "hands off," "be as it will," or "let do." Regardless of its rough translation, this leadership style is marked by a laid-back approach. For groups of highly motivated people who don't need or want micro-managing, laissez-faire leaders might be a natural fit. Groups requiring leaders who possess the skills to motivate and influence followers may suffer at the hands of this type of laissez-faire leader. Some of the negative connotations associated with laissez-faire leaders are that they are disengaged, uninterested, or apathetic.

The Styles theory can offer a great deal of insight into small group leadership. Understanding this framework for describing leadership styles can give a person a useful vocabulary for discussing leadership past, present, and future. However, it is clear that not every leader fits into one of these three styles. Hybrids of these styles exist, so pigeonholing leaders into one style or another may not work. Other theories offer important pieces to the historical and theoretical leadership puzzle.

Situational Theory

In direct contrast to Trait Theory and Transformational Leadership Theory, the Situational Theory of Leadership describes leadership as learned behaviors, not characteristics or traits people are born with. One of the earliest and most cited situational leadership theories is Fiedler's Contingency Model of Leadership Effectiveness (Fiedler, Chemers, & Marah, 1976). This theory rests on the idea that effective leadership occurs when leaders can recognize the type of leader group members need to reach their full potential. Based on the readiness level of group members or followers, leaders take into account the task and relationship needs of their group members and then use the most effective leadership behaviors for these types of followers.

Scholars Hersey and Blanchard continued the work of the situational approach to leadership and have shaped the field's understanding of the interplay between leadership and followership. In

Hersey and Blanchard's Model of Situational Leadership, leaders have a variety of strategies available to them as they interact with their followers and work within and around their followers' readiness levels. Depending on the maturity level of group members, Hersey and Blanchard recommend four distinct leadership styles which they label "telling," "selling," "participating," and "delegating." If you examine Figure 7.10, you will see that Hersey and Blanchard base these four leadership styles on how directive or supportive a leader needs to be based on follower readiness. If a leader needs to be highly directive but does not need to be supportive, then the situation calls for the "telling" style of leadership. If a leader needs to be highly directive and highly supportive, then the situation calls for the "selling" style of leadership. If a leader needs to be highly supportive but not directive, then the situation calls for the "participating" style of leadership. If a leader does not need to be directive or supportive, then the situation calls for the "delegating" style of leadership.

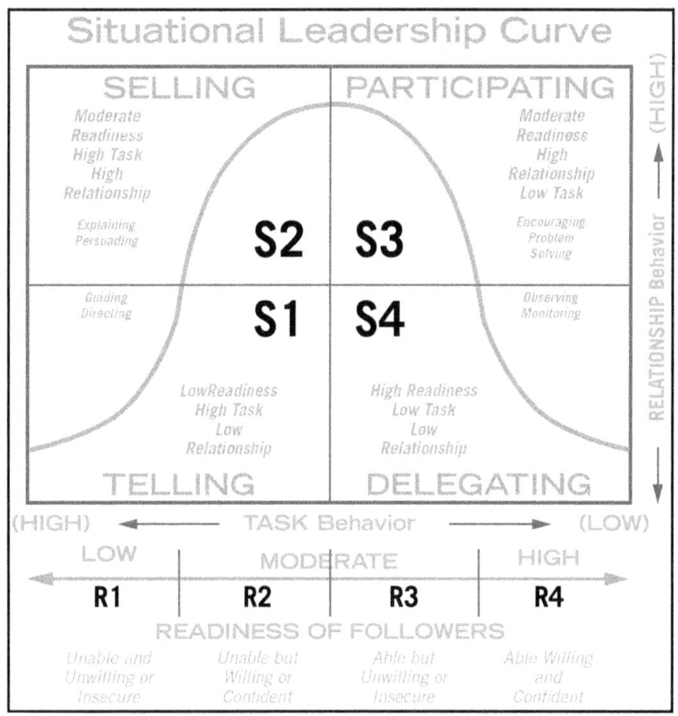

FIGURE 4.14
Hersey and Blanchard's Situational Leadership Model

If Hersey and Blanchard's Situational Theory of Leadership sounds familiar, that is because it has a lot in common with the Style Theory of Leadership. Hersey and Blanchard's "telling" style overlaps with the Lewin, Lippitt, and White's "authoritarian" style; the "selling" and "participating" styles overlap with the "democratic" style, and the "delegating" style overlaps with the "laissez-faire" style. Once these similarities and overlaps are noted, it becomes clear that leaders are not destined to be "autocratic," "democratic," or "laissez-faire" leaders, but individuals can adopt and adjust their leadership styles based on the needs of their group.

Hersey and Blanchard's work reveals that leadership styles, like leadership traits, are not innate and unchangeable. People are not born leaders, and they are not born with only one leadership style. There are many leadership styles that a leader can use, and each of these situational leadership choices may be appropriate for group members based on their readiness level and the larger context or situation.

Functional Theory

This theory focuses on the different roles that small group members can fill in order to develop and maintain relationships within the group and in order to complete the necessary tasks of the group.

The Functional Theory of leadership offers the most insight into small group work. This theory explains how small group members can share leadership by fulfilling many different small group roles. Leadership within this theoretical frame is not static but rather an evolving responsibility that can be taken on by any group member under the appropriate circumstances.

In the Functional Theory of leadership, multiple leaders with different skill sets (such as technical skills or communication skills) that will help the group function effectively may be necessary. Functional Theory could be understood as participatory in nature. Individual group members may interchangeably step in and out of leadership roles as the group works towards achieving its goals. This theory also captures the important and essential role effective communication plays as leadership rotates among the group members. It is through effective communication practices of leaders and followers that groups can come together and work through the group process to achieve group goals.

Summary: the history of leadership theory helps small group communication students and scholars have a holistic understanding of how leadership has been explained and studied. The functional theory currently offers the best insights into leadership for small groups. The "take away" from functional theory should be that anyone can step into leadership roles with the right skills and abilities and that communication is at the heart of effective leadership. Effective leaders also know when to step out of leadership roles to take on other roles in the group when necessary. Now that a theoretical base has been set for understanding leadership, let's consider some specific strategies you can use to become an effective small group leader.

HOW TO BECOME A LEADER

How does a person throw their name into the hat when leadership positions are being decided or are up for grabs? For those individuals interested in stepping into this role, it is important to have a clear understanding of what to do to become a leader. Leadership stretches beyond mere definitions and theoretical foundations, it is about taking information and putting it into action. It is through communication that this action takes place and leadership is possible within small groups. Sitting on the sidelines and never participating in practice doesn't get the team captain badge sewn onto game jerseys. It is a person's conscious efforts, good decision making, and effective communication behaviors and practices that put them in the game. Below are some helpful strategies that individuals interested in becoming a leader within small groups should consider:

- **Take the initiative**—If individuals want to step into leadership roles and positions, it is necessary that they put themselves out there, make themselves noticed and visible, and communicate in ways that complement their desire to become a leader. Demonstrating leadership qualities such as confidence, competence, empathy, and the willingness to lead others can propel hopeful leaders into a new position in their small group.

- **Get involved and stay involved**—It is one thing to take the initiative and make it known that leadership is something an individual desires, but it is another thing to be an active member and to have experiences that strengthen one's candidacy for leadership. Sometimes when small group members do not get or earn the roles they desire, they disengage. Staying active and involved is a sign of leadership, and who knows when the next leader will be needed or called on?

- **Put yourself in good positions**—Being involved is important, but a caveat to "being involved" should be, being involved in the right things. In situations where leadership positions are designated, it is important to be seen by the right people and to make one's work noticed. Individuals who are fixated on certain roles may find themselves stagnating when it comes to progressing into other leadership roles. Aspiring leaders must be strategic in the things they get themselves involved with: strategy is needed both for leadership roles that are designated or in situations where leaders emerge.

- **Work with your heart**—Although becoming a leader may require some careful planning and strategic decision making about what to get involved with, doing work with one's heart is also a very attractive quality of future leaders. People want to get involved with others on projects and in small groups who have a passion, infectious enthusiasm, and devotion towards the tasks of the group. Working with one's heart is the labor of love that is often admired by group members and individuals outside the group as well. It should be clear to others that an individual is doing something because they want to, not because they have to. People perceive this drive and determination in a very positive light.

- **Hone your skills**—Leadership requires a whole host of skills and abilities that are not gained overnight. Individuals looking to step into leadership roles must constantly work on the technical and transferrable skills necessary to be thought of as "leadership material." **Technical skills**, which are often referred to as "hard skills," involve specified abilities in a particular field that have been developed through a combination of education, training, and hands-on experience. Certain small group leadership roles may require specific skill sets to fulfill these roles effectively. **Transferrable skills**, which are often referred to as "soft skills," are skills that are essential to performing job tasks but may not have required specific training or education and are not unique to any one particular field of study or work. Communication skills, organizational skills, and the ability to work well in groups are a few of the other skills traditionally grouped under this concept of transferrable skills.

- **Build strong relationships with others**—Group members are much more likely to work with and for leaders they have built strong relationships with. Initiating, building, and maintaining healthy relationships with group members can also create an environment of social support, increased commitment to group tasks and goals, and group cohesion. Appropriate self-disclosure, a balanced approach to both task and group maintenance roles, and trying to understand group members as both individuals and as contributing group members are ways to work toward creating cohesive relationships. Lastly, group work is much more enjoyable when strong and healthy relationships have been forged which can impact group members' perceptions and memories of small group work.

- **Be persistent**—Not everyone who desires a leadership position or role is assigned that position or rises to leadership within small groups. Hopeful and aspiring leaders have to stay consistently persistent when they want to step into leadership roles.

Even with an aspiring leader's best intentions and efforts, implementing these strategies will not guarantee that an individual will become a leader. These tips should help hopeful leaders conceptualize how to become a leader and to put these constructive practices to work for them. These recommendations should also not be thought of as mutually exclusive or isolated. These strategies should be implemented in combination with each

Leadership requires more than the label of "leader." Effective leadership comes in all shapes and sizes, but communication is at the heart of any leadership style.

FIGURE 4.15

Leaders share their thoughts and opinions with others.

other within small group contexts. In addition to other tips and strategies, these suggestions can be helpful as individuals seek to fulfill leadership positions.

Once individuals have been appointed into a leadership position or have emerged from within a small group or organization as a leader, there are a combination of attributes and communication practices they should demonstrate within their small groups. In his instrumental book on leadership, Bennis (2003) highlights the essential ingredients for effective leadership. According to Bennis, leaders should have or demonstrate:

- **Guiding vision**—Effective leaders must have an understanding of how to arrive at their desired goal or goals. In some cases, effective leaders' divergent and critical thinking allows them to envision the best path for the group to take. In other instances, effective leaders understand the landscape is unpredictable but have experience seeing their way through potentially difficult tasks and shaky environments.
- **Passion**—Leaders who care about and are enthusiastic about the tasks their group is charged with are much more likely to see things through to the end. It is a leader's passion that creates a culture of dedication and drive within the group.
- **Integrity**—Self-knowledge, knowledge, and understanding.
- **Integrity based on trust**—Establish a rapport with people and reinforce that relationship based on trust in the actions a leader takes.
- **Curiosity and daringness**—Leaders who have a healthy dose of curiosity and inquisitiveness can inspire others, foster productivity, and promote divergent thinking.

Leaders who are able to effectively incorporate these ingredients into their leadership potentially lay a sound and stable foundation for small group work. When leaders act as visionaries for the group and are not blinded by their own ambition or arrogance, are passionate about the work they are doing and the people they are doing it with, have integrity and have created trust amongst group members, and are willing and can successfully get others on board to be curious and unconventional, small groups can be highly functional and productive. Campaign organizers who use these ingredients to motivate their work teams and small groups are prime examples of how these elements are used. These ingredients can help aspiring leaders to create something great.

In addition to these very important ingredients for leadership, a few others could be added to make this a recipe for effective leadership. These additional elements are:

- **Empathy**—Although empathy was mentioned in passing in a previous section, it can't be stressed enough how this communicative behavior can produce catharsis interpersonally and within small groups. **Empathy** is the act of perspective taking where an individual tries to understand a specific event or series of events through another person's point-of-view while considering their current position and life circumstances. Leaders who are metaphorically able to step into the shoes of others often are afforded a vantage point that can reveal much needed insight into their leadership style with these group members. Empathy, on some level, embodies what Daniel Goleman (2005) describes as "emotional intelligence." People, and especially leaders, must demonstrate emotional intelligence if they want to truly listen to their followers and provide them the feedback, resources, or help they need to accomplish their tasks or solve their problems. On some level, the human brain is wired to sense the emotional states of others (Goleman, 2007). Being receptive to this connection and open to others makes empathy a potent ingredient to successful leadership.
- **Effective Communication**—The effectiveness of communication practices and behaviors of leaders, and all small group members for that matter, cannot be stressed enough. This is especially true for leaders. Hopefully it is now clear that anything and everything a person does potentially has meaning for others. It is what a person does which allows all parties involved to create a shared meaning or understanding. Through communication it is possible for co-communicators to create ideas of integrity and demonstrate their attributes through their verbal and nonverbal communication.

There are infinite variables to consider when leading others, and it would be ostentatious to think anyone is capable of considering all factors. However, the ingredients, strategies, and practices mentioned above will help any leader be more effective in their small groups. When reading about how-to-do something, it is often helpful to consider what-not-to-do as well. By being aware of potentially destructive and counterproductive behaviors by people in leadership positions, people can communicate in ways to avoid these potentially damaging behaviors. Hackman and Johnson (2013) outline the "bad" or "toxic" side to leadership by identifying the following characteristics of poor or ineffective leaders:

- **Selfish**—Being self-centered, ego-centric, and/or narcissistic
- **Cognitive Errors**—Poor decision making
- **Environmental Factors**—External forces that create barriers or situations for ineffective leadership
- **Incompetent**—Lacking the desire or skill to be effective
- **Rigid**—Inflexibility, stubbornness, and unwillingness to change
- **Intemperate**—A combination of lack of self-control and followership that is unwilling or unable to intervene
- **Callous**—Cold, uncaring, and/or unkind
- **Corrupt**—Unethical behaviors such as lying, cheating, or stealing driven by self-interest
- **Insular**—They minimize, disregard, or ignore the impact of their actions (both intentional and unintentional actions)
- **Evil**—Intentional acts to inflict physical and/or psychological pain

FIGURE 4.16

It is easy to spot how these characteristics could breed contempt and frustration among group members. When leaders communicate these different characteristics verbally and non-verbally to their group members it can negatively impact their small group. These characteristics may be communicated directly and explicitly, but they might also be communicated indirectly and implicitly through unintentional messages. Leaders who are conscious of their communication practices and take on an other-orientation in their leadership will avoid many of these "toxic" behaviors. When leaders are able to put the group, group tasks, and group goals in front of concerns for themselves, issues of selfishness, lack of control, and corruption can become non-issues. What separates effective leaders from ineffective leaders are a number of characteristics and behaviors that revolve around being mindful, collaborative, flexible, and conscious of their communication practices.

As people step into leadership roles, they should be cognizant of their communication and the meanings they are helping to create with their group members by their words and actions. Let the essential ingredients of effective leaders and the additional tips in this chapter, and this entire book, guide the way leadership is created in small groups. Remember, there isn't a "right way" to lead. However, there are a lot of ways leaders can get off the path while trying to help their group accomplish their goals.

Summary

This chapter covered the difference between leaders and leadership, explained how leaders enter into groups, covered the five major theories traditionally used to study leadership, and highlighted some strategies for becoming an effective leader. Leadership is a lot more complicated than people just calling themselves leaders and bossing others around. Effective leadership encompasses individuals being fluid, adaptable, and willing to do whatever it takes to help the group succeed. Communication is at the heart of effective leadership, and if leaders cannot communicate their ideas clearly to group members and effectively listen to the ideas of others, a whole host of issues can arise.

In addition, this chapter went over the different categories of roles and the different roles of individual group members. Remember, communication is at the heart of all group work, and the ways in which group members behave as they work towards their goals will greatly influence the group process including how tasks are approached and completed as well as how interpersonal relationships within small groups are built and maintained. For the last time, there isn't a right way to lead or participate in groups. There are a lot of destructive and counterproductive behaviors that can be avoided with this newfound understanding of leadership and roles.

Glossary

Autocratic leaders: People who have the resources of power and authority to use as a controlling factor of group interaction and decision-making.

Democratic leaders: Leaders that promote a culture of equality and participation within a group.

Designated leaders: These leaders are appointed or assigned by both/either the group members or outside entities such as upper management, specific offices, or people in greater positions of power.

Emergent leaders: People who, for a variety of reasons, achieve their place as a leader within a small group.

Empathy: The act of perspective taking where an individual tries to understand a specific event or series of events through another person's point-of-view while considering their current position and life circumstances.

Expert power: One of the five basic power resources. A person with special knowledge or training has expert power.

Extrinsic rewards: Incentives such as money, gifts, or recognition that can be used to motivate people to accomplish tasks or reach goals.

Formal roles: The duties and responsibilities that are assigned to an individual or a position within a group.

Functional Theory: Created by Dennis Gouran and Randy Hirokawa, this theory focuses on how the group functions and the behaviors that members enact.

Intrinsic motivation: The inner drive that people have to accomplish tasks or reach goals. Extrinsic rewards can reduce or eliminate intrinsic motivation.

Leader: A designated or emergent person or people who are held responsible for group members and the group's task or charge.

Leadership: The ability of individuals working with others to think and behave (through communication) in intentional and unintentional ways that potentially influence the thoughts and behaviors of others in their pursuit to accomplish a shared goal or goals.

Legitimate power: One of the five basic power resources. A person who is appointed or elected to a leadership position has legitimate power.

Personal power: One of the five basic power resources. A person with charisma, moral virtue, wisdom, and other positive personal attributes has personal power.

Power imbalances: Power imbalances occur when one or a few people hold(s) power and other parties feel powerless.

Punishment power: One of the five basic power resources. A person with the ability to impose penalties or punishments has punishment power.

Resistance: Resistance is a response to a power imbalance. People who feel that they do not have enough power may resist those who have more power.

Reward power: One of the five basic power resources. A person with the ability to provide favors or incentives to others has reward power.

Trait Theory: Based on various research, asserts that successful leaders tend to have a certain set of attributes or traits.

Works Cited or Consulted

Asch, S.E. (1956). Studies of independence and conformity: A minority of one against a unanimous majority. *Psychological Monographs,* 70(9). (*One of the first research articles on conformity.*)

Benne, K., & Sheats, P. (1948). Functional Roles of Group Members. *Journal of Social Issues,* 4(2), 41–49. (*One of the first research articles pointing out the importance of small group roles.*)

Bennis, W. (2003). *On Becoming a Leader: The Leadership Classic Updated and Expanded* (2nd ed.). New York, New York: Basic Books. (*Respected leadership expert Warren Bennis updates his classic treatise on what it takes to be an effective leader.*)

Bormann, E. (1975) *Discussion and Group Methods: Theory and Practice* (2nd ed.). New York: Harper and Row. (*In this 1970s textbook, Ernest Bormann describes The Minnesota Studies and explains how researchers identified and labeled the stages of emergent leadership in discussion groups.)*

Fiedler, F.E., Chemers, N.M., & L. Mahar, L. (1976). *Improving Leadership Effectiveness: The Leader Match Concept.* New York, New York: Wiley. (*Fiedler, Chemers, and Mahar refine and improve their leadership training method which has leaders match their leadership style to their job situations.*)

French, R.P., John, & Raven, Bertram. (1959). The bases of social power. In Cartwright, D. (Ed.), *Studies in social power* (pp. 150–167). Ann Arbor, MI: Institute for Social Research. (*The original research article that introduced the idea of five power resources.*)

Frey, R., Larry. (1994). *Group communication in context: Studies of natural groups.* Mahwah, NJ: Lawrence Eribaum Associates Inc. (*A book-length work which explores the characteristics of natural groups and how they differ from small groups in labs and classrooms.*)

Goleman, D. (2006). *Emotional Intelligence: Why it Can Matter More than IQ* (10th Anniversary Edition). New York, New York: Bantam Books. (*A groundbreaking work that provides solid evidence for the importance of emotion management. Chapter 10 focuses on "managing with heart."*)

Goleman, D. (2007). *Social Intelligence: The New Science of Human Relationships.* New York, New York: Bantam Books. (*In his follow-up to Emotional Intelligence, Goleman uses the latest findings in brain science and biology to argue that our interpersonal relationships are crucial for our well-being. He gives business leaders and teachers insights into how to inspire the best in those they lead.*)

Gouran, Dennis and Hirokawa, R. (1983). The role of communication in decision-making groups: A functional perspective. In Mary Mander (ed.) *Communications in Transition* (pp. 168–185). New York: Praeger. (*A useful chapter explaining the functional theory of small group decision making.*)

Hackman, M., & Johnson, C. (2013). *Leadership: A Communication Perspective* (6th ed.). Long Grove, Illinois: Waveland Press. (*Michael Hackman and Craig Johnson update their best-selling textbook that stresses the importance of communication competence in leadership. If there is one book to own related to leadership in small groups, this is it.*)

Hammer, M.R., Bennett, M.J., & Wiseman, R. (2003). The intercultural development inventory: A measure of intercultural sensitivity, *International journal of intercultural relations, 27*, 421–443. (*The first version of the Intercultural Conflict Style Inventory which recognizes different cultural approaches to conflict.*)

Lewin, K., Lippitt, R. and White, R.K. (1939). Patterns of aggressive behavior in experimentally created social climates. *Journal of Social Psychology*, 10, 271–301. (*An early article that examines the effects of autocratic, democratic, and laissez-faire leadership.*)

Miller, G.R., & Steinberg, M. (1975). *Between people: A new analysis of interpersonal communication.* Chicago: Science Research Associates. (*Miller and Steinberg introduce the idea of pseudo conflict, simple conflict, and ego conflict in this book focusing on interpersonal communication.*)

Rothwell, J.D. (2013). Power in groups: A central dynamic. In *In mixed company: Communicating in small groups and teams* (8th ed.) (pp. 300–343). Wadsworth Cengage Learning. (*Rothwell devotes an entire chapter of his small group communication textbook to the dynamics of power in small groups.*)

Shannon, C.E., Weaver, W. (1949). *The mathematical theory of communication.* Urbana, IL: University of Illinois Press. (*A work that helped to establish the study of Communication as a social science field with precise technical terms.*)

Thomas, W., Kenneth, & Kilmann, H., Ralph. (n.d.). An overview of the Thomas-Kilmann conflict mode instrument (TKI). Retrieved March 24, 2016, from http://www.kilmanndiagnostics.com/overview-thomas-kolmann-conflict-mode-instrument-tki. (*Thomas and Kilmann provide a brief explanation of the five conflict management strategies that their diagnostic tool is designed to identify.*)

Tuddenham, R.D., MacBride, P., and Zahn, V. 1958. The influence of the sex composition of the group upon yielding to a distorted norm. *Journal of Psychology*, 46, 243–251. (*Read Tuddenham's initial published research on the attitudes and characteristics of conformists.*)

Weinberg and Gould, 2011. *Foundations of sport and exercise psychology*, (5th ed.), Champaign, IL: Human Kinetics. (*A best-selling introductory textbook on exercise and sports psychology.*)

Chapter 5:

Diversity in Groups

© Andresr, 2013. Used under license from Shutterstock, Inc.

Chapter Objectives

- Identify dimensions on culture that affect communication in groups.
- Understand obstacles to effective group communication including ethnocentrism, sterotyping, prejudice, discrimination, and the "isms."

To understand how culture may affect your communication in groups, it's important to examine methods to discern distinctions in cultures to help you understand.

We will look at Hofstede's Dimensions on Culture and Hall's Time Orientations and linguistic relativity. By comprehending these dimensions, you will gain knowledge as to how to communicate with your group members.

Finally, this chapter identifies barriers to effective communication in groups including ethnocentrism, stereotyping, prejudice, discrimination, and the "isms."

*Hofstede's Value Dimensions

Gerard (Geert) Hofstede is a Dutch social psychologist who worked for IBM International in the 1960s and the 1970s. As a researcher for IBM, he was able to access tens of thousands of employee surveys in order to analyze and identify national values in over 40 different countries. Over the last four decades, his research has yielded six cultural value dimensions that are now widely recognized and discussed in the fields of cross-cultural psychology, international business, and intercultural communication. Anyone working in these fields should have some familiarity with Hofstede's categories and the vocabulary he developed to describe and discuss different national values.

Hofstede's biography and a list of his published work can be found on his official website, www.geerthofstede.nl. According to his official website, a revised and expanded third edition of his book Cultures and Organizations (McGraw-Hill, New York, 2010) contains the latest iteration of his cultural dimensions. We will provide a very brief, very general summary of Hofstede's value dimensions in order to acquaint you with Hofstede's value dimension categories.

Hofstede's Value Dimensions	
1. Individualism	1. Collectivism
2. High-Power Distance	2. Low-Power Distance
3. High Uncertainty Avoidance	3. Low Uncertainty Avoidance
4. Masculinity	4. Femininity
5. Long-Term Orientation	5. Short-Term Orientation
6. Indulgence	6. Restraint

FIGURE 5.1

Hofstede has identified six different cultural value dimensions.

Individualism vs. Collectivism: In this value dimension, Hofstede is not referring to communist collectives, but to how much individuals are integrated into groups. People from individualistic societies value personal achievement and individual autonomy, whereas people from collectivistic societies value social cohesion and social stability.

High-power distance vs. Low-power distance: In cultures with high-power distance, less powerful members of organizations and institutions are likely to accept and expect that power is distributed unequally, whereas in cultures with low-power distance, members accept and expect more consultative and democratic power relations. High-power distance cultures are hierarchical, whereas low-power distance countries are egalitarian.

High uncertainty avoidance vs. Low uncertainty avoidance: In cultures with high uncertainty avoidance, people try to minimize unknown and unusual circumstances by implementing and following rules and regulations, whereas in cultures with low uncertainty avoidance, people accept and operate well in unstructured environments and changing situations with few rules or regulations. High uncertainty avoidance cultures expect an "official" voice or explanation, whereas low uncertainty avoidance cultures are comfortable with the expression of multiple viewpoints and opinions.

Masculinity vs. Feminity: Masculine cultures value competitiveness, assertiveness, materialism, ambition, and power, whereas feminine cultures value relationships, emotional sensitivity, and the quality of life. In masculine cultures, the differences in sex and gender roles tend to be more pronounced and less fluid than in feminine cultures. In feminine cultures, the differences between gender roles are less pronounced and more fluid, and both males and females value care and concern for others.

Long-term orientation vs. Short-term orientation: Cultures with a long-term orientation value the future benefits that come through persistence, saving, and the ability to adapt, whereas cultures with a short-term orientation focus on the past or present and value respect for tradition, preservation of face, reciprocation, and fulfilling social obligations.

Indulgence vs. Restraint: Indulgent societies tend to allow relatively free gratification of basic physical human desires, whereas restrained societies tend to regulate the gratification of basic human physical desires by strict norms.

Hofstede's work has provided a framework for discussing and thinking about cross-cultural communication. Many other researchers have supplemented Hofstede's original work, so you can now access charts and graphs that place most of the countries of the world on Hofstede's value dimensions. You can also take surveys that will reveal your personal value dimension scores. Both individuals and countries can be compared to one another in order to gain a better understanding of where they fall on Hofstede's value dimensions.

FIGURE 5.2

FIGURE 5.3

Hall's Two Types of Time Orientations

Although chronemics (the study of the way different cultures view and use time) is an appropriate topic for our chapter on nonverbal communication (Chapter 6), we will introduce here E.T. Hall's distinction between two different types of time orientation because these two different time orientations lead cultures to value different things.

Robert Kohls pointed out in his monograph that Americans value time and its control. When he made this observation in the 1980s, Kohls was very likely drawing upon the groundbreaking work of E.T. Hall that was mentioned in Chapter 1 of this textbook. In Chapter 1, we noted that E.T. Hall is credited with the establishment of Intercultural Communication studies in the 1960s, including the establishment of the study of the way cultures use space (proxemics) and the study of the way cultures use time (chronemics).

When he initiated the study of the way cultures view and use time, E.T. Hall coined technical terms for two different time orientations: some cultures, Hall asserted, were "monochronic," whereas other cultures were "polychronic." This distinction is now widely accepted.

On the one hand, monochronic cultures have a time orientation that views time as linear. People in monochronic cultures view time as something that can be segmented into precise units that can be used or spent. Consequently, monochronic cultures value time and its control very highly.

Polychronic cultures, on the other hand, have a time orientation that views time as circular or reoccurring. Since time is viewed as something that reoccurs or repeats, polychronic cultures do not view time as a valuable commodity. Instead, they subordinate their use of time to their relationships with other people. Polychronic cultures value human interaction and human relationships. The following table presents some of the differences between monochronic and polychronic people.

People in Monochronic Cultures	People in Polychronic Cultures
1. Do one thing at a time	1. Do many things at once
2. Adhere to plans and schedules	2. Change plans and schedules often and easily
3. Take deadlines seriously	3. View deadlines as objectives that may or may not be achieved
4. Are committed to task completion	4. Are committed to people and to relationships
5. Value promptness and being on time	5. Value socializing

FIGURE 5.4
Different time orientations lead to different behaviors and different cultural values

LINGUISTIC RELATIVITY AND HIGH- AND LOW-CONTEXT COMMUNICATION STYLES

Edward T. Hall is considered the father of Intercultural Communication. Hall was an anthropologist and cross-cultural researcher. Hall was fascinated by the ways in which people interact with one another. In his work, first on Navajo and Hopi reservations in the 1930s then later in Europe, the Middle East, and Asia, Hall came to understand that people use language differently, based on the values and needs of their culture. In the 1950s while he was an intercultural trainer for the state department he developed the concepts of high- and low-context culture in order to help American Foreign Service personnel better understand the ways people use language and do not use language in their interactions.

Low Context

It is assumed that communicators do not share a previously established context. Thoughts and ideas must be explained clearly, and meanings must be fully expressed in order to assure that everyone in the communication encounter grasps the contexts. For low-context communicators communicating unambiguously is important. High-context communicators often find low-context communicators to be wordy or micromanaging.

Some Low-Context Cultures	
Australian	Hebrews/Jews (Israel, Europe, North America)
Dutch (Netherlands)	New Zealand
English Canadian	Scandinavia
English	Switzerland
Finnish (Finland)	United States (other than parts of Southern US)
German	

High Context

It is assumed that communicators share a previously established context. As a result, it is unnecessary, and often annoying to explain every detail. For high-context communicators, shared contexts build mutual respect. High-context communicators respect the other person's understanding of situations and leave understanding to the other person. Low-context communicators often find high-context communicators to be confusing and ambiguous.

Some High-Context Cultures			
African (most)	Greek	Japanese	Southern US
Arab	Hawaiian	Korean	Spanish
Brazilian	Hungarian	Latin Americans	Thai
Chinese	Indian	Nepali	Turkish
Filipinos	Indonesian	Persian (Iran)	Vietnamese
French Canadian	Italian	Portuguese	South Slavic
French	Irish	Russian	

High/Low Context is about *how we process information (what we value as important)* more than it is about behaviors.	
High Context is where much of the meaning comes from between the lines.	**Low Context** is where much of the meaning comes from what is explicitly verbalized. (KapplerMikk, 2012)

Both high- and low-context communication styles exist in US culture to varying degrees. Whenever we can depend on a previously established context, we tend to fall into the shorthand of high-context communication. Whenever we know that we do not share previous contexts with someone or a group of people, we rely on the explicit directness of low-context communication style.*

**NONVERBAL COMMUNICATION AND CULTURE

Since many small groups today are composed of people form different cultures, it pays to be aware of different cultural behaviors and expectations related to nonverbal communication. First, some people are from high-contact cultures, whereas other people are from low-contact cultures. People from high-contact cultures prefer and are comfortable with a high degree of physical contact and touching. They may also have little need for, or notion of, personal space—they may sit or stand very close to other people. People from low-contact cultures, on the other hand, often do not like to be touched, and they may get uncomfortable if you "pop" their personal space bubble by getting too close.

Second, some people are from low-context cultures, whereas other people are from high-context cultures. People from low-context cultures focus primarily on verbal messages sent through the auditory channel. They tend to "take you at your word" and believe that what you say is what you mean. People from high-context cultures, on the other hand, focus not only on verbal messages sent through the auditory channel, but they also take into consideration other messages sent simultaneously through paralanguage and the visual and tactile channels.

High-context people do not always say what they mean. Instead, they expect you to pay attention to their nonverbal messages in order to correctly interpret their verbal messages. They may say, "I will try to do that," but they expect you to understand that their body language is telling you, "No."

When you are working in a small group that is culturally diverse, be sensitive to high-contact/low contact and low context/high context differences. Since we Americans are mostly low-contact people, we need to make allowances for people from high-contact cultures. People from some Latin American and Asian countries may stand or sit closer to us than we expect, but they are not intentionally invading our space.

Similarly, since we Americans are mostly low-context communicators, we need to pay particular attention to the nonverbal communication of people from high-context cultures, and we need to realize that they are not intentionally misleading us when they do not verbalize what they actually mean.

*From *Intercultural Communication: Building Relationships and Skills* by Helen Acosta, Mark Staller, Bryan Hirayama.

FIGURE 5.5

People from high-contact cultures have little sense of "personal space."

FIGURE 5.6

Sex and gender differences affect the way men and women communicate.

The high contact/low contact and low context/high context differences can also be applied to males and females. Generally, men tend to be more low contact than women, and men also tend to be more low context than women. If you are a woman working in a small group with men, give them their space, and try to send accurate verbal messages. If you are a man working with women, pay close attention to their nonverbals. If popular author John Gray is right in claiming that men are from Mars and women are from Venus, then interplanetary peace and effective small group communication depends on a sensitivity to sex and gender differences.**

Barriers to Effective Communication in Groups

Several factors related to diversity may become obstacles to effective group communication. A discussion of these barriers follows including ethnocentrism, stereotyping, prejudice, discrimination, and the "isms."

*ETHNOCENTRISM

"Ethnocentrism" is a broader term than "racism." Whereas the term "racism" refers to the belief in the inherent superiority of one's own racial group, "ethnocentrism" refers to the belief in the inherent superiority of one's own ethnic group or culture. If you are ethnocentric, you assume that people like you and cultures like your culture are good, desirable, and superior, whereas people that are different from you and cultures that are different from your culture are bad, undesirable, and inferior.

It is not necessarily wrong to conclude that some aspects of your culture are superior or better than some aspects of other cultures: human beings can and should make value judgments and moral evaluations. However, you are guilty of ethnocentrism when you assume that your culture is superior just because it is *your* culture.

**From *Small Group Work in the Real World: A Practical Approach* by Mark L. Staller, Andrea Thorson, Bryan Hirayama. Copyright © 2017 by Kendall Hunt Publishing Company. Reprinted by permission.

Ethnocentric evaluations are made without undertaking the mental work of looking through different cultural lenses or attempting to understand different cultural worldview frameworks. It is unfair to judge or evaluate another culture with your own cultural criteria and without having a clear understanding of the beliefs, values, and motives that are driving the people in a culture. This is the principle behind the Native American proverb "Do not judge a person until you have walked two moons in their moccasins."

You should not assume that everyone has the same way of viewing the world, or that different cultures value the same things equally. When you have made the effort to understand people and cultures at a deep level, when you have comprehended their worldview frameworks and value orientations, then you have earned the right to make responsible value judgments and moral evaluations.

Embodied Ethnocentrism

To be an effective group member, you need to decrease your ethnocentrism, but it is unreasonable to think that you can completely eradicate all ethnocentrism, especially "embodied ethnocentrism." Human beings feel comfortable in places that they recognize as their own—this is "embodied ethnocentrism." We often prefer and highly value our own houses, neighborhoods, and countries.

Even though there is nothing inherently superior about your house and neighborhood, you may have a strong preference for and allegiance to this physical space. In fact, according to many objective standards, your house or neighborhood may be obviously inferior to other houses or neighborhoods, and yet you may still prefer your house and your neighborhood, and you may value them highly, because they are "home."

Just as we live in a neighborhood and have a sense of belonging to our "home," we live in a country and have a sense of belonging to that country or homeland. The US national anthem refers to America as the "land of the free and *home* of the brave." The Canadian national anthem refers to Canada as "my *home* and native land." National anthems like these are played for the top-placing athletes at the International Olympics, and many Olympic athletes take great pride and pleasure in representing their respective countries. Although human beings may have a cosmopolitan perspective, they still have a need to belong somewhere on the earth—a homeland.

STEREOTYPING

Stereotypes are offensive because they assume sameness where sameness does not exist. When someone says "White people can't dance," the word "all" is implied: "(All) White people can't dance." If you are a white person who can bust a move and dance proficiently, your individual skill has been denied because you have been placed in the category of "Nondancing white people."

Even "positive" stereotypes are offensive, for the very same reason. When someone makes a positive assumption about a person based on a stereotype, they are still assuming sameness where sameness does not exist, and they are ignoring that person's individual personhood. Even the "positive" stereotype "(All) Asians are good at math" may be offensive to Asians, especially to Asians who are not good at math.

Stereotypes that assume sameness among a group of people are at the heart of many bad attitudes and behaviors. We will revisit the iceberg metaphor and image once more to clarify the relationship between stereotypes, ethnocentrism, prejudice, and discrimination. Stereotypes are false beliefs. These false beliefs can lead to ethnocentrism, the belief that one's own culture is superior to other cultures. Ethnocentrism can lead to prejudice, an unjustified attitude of dislike, disdain, and even hatred for other people. Prejudice often leads to discrimination, the unfair treatment of others.

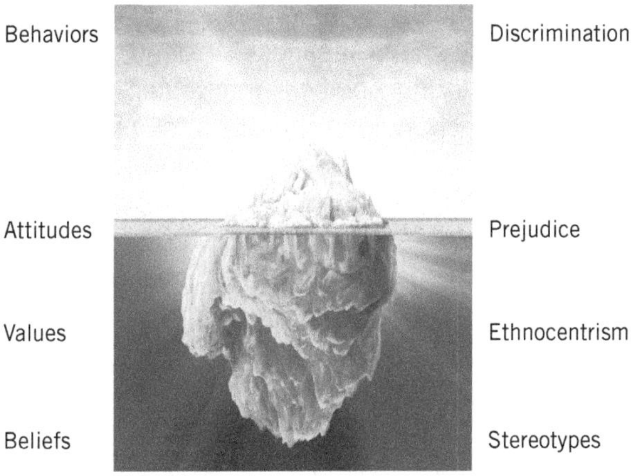

Behaviors — Discrimination
Attitudes — Prejudice
Values — Ethnocentrism
Beliefs — Stereotypes

FIGURE 5.7

Distinguishing Valid Generalizations from Invalid Stereotypes

In order to talk about national cultures or co-cultures at all, you need to make generalizations about these cultures. For example, in order to talk about what Americans are like, you need to make statements or assertions that apply to the majority of Americans. And in order to talk about what American men and women are like, you need to make statements or assertions that apply to the majority of American men and women. If you could not make generalizations, you could not even begin to think or talk about cultures.

However, when you speak about characteristics or attributes that apply to a large group of people, it is very easy to fall into stereotyping. When talking about Americans, you may find yourself and others stereotyping people and saying things like "Americans are materialistic" or "Americans are religious." When talking about men and women, you may find yourself and others stereotyping people and saying things like "Men like to drink beer" and "Women like the color pink."

How can you talk about cultures without stereotyping people? You need to clearly distinguish valid generalizations from invalid stereotypes. There are two major differences. First, valid generalizations are qualified with words and phrases such as "most," "many," "the majority of," "often," "generally," and so on, whereas invalid stereotypes use or imply universal terms such as "all," "every," "always," "never," and so on.

When speaking about people groups or dominant cultures, make sure you qualify your generalizations and assertions with words like "most," "many," and "the majority of" in order to leave room for cultural "deviants"—people who violate the cultural norms and do not fit into the mental category you are creating. Generalizations about cultures are almost always a matter of probability, not certainty. Universal deductive thinking (the method used in classic Euclidian Geometry) is not a good model for thinking and talking about people and cultures. Individuals in a culture vary, and some will not be included in the generalizations you must construct in order to make sense of the world.

Second, valid generalizations are based upon evidence, whereas invalid stereotypes are assumed and applied without evidence. The valid generalization "Most Americans are acquisitive" can be backed up with plenty of evidence—just look at the plethora of material possessions found in the majority of American homes. However, even this valid generalization can lead to invalid stereotyping if it is applied to an individual American without any corroborating evidence. Just because Janice is an American, and just because most Americans are acquisitive, you should not *assume* that Janice is also acquisitive.

When you learn the general qualities or attributes of people in a culture or co-culture, do not apply these generalizations to an individual person without supporting evidence. For example, although it is true that many Japanese prefer to be indirect in conflict situations, you should not automatically assume that your classmate Yuriko prefers to be indirect in conflict situations merely because she is Japanese. Instead, you should use your general knowledge about Japanese culture as a starting point for interacting with Yuriko in a conflict situation: there is a good chance she prefers an indirect approach to conflict, but she may deviate from this cultural norm.

Remember, to avoid stereotyping, there are two steps you must take: 1) qualify your generalizations and assertions with words such as "most," "many," and "the majority of," and 2) do not apply a generalization to an individual without evidence or corroboration.

PREJUDICE, DISCRIMINATION, AND "ISMS"

Assuming that people are the same, or that we should act like they are the same when they are in fact different, can lead to unconscious, unintentional prejudice and discrimination. Some well-intentioned people trying to avoid or decrease prejudice and discrimination actually promote prejudice and discrimination when they assert that people are "basically the same" and that differences among people "do not really matter."

This was the approach taken by many feminists in America in the 1960s and 1970s. Many feminists advocating for equal rights for women made the mistaken claim that women were "just the same as men" and therefore should be treated equally. However, in her groundbreaking book In A Different Voice (Harvard University Press, 1982), feminist Carol Gilligan pointed out that women have different biological and cultural influences that cause them to view morality somewhat differently than men. Men are taught to follow abstract rules and seek for justice, whereas women are taught to value relationships and an ethic of care, so the path of moral development may be different for men and women.

FIGURE 5.8

Males and females are different, but equal

If we impose a "male" model of moral development on women (as psychologists had done until Carol Gilligan's work was published) and assume that women's moral development is exactly the same as men's, we will evaluate female deviations from the male model as problematic, and we will view female moral development as inferior. Similarly, medical studies that use male subjects as the biological norm and that do not distinguish between male and female physiology will make female physical development seem abnormal or aberrant.

Certainly early feminists were trying to benefit women, but their insistence on sameness actually helped to contribute to the devaluation of females who deviated from the dominant male norm. It now seems much wiser to say that men and women are different, but equal. Women are not "just the same as" men: they are not biologically, psychologically, or culturally the same, and to treat them as such makes their differences seem inferior and undesirable.

When dealing with race and racism, an approach which overemphasizes sameness is the notion of colorblindness: some well-intentioned people assert that we should not pay attention to the color of a person's skin. We should, they claim, be "colorblind" and realize that people are, underneath their skin, "just the same."

However, skin color, and the way people are treated because of their skin color, is an important part of our lived experience that creates who we are as human beings. When we overemphasize sameness and do not recognize differences, we can assume that minority ethnic or racial groups in a culture have had the same experiences and privileges as the majority ethnic or racial group—this is clearly not the case.

Differences in race or skin color can lead to very different experiences and attitudes. Although all American citizens belong to the same national culture, they belong to different co-cultures determined in part by their age, sex, socioeconomic status, and race. These differences need to be acknowledged, or else unconscious discrimination can result. For example, minority advocates point out that standardized questions on educational aptitude tests sometimes have a "white bias" that favors students who are part of the dominant white culture. Discrimination is often motivated or caused by prejudice, but sometimes it is unintentionally caused by the assumption of sameness when important differences exist.

These barriers to communication—ethnocentrism, sterotyping, prejudice, and discrimination—can greatly affect group interaction and dynamics. Awareness may lead your group to better decision-making or problem-solving.

Glossary

High-context communication style: It is assumed that communicators share a previously established context. As a result, it is unnecessary, and often annoying to explain every detail. For high-context communicators shared contexts build mutual respect.

Interpretation: The work of professional interpreters who must instantaneously hear, understand, and transfer information from one language to another.

Language families: Languages that share a common origin.

Language isolates: Languages that developed in isolation from other languages and share no common root.

Linguistic relativity: The school of thought concerned with the notion that language influences our perceptions in substantial ways.

Linguistic universalism: The school of thought concerned with the notion that languages are substantially similar and influence thought in similar ways.

Low-context communication style: It is assumed that communicators do not share a previously established context. Thoughts and ideas must be explained clearly, and meanings must be fully expressed in order to assure that everyone in the communication encounter grasps the contexts.

Phonetics: The sounds of words and the ways we transcribe the sounds of words.

Pragmatics: The study of the language ambiguities that can only be explained through contextual understandings of time, place, relationship, and manner of utterance.

Sapir–Worf hypothesis: Based on the work of Edward Sapir and his student, Lee Worf, the Sapir–Worf hypothesis was developed by Roger Brown and Eric Lenneberg who turned Sapir and Worf's notion that language influences thoughts and behaviors into a testable hypothesis.

Semantics: The study of the meanings of words and sentences and the relationships between the meanings of words and the meanings of the sentences they exist within.

Syntactics: The study of the rules that govern the structure of any language—rules about ways in which words are put together to form phrases, clauses, or sentences.

Tonal languages: Languages in which meaning is dependent on the combination of word and tone.

Translation: A text transferred from one language to another, with efforts made to maintain the underlying meanings of the original text that are culturally bound.

Works Cited or Consulted

Abumrad, J., & Krulwich, R. (2011, January). *Birds-eye view.* Retrieved from NPR's Radio Lab website: http://www.radiolab.org/story/110193-birds-eye-view/

Adelman, J., & Suga, M. (2013, November). *Japan won't set dates for restarting 50 idled nuclear reactors.* Retrieved from Business Week website: http://www.businessweek.com/news/2013-11-18/japan-won-t-set-dates-for-restarting-50-idled-nuclear-reactors

Boroditsky, L. (2010, July 23). *Lost in translation: New cognitive research suggests that language profoundly influences the way people see the world; a different sense of blame in Japanese and Spanish.* Retrieved from Wall Street Journal website: http://online.wsj.com/news/articles/SB10001424052748703467304575383131592767868

Bowers, J. S., & Pleydell-Pearce, C. W. (2011, July 20). *Swearing, euphemisms, and linguistic relativity.* Retrieved from PLOS ONE website: http://www.plosone.org/article/info%3Adoi%2F10.1371%2Fjournal.pone.0022341

Chen, M. K. (2013). The effect of language on economic behavior: Evidence from savings rates, health behaviors, and retirement assets. *American Economic Review, 103*(2), 690–731. doi:10.1257/aer.103.2.690

Committee of Experts. (2010, April 21). *European charter for regional or minority languages: Application of the charter in the United Kingdom, 3rd monitoring cycle.* Retrieved from Council of Europe website: http://www.coe.int/t/dg4/education/minlang/report/EvaluationReports/UKECRML3_en.pdf

Crawford, J. (2012, February). *Language legislation in the USA.* Retrieved from Issues in US Language Policy website: http://www.languagepolicy.net/archives/langleg.htm

Ethnologue: Languages of the World. (2014a, Spring). *Basque: A language of Spain.* Retrieved from Ethnologue: Languages of the World website: http://www.ethnologue.com/language/eus

Ethnologue: Languages of the World. (2014b, Spring). *China.* Retrieved from Ethologue: Languages of the World website: http://www.ethnologue.com/country/CN/status

Fausey, C. M., & Boroditsky, L. (2011). Who dunnit? Cross-linguistic differences in eye-witness memory. *Psychonomic Bulletin & Review, 18*(1), 150–157.

Greene, R. L., Boroditsky, L., & Liberman, M. (2010, December 13–23). *Language: This house believes that the language we speak shapes how we think.* Retrieved from The Economist website: http://economist.com/debate/overview/190

Jamison, A. (2010, March 31). *French government picks new words to replace English.* Retrieved from The Telegraph UK website: http://www.telegraph.co.uk/news/worldnews/europe/france/7540588/French-government-picks-new-words-to-replace-English.html

KapplerMikk, B. (2012, July 12). *High vs low context communication.* Portland, OR: Summer Institute for Intercultural Communication.

Kingston, J. (2013, November 30). *Opinion: Imagining post-nuclear Japan.* Retrieved from The Japan Times website: http://www.japantimes.co.jp/opinion/2013/11/30/commentary/imagining-post-nuclear-japan/#.UpuWSsRDsa8

Marcus, G. (2012, December 7). *Happy Birthday, Noam Chomsky.* Retrieved from The New Yorker website: http://www.newyorker.com/online/blogs/newsdesk/2012/12/the-legacy-of-noam-chomsky.html

Stephens, R., & Umland, C. (2011). Swearing as a response to pain—Effect of daily swearing. *The Journal of Pain, 12*, 1274–1281.

Swoyer, C. (2010, Winter). *Sapir–Whorf hypothesis.* Retrieved from Stanford Encyclopedia of Philosophy website: http://plato.stanford.edu/entries/relativism/supplement2.html

Tesafe, W. (2007). Laguu in the Oromo society: A sociolinguistic approach. In A. Amha, M. Mous, & G. Sava (eds.), *Omotic and Cushitis language studies.* Collogne: Rüdiger Köppe Verlag.

Trafton, A. (2008, June 24). *MIT-led team finds language without numbers.* Retrieved from MIT News website: http://web.mit.edu/newsoffice/2008/language-0624.html

University of Hawaii, Manoa. (2014, March 9). *Endangered languages: Why so important?* Retrieved from The Endangered Languages Project website: https://docs.google.com/document/d/19MvWf22roO_egGdcma1rSAplMrQitKskxL3xn0gBgSU/edit).*

Chapter 6:

Interaction: Verbal and Nonverbal Communication and Listening in Groups

Chapter Objectives

- Understand the general characteristics of effective communication.
- Learn how to send clear and supportive messages to your group.
- Distinguish between verbal, nonverbal, vocal, and nonvocal communication.
- Identify types of nonverbal communication.
- Comprehend the listening process and how listening barriers and poor listening behaviors affect group communication.

Communication is the "glue" that holds a small group together. When small group members use their communication skills to develop and maintain relationships with one another, they create a cohesive small group with strong interpersonal ties. Communication is also a crucial factor in effectively completing small group tasks. To carry out and complete tasks effectively, small groups need competent communicators that can send and receive concise and clear messages.

FIGURE 6.1

This chapter will give you the knowledge and point out the skills you need to communicate effectively in your small group.

GENERAL PRINCIPLES OF EFFECTIVE COMMUNICATION

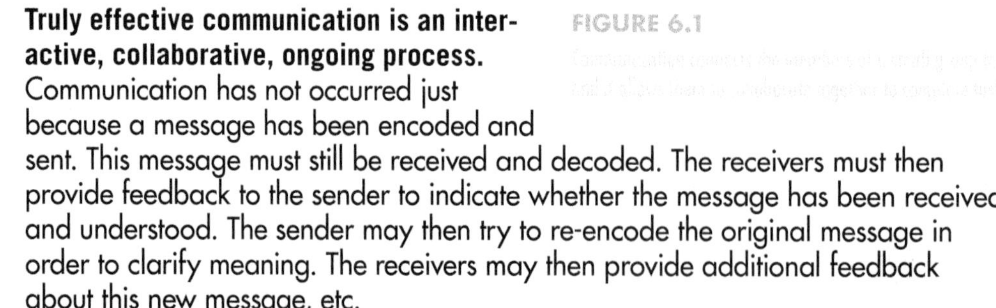

1. **Truly effective communication is an interactive, collaborative, ongoing process.** Communication has not occurred just because a message has been encoded and sent. This message must still be received and decoded. The receivers must then provide feedback to the sender to indicate whether the message has been received and understood. The sender may then try to re-encode the original message in order to clarify meaning. The receivers may then provide additional feedback about this new message, etc.
2. **Effective communicators provide clear, unambiguous messages.** Although there are rare occasions when unclear, ambiguous messages are appropriate, small group members trying to complete tasks need to send easy-to-understand messages. Since the encoding and decoding processes are complicated, effective communicators strive to give clear messages that can be easily transmitted and understood.
3. **Effective communicators tailor their messages to their particular audiences.** They are aware of, and sensitive to, similarities and differences in their various communication partners, and they adjust their messages accordingly. The diversity in a small group requires people to communicate differently with different group members.
4. **Effective communicators choose the correct communication channels for their messages.** The most carefully crafted messages still need to be sent through the proper channels. No matter how clear a message may be, an ineffective or inappropriate communication channel will still hinder communication.
5. **Effective communicators seek for and provide feedback concerning messages.** Effective senders ask for and pay attention to feedback from their receivers, and then they repeat or adjust their messages accordingly. Effective receivers decode messages, and then they give feedback in order to share the meanings they have assigned to these messages.

6. **Effective communicators work together to reduce or eliminate communication noise.** Any external distractions in the communication environment or in the communication channels are dealt with. A supportive communication climate that encourages the open exchange of information is established. Communicators acknowledge and process distracting thoughts and feelings in order to focus their attention on the messages being sent and received.
7. **Effective communicators are mindful of both the content aspect and the relational aspect of their messages.** They realize that competent communicators skillfully share their messages in ways that establish and maintain good relationships with other communicators. Therefore, they consider not only the content of their messages, but they also pay attention to the manner in which they convey these messages verbally and nonverbally.

FIGURE 6.2

GENERAL PRINCIPLES OF EFFECTIVE COMMUNICATION
1. Effective communication is an interactive, collaborative, ongoing process.
2. Effective communicators provide clear, unambiguous messages.
3. Effective communicators tailor their messages to their particular audiences.
4. Effective communicators choose the correct communication channels for their messages.
5. Effective communicators seek for and provide feedback concerning messages.
6. Effective communicators work together to reduce or eliminate communication noise.
7. Effective communicators are mindful of both the content aspect and the relational aspect of their messages.

Gaining Communication Competence

Knowing the general characteristics of effective communicators can help you gain **communication competence**. Communication competence is the ability to communicate effectively in a given context. Communication competence is *not* a trait that you either have or do not have. Communication competence is a state that you achieve more or less frequently. In other words, sometimes you communicate effectively, and sometimes you do not. Sometimes you pay attention to your relational messages, and sometimes you do not. Sometimes you choose the appropriate communication channel for your message, and sometimes you do not.

In your small group communication class, you will have many opportunities to make communication decisions and to practice communication skills. Every time you make a good communication decision or effectively use a communication skill, you are increasing your communication competence. As you increase your communication competence, you are becoming a more valuable group member, and you are increasing the likelihood that your small group as a whole will experience success.

As you work together with other small group members, realize that effective communication is the product of motivated, knowledgeable, and skillful communicators. Every small group member involved in the collaborative communication process must have the desire to communicate, the knowledge of how to communicate effectively, and the necessary communication skills. If any person in your small group lacks motivation, knowledge, or skill, the communication in your small group will be hindered.

Communicating Clear Verbal Messages

Three practical tips for communicating clear verbal messages include: 1) be specific, 2) be succinct, and 3) be aware of the four levels of language.

First, be specific. If you want to send clear verbal messages, avoid general, abstract, vague language. For example, do not say, "We need to have better meetings." What exactly do you mean? If you want your small group members to change their behaviors, you need to describe the specific behaviors that need to change.

Instead of saying, "We need to have better meetings," be specific and say, "We need every member to show up on time to our next meeting with their assigned work completed, we need to set an agenda, and we need to a assign a meeting chair and timekeeper." The second statement is much more specific, and it clearly sets forth the behaviors that need to occur. Specific language is not always necessary or desirable, but it is very helpful if you are trying to clearly communicate about small group processes or goals.

Second, be succinct. Give as many specific details as is necessary, but no more. One drawback of small group work and discussion is the amount of time that it takes for every member to participate and share their thoughts and opinions. Since we are so conditioned by modern technology for very rapid, almost "instantaneous" communication, the slow pace of face-to-face small group discussions can be excruciating for "time-oriented" listeners who expect speakers to "get to the point" quickly.

FIGURE 6.3

There are four levels of language: phonetic, semantic, syntactic, and pragmatic.

When you are speaking to your small group, omit extraneous details that slow down the transmission of your essential message. Your small group members will appreciate your succinct remarks that free up time for further group discussion. Too much information will clutter, not clarify, your message.

Third, be aware of the four levels of language. The four levels of language are 1) the phonetic level, 2) the semantic level, 3) the syntactic level, and 4) the pragmatic level. Miscommunication and misunderstanding can occur on any of these four levels.

Phonetic level: The phonetic level of language is the simplest, most basic level of language. It involves the sounds that combine together to form words. In written language, these sounds are often represented by letters. In spoken language, these sounds are vocalized. To communicate clearly with your small group members, you need to articulate your sounds clearly and pronounce your words correctly. Do not mumble. Do not cut off the ends of your words or run your words together. Speak clearly in order to communicate clearly.

Semantic level: The second level of language, the semantic level, involves words and their meanings. Semantic confusion occurs when people assign different meanings to the same word. Do not assume that your small group members will assign the same meanings to your words as you do. Take time to define and to clarify the meanings of the words you use in order to communicate clearly with your small group.

If you are working with people who speak English as a second language, avoid idiomatic sayings and colloquial expressions that will lead to semantic confusion. Native English speakers may know what it means to "bury the hatchet" or to "pick a bone" during a group discussion, but a group member speaking English as a second language may be stumped by these expressions.

Syntactic level: The third level of language, the syntactic level, involves how words are put together into sentences. Syntactic confusion occurs when people violate grammar rules or punctuate sentences incorrectly. One misplaced comma can change the entire meaning of a sentence. Syntactic misunderstandings are most likely to arise in small group communication when you are sending or receiving emails or text messages.

Pragmatic level: The fourth level of language, the pragmatic level, concerns the context of a communication. Certain words or phrases may be appropriate or inappropriate depending on the communication context. Where is the communication occurring? Who is speaking to whom? Who might be listening in on the communication?

In your small group discussions, you need to consider the pragmatic level of language. What might be a perfectly acceptable message to voice among your closest friends may not be an appropriate verbal message to voice in your small group communication class. Violating the pragmatic rules of language can negatively affect your small group relationships, and it can distract others from the core of your verbal message.

THE FOUR LEVELS OF LANGUAGE
1. **The phonetic level:** the sounds and letters that combine together to form words
2. **The semantic level:** the meaning of words
3. **The syntactic level:** how words are put together into sentences
4. **The pragmatic level:** the context of a communication

Creating a Supportive Communication Climate

Imagine you wake up one Saturday and pull back the curtains of your bedroom window to discover a balmy, pleasant day. The sky is clear and blue. The sun is shining brightly, but not too brightly. A slight breeze is blowing through the green trees of your neighborhood. What would you feel like doing? Perhaps you might decide to go for a long bike ride, or you might decide to mow your lawn, or you might sit outside and visit with your neighbors.

Now imagine you wake up on another Saturday morning and pull the curtains back to discover that a frigid weather front has arrived. Ominous, dark clouds fill the sky. Turbulent winds are blowing. Sleet is pummeling the ground outside. Now what would you feel like doing? You might decide to stay inside, turn up the heat, and read a good book, or you might pull the bedcovers over your head and burrow in for a long morning snooze.

Just as the weather and the climate outside affects your behavior (Systems Theory), the communication climate that you create in your small group will affect the behavior of your small group members. If you and your group members create a warm, supportive communication climate, people will want to speak up and participate in you small group discussions. However, if a cold, defensive atmosphere exists in your small group, group members will "shut down" and withdraw themselves from small group discussions.

We have very little control over the weather, but we have a fair amount of control over the communication climate that exists in our small groups. We create a defensive or a supportive communication climate through the responses we give to others and through the communication behaviors we use with others.

DISCONFIRMING RESPONSES VERSUS CONFIRMING RESPONSES

In 1969, Social scientist Evelyn Sieburg identified several responses that she labeled either "disconfirming" responses or "confirming" responses. Disconfirming responses are responses that create a defensive communication climate because they make people value themselves less, whereas confirming responses create a supportive communication climate because they make people value themselves more.

Over the course of a decade, Sieburg worked with Carl Larson to clearly identify and categorize these two different types of responses. Their seminal work has yielded to our understanding seven disconfirming responses and five confirming responses.

Seven Disconfirming Responses

The following disconfirming responses should be avoided in small group discussions because they will create a defensive communication climate in which people feel ignored or devalued.

1. **Impervious responses:** Speakers do not acknowledge in any way that someone else has just spoken. They are "impervious" to the preceding remark, and they proceed with their own remarks as if the previous speaker had made no comment at all.
2. **Interrupting responses:** Speakers "barge in" while another person is still speaking. Instead of waiting for a person to complete his or her thought, they cut the person off in order to present their own thoughts.
3. **Irrelevant responses:** Speakers respond to a remark by introducing a totally unrelated topic, or by returning to a topic that they had introduced before. They act as if they are unaware of the conversation that has just occurred.
4. **Tangential responses:** Speakers acknowledge a comment, but then they quickly take the discussion in a different direction. After briefly acknowledging a remark, they "go off on a tangent."

5. **Impersonal responses:** Speakers talk in vague generalities or clichés, and they act as if they are addressing no one in particular. Their responses lack first-person "I" statements, and they are filled with impersonal, abstract discourse removed from the people sitting around the table.
6. **Incoherent responses:** Speakers give responses that lack any apparent coherent meaning. They speak in garbled, incomplete sentences, or their responses ramble with much backtracking, side comments, and verbal clutter.
7. **Incongruous responses:** Speakers give verbal responses that are out of synch with or contradict their nonverbal cues. These incongruous verbal and nonverbal messages create confusion and uncertainty.

Five Confirming Responses

In contrast to the seven disconfirming responses listed above, the five following confirming responses can help to create a supportive communication climate in which group members feel acknowledged and valued.

1. **Direct acknowledgment:** Speakers respond directly to a previous remark. They acknowledge that the remark was made, and their responses directly relate to the remark.
2. **Agreement about content:** Speakers verify that they understand the content of a previous remark. They may not agree with the remark, but their response demonstrates that they fully comprehend what another group member has said.
3. **Supportive responses:** Speakers attempt to empathize with, support, or encourage another group member. Their responses indicate good will and positive regard for the person who has just spoken.
4. **Clarifying responses:** Speakers try to clarify the meaning or intention of a previous remark. Their responses may include requests for more information, prompts to expand the original remark, or paraphrases to check for understanding.
5. **Expressions of positive feeling:** Even if they disagree with a previous remark, speakers express positive feelings about the discussion that is occurring or the people that are involved in the discussion.

DISCONFIRMING RESPONSES	CONFIRMING RESPONSES
1. Impervious responses	1. Direct acknowledgment
2. Interrupting responses	2. Agreement about content
3. Irrelevant responses	3. Supportive responses
4. Tangential responses	4. Clarifying responses
5. Impersonal responses	5. Expressions of positive feeling
6. Incoherent responses	
7. Incongruous responses	

DEFENSIVE AND SUPPORTIVE CLIMATES

Whereas Sieburg and Larson focused on specific types of disconfirming and confirming responses that could create a defensive or supportive communication climate, Dr. Jack Gibb focused for several years on general defensive and supportive behaviors. His research has yielded what we now call the Gibb categories; six defensive behaviors and their contrasting supportive behaviors.

THE GIBB CATEGORIES

Defensive Behaviors	Supportive Behaviors
1. Evaluation	1. Description
2. Control	2. Problem Orientation
3. Strategy	3. Spontaneity
4. Neutrality	4. Empathy
5. Superiority	5. Equality
6. Certainty	6. Provisionalism

As you work together with others in your small group to create a supportive climate, in addition to monitoring the types of verbal responses that are given, be on the alert for these general communication behaviors. The first behavior in each of the following pairings will lead to a defensive climate, whereas the second behavior will create a supportive climate.

Evaluation versus Description

Evaluation: Sometimes you will need to evaluate ideas generated in your small group discussions. For example, after your group has brainstormed possible solutions to a problem, your group will then need to evaluate these solutions in order to select the best one. However, when a small group member continually evaluates and comments on the remarks of other members, a very unpleasant climate is generated. People will not want to speak up and share their ideas if their remarks are met with comments like, "That's a stupid idea," or, even worse, "You are an idiot!" An overly-critical group member can have a chilling effect on small group discussions.

Description: The antidote to evaluation is description. Instead of making evaluative, judgmental "you" statements in your small group discussions, offer descriptive "I" statements. When someone offers an idea or opinion, describe your thoughts and feelings about the person's comment. You can also paraphrase and "describe" their idea in your own words to make sure you understand what they are saying. Most people want to be understood, not evaluated and criticized.

Control versus Problem Orientation

Control: Since some people avoid small group work because they fear a loss of control, they are likely to get quite defensive if another group member announces, "This is how we are going to do our project." This pronouncement is a "controlling" communication that sends the message that others are expected to do things the way the speaker wants, and that their opinions and wishes do not really matter. A controlling small group member can quickly alienate others in the group.

Problem Orientation: When you approach small group tasks and projects with a "problem orientation," you do not try to impose your will or your ideas on others; instead, you ask other members to join you in problem solving. Instead of "commanding" others (with controlling communication), you invite others to collaborate with you. A supportive climate is created because people feel like you are addressing them as partners on a problem-solving quest, and not as servants or underlings who must carry out your wishes.

Strategy versus Spontaneity

Strategy: Strategy is expected in a football game or a chess match, but your small group members do not want you to treat them as if they are just "x"s and "o"s or chess pieces. No one likes to be "played," so when people think that you are manipulating them through strategic, "scripted" communication, they will get defensive.

Spontaneity: Being "spontaneous" does not mean that you never put any thought into what you say or that you just say whatever pops into your mind; it means that you are willing to enter into a small group discussion without a pre-planned script or a hidden agenda. Instead of using your communication skills to manipulate others, you will use them to clearly convey your ideas to others so you all can engage in an open, honest, give-and-take conversation.

Neutrality versus Empathy

Neutrality: Although neutrality is sometimes a positive thing, "neutrality" as a Gibb category is a behavior that leads to a defensive communication climate. If you come across as indifferent or unconcerned about your small group or its members, they will feel devalued.

Empathy: Empathy is the supportive response that counteracts neutrality and indifference. If a small group member self-discloses that a family member is critically ill or that they are struggling in their college classes, you should show care and concern for this member. This care and concern can be communicated by your facial expression and body posture, as well as by your verbal response.

Superiority versus Equality

Superiority: A small group member with a superior attitude puts others on the defensive and undermines his or her small group relationships. A superior, patronizing attitude sends the message, "I am better than you." Who wants to work with, or be in a relationship with, someone who thinks this way?

Equality: Although you may be smarter, or more knowledgeable, or better looking, or more athletic than other small group members, you need not project a sense of superiority. Instead, you can send the message that your small group members have equal worth and value as human beings. When you think of, and treat, your small group members as equals, you help to create a supportive small group environment.

Certainty versus Provisionalism

Certainty: Although certainty is a good feeling, when small group members present their ideas or proposals with certainty, as though they could not possibly be wrong, they put other group members on the defensive. Ironically, the more "certainly" an idea is presented, the more resistance it is likely to receive. After all, if an idea or proposal "cannot possibly be wrong," then what is being implied about all the ideas and proposals of other group members?

Provisionalism: You are more likely to receive support for an idea or proposal if you present it with some degree of provisionalism. If you leave room for the possibility that your idea or proposal may be improvable (and that the ideas and proposals of other group members may have some merit), you create a supportive communication climate where your idea or proposal has a good chance of being discussed and, if it truly has merit, accepted.

The Gibb categories and Sieburg and Larson's categories of disconfirming and confirming responses reveal that your communication behaviors have a strong influence on your small group communication climate, for better or worse. Do not be a "Mr. Freeze" who has a chilling effect on small group discussions. Instead, be a "Little Miss Sunshine" who helps to create a warm, comfortable group climate.

Mr. Freeze, or . . .

Little Miss Sunshine?

The Difference Between Verbal and Nonverbal Communication

To clearly distinguish between verbal and nonverbal communication, we need to complicate these two categories a bit. Figure 6.7 reveals that communication can be verbal or nonverbal *and* vocal or nonvocal. Thus, there are four categories to distinguish between different types of communication: communication can be 1) verbal and vocal, 2) verbal and nonvocal, 3) nonverbal and vocal, or 4) nonverbal and nonvocal.

	Verbal Communication	**Nonverbal Communication**
Vocal Communication	Speaking words and sentences	Laughing, grunting, sighing Paralanguage: voice rate, volume, pitch, etc.
Nonvocal Communication	Writing, texting, and signing	Body position and posture, body movement, facial expressions, eye contact, etc.

FIGURE 6.4

These are four main categories of human communication.

Verbal communication is communication expressed in human language. If you are communicating with words (nouns, pronouns, prepositions, adjectives, adverbs, and verbs), you are communicating verbally. Words can be vocalized, but they can also be encoded in visual symbols, so verbal communication can occur through the visual channel as well as the auditory channel. You may decide that some verbal messages should be written out and shared in letters, emails, or text messages. If you have a deaf members in your small group, you may need to "sign" some words using sign language. If you have deaf members read Braille, they can also receive verbal communication through the tactile channel.

Vocal communication is communication expressed through the voice. Human beings use their diaphragms, vocal chords, and mouths to communicate vocally. Often we vocalize words, but sometimes we vocalize sounds that are not words. For example, you can communicate with members of your small group through the use of chuckles, grunts, exasperated sighs, and "oohs and aahs" of surprise.

FIGURE 6.5

If you use verbal, vocal communication in your small group, you speak words with your mouth that travel through the auditory channel. The vocalized sounds of these words are heard and decoded by your listeners. Be aware that when you vocalize words in your small group, you are also sending vocal, nonverbal messages at the same time. Your voice volume, your rate of speech, and your tone of voice also communicate messages to your audience. These vocal, nonverbal elements are called paralanguage. When you speak in your small group, you need to pay attention not only to *what* you say, but also to *how* you say it.

When you use nonverbal, nonvocal communication in your small group, you will usually forgo the auditory channel and send messages instead through the visual and tactile channels. You can communicate through your use of space, your posture, your touch, your body movement, etc. Nonverbal, nonvocal communication is usually what people are referring to when they use the term "nonverbal" communication.

Now that we have clearly distinguished verbal communication from nonverbal communication, let's note some other important differences between these two primary communication types.

NONVERBAL COMMUNICATION VERSUS VERBAL COMMUNICATION

1. **Whereas verbal communication is intermittent, nonverbal communication is continuous.** Nonverbal communication occurs twenty-four hours a day, seven days a week. If people can see you, you are communicating with them through your nonverbals whether you want to or not. Nonverbal communication is why you cannot not communicate with your small group. If you sit silently in your small group with your arms crossed and your head turned away from the group in an attempt to stop communicating, your group members can still receive many messages from this nonverbal behavior.

2. **Whereas most verbal communication is conscious and intentional, nonverbal communication is often unconscious and unintentional.** We usually choose the words we use to express our ideas, but we are often unaware of our nonverbal behaviors. When you are participating in a small group discussion, you need to tune in to the unintended messages that you are sending to others with your facial expressions, your body movement, and your paralanguage.
3. **Nonverbal communication is more believable than verbal communication.** If there is a contradiction between your verbal communication and your nonverbal communication, your small group members will most likely believe your nonverbal communication because "actions speak louder than words." For example, if you say, "I'm not angry," but your hands are clenched, your voice volume is loud, and your brow is furrowed, your group will think you are angry despite your words.

FIGURE 6.6
[illegible]

4. **Nonverbal communication is used more often than verbal communication to send relational messages.** You rarely interrupt a small group discussion to say to another member, "I do not find you very interesting," or, "I respect and admire you." However, you are often sending these sorts of relational messages with your nonverbal communication. While your vocalized words will often relate to the group task at hand, your paralanguage, facial expressions, and body language will communicate how you think and feel about your other group members.

Now that we have compared nonverbal and verbal communication, the importance of nonverbal communication should be obvious. We must pay attention to our nonverbal communication because 1) nonverbal communication is continuous, 2) nonverbal communication is often unconscious and unintentional, 3) nonverbal communication is more believable than verbal communication, and 4) nonverbal communication is often used to send relational messages.

Since nonverbal communication is so important, let's take a closer look at some specific nonverbal elements and how they affect small group communication in particular. Let's consider use of space, body position and body posture, facial expressions, eye contact, personal appearance, and paralanguage.

Use of Space

It matters where you sit in your small group. "Small group ecology" is a ripe area for social science research. Researchers have discovered that where small group members sit affects their relationships, their communication patterns, and their leadership roles.

If you want to develop stronger relationships with certain small group members, sit across from them, not beside them. If you sit across from people, you will be able to establish good eye contact, and your communication interactions will increase.

If your small group is using a rectangular table, you can sit at the end of the table in the traditional "leader" position, or you can sit in the middle of the long side of the table and more easily lead the small group discussion by being in the center of the communication flow. Researchers have discovered that those who sit where they can most easily interact with others have the most communication interactions, and that small group members who have the most communication interactions often emerge as small group leaders.

For example, if, in a five-member group, three members sit on one side of a table and two members sit on the other side, the two members on the one side of the table are more likely to emerge as the small group leaders. Why? Because they are facing three other group members and are therefore more likely to have more communication interactions than the three members on the other side of the table.

Group members who sit at the corners of a table tend to have the least communication interactions. If you are trying to get low-participating members more involved, suggest or request that they sit in the middle of one side of the table. Conversely, if one member tends to dominate the small group discussions, place them at a corner of a rectangular or square table, or find a circular table that will encourage more equal participation.

However, if you ask your small group members to change seats or tables, be aware that human beings, like other animals, are territorial. Just as dogs, for example, mark and defend their territory, your small group members will become accustomed to sitting in a certain place in your small group, and they may even "mark" their territory with books, drink cups, and other personal items. If group members have well-established "territories" in your small group venue, you may experience resistance if you ask them to change places or locations without a reason or explanation.

FIGURE 6.7
Where you sit at a table matters

FIGURE 6.8
Like dogs, human beings are territorial

Body Position and Body Posture

In addition to *where* you sit in your small group, you need to consider *how* you sit. First, think about the way you position your body: try to position yourself so you can see and interact with all your small group members. You want to send the nonverbal message that you are ready and willing to communicate with everyone in your group. Make sure you are not turned away from other group members, or they may think that you are giving them the "cold shoulder."

Second, think about your posture. Your posture is how you hold your body when you stand or sit. Doctors and physical education teachers encourage good posture for health benefits, but there are also "good" and "bad" postures for small group communication. If you slump forward in your seat and lay your head on your desk, or if you sprawl out in your seat and prop your feet up on a table, your group members may get the negative message that you are not very interested in what they have to say. If you want your posture to signal that you are paying attention and are interested in the group conversation, sit up straight in your seat and lean slightly toward people as they speak.

FIGURE 6.9

Hand Gestures

In 1969, Paul Ekman and Wallace Friesen identified five major types of nonverbal behaviors: 1) emblems, 2) illustrators, 3) affect displays, 4) regulators, and 5) adaptors. Although these five categories apply to many nonverbal behaviors, we will introduce them here because they are especially useful in describing and analyzing hand gestures.

Emblems: Emblems are nonverbal symbols that take the place of verbal symbols. Your hand gestures are being used as emblems when you make a circle with your index finger and thumb to indicate that everything is going okay or when you give a "thumbs up" or a "thumbs down" to indicate your agreement or disagreement with a proposal.

Illustrators: Illustrators are nonverbal symbols that emphasize or reinforce a verbal message. Your hand gestures are being used as illustrators when you raise your upturned palms as you talk about increasing success or when you shake your fist to reinforce your forceful verbal message.

FIGURE 6.10

Hand gestures can be used as emblems, illustrators, affect displays, regulators, or adaptors.

Affect displays: Affect displays are nonverbal cues that signal the emotional state of a communicator. Your hand gestures are being used as affect displays when you place your palms on your cheeks to indicate surprise or when you brush the back of one hand across your forehead to indicate relief.

Regulators: Regulators are nonverbal cues that help control the flow of communication. They indicate that people should start or stop sending verbal messages. Your hand gestures are being used as regulators when you raise your hand to ask a question or when you place your index finger in front of your lips to indicate that everyone should be quiet.

Adaptors: Adaptors are nonverbal behaviors that help people adapt or adjust to their environment. Your hand gestures are being used as adaptors when you scratch an itching nose or when you fan your face because you are overheating.

FIVE TYPES OF NONVERBAL BEHAVIORS
1. **Emblems:** Nonverbal symbols that take the place of verbal symbols.
2. **Illustrators:** Nonverbal symbols that emphasize or reinforce a verbal message.
3. **Affect displays:** Nonverbal cues that signal the emotional state of a communicator.
4. **Regulators:** Nonverbal cues that help control the flow of communication.
5. **Adaptors:** Nonverbal behaviors that help people adapt to their environment.

Knowing about the different types of nonverbal behaviors can help you interpret other people's hand gestures more accurately. Adaptors reveal that a person's hand gesture may not always carry a deep meaning—a nose may be scratched because it itches, and not because a message is purposely being sent.

Facial Expressions

Facial expressions primarily indicate the emotional state of a person. Human beings are biologically programmed to read out the emotional state of anything that looks like a human face. We ascribe emotions to cartoon faces and computer emoticons even though these "faces" do not belong to human beings.

FIGURE 6.11

Another remarkable fact about facial expressions is that they are universal communicators of emotion—regardless of time and place, communication researchers have discovered that there are basic facial expressions that correlate with basic human emotions. All human beings seem to display the same basic facial expressions when they experience surprise, fear, anger, disgust, and happiness.

When you communicate face-to-face with your small group members, be aware of your facial expressions, and pay attention to the facial expressions of others. Your facial expressions should match the tone and content of your verbal communication. If you verbally claim that you are delighted by an idea presented by a group member, your face should also register a look of delight. Remember, nonverbal communication is more believable than verbal communication. If there is a contradiction between your words and your facial expression, your facial expression will trump your verbal message.

Some people try very hard to "mask" their emotions by maintaining a neutral or "inscrutable" facial expression or by consciously using a facial expression that does not match their emotional state. You can ascertain their true emotional state by looking for "micro-expressions," fleeting, very brief facial expressions that appear when people momentarily lose control of their conscious facial facades.

FIGURE 6.12

A direct gaze indicates that it is our turn to speak.

Eye Contact

Eye contact is the main nonverbal indicator that is used to regulate interpersonal and small group interactions. We do not usually raise our hands to take part in a conversation. Instead, we usually enter into a conversation when we are "invited" by the direct eye contact of a speaker.

Although we Americans use a fair amount of eye contact, we do not actually stare directly at the people to whom we are speaking. Instead, our gaze "bounces around" as we look into the eyes of our interlocutors and then look away. When we are done speaking, we then look directly at a person to indicate that it is now their turn to speak.

To verify this fact, watch what happens in a crowded room when a speaker asks for a volunteer—people will avert their gaze if they do not want to volunteer or get involved. As an instructor, I have discovered that if I look directly at a student when asking a question, that student will very likely be the one to give an answer.

You too can get low participators more involved in group discussions by using effective eye contact. You can give verbal encouragement and invitations to them, but you can also increase their participation merely by looking directly at them as you finish verbalizing a thought.

Personal Appearance

As you seek to form working relationships with your small group members, remember that personal appearance is a factor in interpersonal attraction. Group members may be attracted to you and want to get to know you better because of the way you look. Conversely, some group members may by turned off by the way you present yourself in public. Your clothing and grooming choices affect your relationships with your small group members.

If your small group has to make a public appearance, you can increase small group cohesiveness and signal that you are a "tight" group by asking your members to dress in a similar manner. Your small group could design and wear a team t-shirt or outfit, or your group members could agree to coordinate their clothing colors or styles. If your group is making a public presentation, members may want to dress professionally to gain credibility as public speakers.

FIGURE 6.13
You can signal that your group is "tight" by dressing in a similar manner.

Paralanguage

As you speak and listen to each other in your small group, remember to pay attention to the paralanguage that accompanies your vocalized verbal communication. Voice volume, voice inflection, rate of speech, and voice quality add another dimension to your vocalized words. *How* you say *what* you say has a significant effect on your overall message and how it is received. If your vocalized verbal message is filled with awkward pauses or lots of verbal clutter ("uhs," "umms," and "ya knows"), your small group members may not take it as seriously as a vocalized verbal message that is smoothly articulated.

In addition to reinforcing vocalized, verbal messages, paralanguage also sends messages about how you feel about the other people in your small group. Make sure your paralanguage communicates interest in, attention to, and respect for your small group members.

INTERPRETING NONVERBALS

As we wrap up this section on nonverbal communication, we want to make one final distinction between verbal and nonverbal communication—nonverbal communication is more ambiguous than verbal communication. You should pay attention to the nonverbal communication of other people, but you need to realize that you can easily misinterpret nonverbal cues. Someone may frown because they are concentrating, and not because they are displeased with you. Someone may turn away from you because they didn't hear you speak, and not because they are trying to snub you.

When you interpret the nonverbal cues of others, take all of their behaviors into account, and do not take one nonverbal cue out of context. In addition, you do not need to guess about the nonverbal cues of others. When a nonverbal cue is ambiguous, you can directly ask for clarification.

Listening

This section on listening bridges the sections on nonverbal and verbal communication because listening goes beyond hearing the words of others. The Chinese pictograph for listening, "ting," is composed of four symbols meaning "eye," "ear," "heart," and "attention." Westerners who value

FIGURE 6.14

speaking can learn from Easterners who value listening. To truly listen to your other group members, you must attend to their words, pay attention to their nonverbal cues, and open your mind and heart to their messages.

Epictetus said, "We have two ears and one mouth so we can listen twice as much as we speak." The need for effective listening is especially great in small groups. If every member of your small group is fully participating in your small group discussions, each individual member should be spending much more time listening to other group members than speaking. For example, if there are six members in a small group, each member should be speaking approximately one-sixth of the time, and five-sixths of each member's time should be devoted to listening.

Ironically, although listening is the communication activity human beings engage in the most often, this crucial communication skill is taught the least. In the American education system, there are required courses in reading and writing and even public speaking, but there are no courses devoted to teaching the skill actually used more often than any other communication skill—listening.

This lack of training in listening is unfortunate because we often misunderstand or completely miss the messages of others as a result of several general listening barriers or specific poor listening behaviors.

THREE LISTENING BARRIERS

There are three listening barriers that can affect our ability to receive and process the messages of others. These three barriers are: 1) hearing problems, 2) communication noise, and 3) information overload.

1. **Hearing problems:** If you have a small group member who often asks others to repeat their messages or consistently misunderstands the vocal messages of others, perhaps this person has a hearing problem. Hearing deficiencies often go undiagnosed, and sometimes people do not want to reveal that they have a hearing deficiency. If small group members have major hearing deficits, they may use hearing aids. If their hearing loss is severe or total, they may need to use an interpreter. Small groups with deaf members need to adjust their communication behaviors to ensure that everyone in the group can participate fully in group discussions.
2. **Communication noise:** The transactional model of communication presented at the beginning of this chapter introduced to you the concept of communication noise. There are three types of communication noise: 1) physical noise, 2) physiological noise, and 3) psychological noise. The term "noise" encompasses more than distracting sounds. Communication noise also refers to distracting visual stimuli, distracting body states and conditions, and distracting thoughts and feelings. Obviously, eliminating distracting communication noise will improve your ability to hear and listen effectively.

3. **Information overload:** In this "information age" that we live in, a very common listening barrier is information overload. When too much information is shared at once, our mental circuits become overloaded and we are unable to process any messages. Information overload is sometime referred to as the "Charlie Brown Effect." In the Charles Schultz cartoon, the character Charlie Brown sits in the back of his class, and when his teacher speaks, all Charlie Brown hears is, "Waa, waa, waa . . . waa, waa, waa. . . ."

FIGURE 6.15

Watch out for information overload in your small group discussions, especially if several people are speaking at the same time. Information overload may kick in, and you will discover the truth in the lyrics of the Neil Young song, "Everybody's talkin' at me, I don't hear a word they're sayin'."

EIGHT INEFFECTIVE LISTENING BEHAVIORS

Whereas the three listening barriers we have mentioned are outside factors that sometimes impinge on our ability to listen, the following eight ineffective listening behaviors are much more within our control. We sometimes listen poorly due to 1) stagehogging, 2) pseudolistening, 3) selective listening, 4) insulated listening, 5) ambush listening, 6) defensive listening, 7) prejudging, and 8) rehearsing a response. As we describe each of these ineffective listening behaviors, see if you recognize yourself in any of these descriptions.

1. **Stagehogging:** Stagehogging occurs when we interrupt others or dismiss what they are saying in order to present our own ideas or examples. If one small group member, for example, is sharing a personal experience, stagehogs will interrupt or ignore this personal experience in order to present their own experiences (which they evidently think are much more interesting or important). In addition to being poor listeners, stagehogs are also annoying: at the end of Chapter 3 of this textbook, stagehogs made it onto the "Top Ten" list of difficult people to have in a small group.

2. **Pseudo listening:** Pseudolistening occurs when we act like we are listening but our minds are far away. Pseudolisteners may nod their heads and scratch their chins to give the appearance of listening, but in reality they may not even be receiving the messages sent by others.

3. **Selective listening:** Selective listening occurs when we only listen to the topics which interest us. Selective listeners "select" or focus only on their favorite ideas or topics. If others are discussing these particular topics, they will pay attention; otherwise, they zone out.

4. **Insulated listening:** Insulated listening is the opposite of selective listening. Insulated listening occurs when we purposely "tune out" topics or ideas we do not like or find objectionable for some reason. In a small group discussion, insulated listeners may ignore verbal messages they do not like, or they may ignore any messages sent by particular group members they do not like.

5. **Ambush listening:** Ambush listening occurs when we listen primarily to gain "ammunition" which we can use against other people. Like a prosecutor cross-examining a hostile witness, ambush listeners process the messages of others primarily because they want to attack what others are saying. Since very few people willingly subject themselves to being attacked, ambush listeners have a chilling effect on small group discussions.

6. **Defensive listening:** Defensive listening occurs when we assume that whatever others say somehow reflects negatively on ourselves. Defensive listeners often have low self-esteem, so they tend to interpret the messages of others as personal attacks. Since they are so focused on these perceived attacks or slights, defensive listeners often miss the point of what others are actually trying to communicate.

7. **Prejudging:** Prejudging occurs when we determine ahead of time that a message will be problematic. Our expectation causes us to overlook the actual content of the message. In small group discussions, we have to overcome the temptation to assume that a particular person or topic will be boring, offensive, too complicated, or too controversial. Instead of prejudging the messages of others, we need to listen carefully, and we need to encourage open, honest, supportive communication.

FIGURE 6.16

[illegible]

8. **Rehearsing a response:** When we rehearse responses to messages, we stop paying attention to what people are saying. Our desire to craft good responses interferes with our ability to fully receive the messages of others. No matter how well-crafted our responses are, if we do not comprehend what people are actually saying, our responses will miss the mark.

THE FIVE STEPS OF THE LISTENING PROCESS

Now that you know three general listening barriers and eight specific ineffective listening behaviors, we will help you combat these barriers and behaviors with a knowledge of the five steps of the listening process and ten steps you can take to be a more effective listener. First, let's quickly describe the five steps of the listening process.

A basic knowledge of the listening process can help you become a better listener. Listening is composed of at least five steps: 1) **hearing**, 2) **attending**, 3) **understanding**, 4) **responding**, and 5) **remembering**.

First, you must receive the auditory and visual signals of a message. Sound waves must reach your inner ear and images must enter into your eyes. Second, your mind must focus on and select the auditory and visual stimuli that you will interpret. Third, you must decode and interpret the messages that you receive. Fourth, you must respond to these messages verbally and nonverbally. Fifth, you must remember the messages that you have received.

THE FIVE STEPS OF THE LISTENING PROCESS
1. **Hearing:** receiving auditory and visual signals
2. **Attending:** focusing on and selecting signals to be interpreted
3. **Understanding:** decoding and interpreting auditory and visual signals
4. **Responding:** providing verbal and nonverbal feedback and responses
5. **Remembering:** recalling and retransmitting the messages of others

When you learn the five steps of the listening process, you realize that good listening involves much more than understanding the messages of others. Before you can understand a message, you must hear and attend to the message. After you understand a message, you must respond to and remember the message.

If you do not think that responding to and remembering a message is part of the listening process, ask people to describe what a good listener does—they will describe people who give appropriate feedback and are able to recall messages. You "prove" that you have listened to others by responding appropriately and remembering faithfully.

TEN STEPS TO TAKE TO BECOME A BETTER LISTENER

Now that you know the five steps or stages of the listening process, you are ready to learn ten steps you can take to become a better listener. Listening barriers can be overcome and ineffective listening behaviors can be eliminated if you take these ten steps.

1. Check your hearing equipment. Before a concert, musicians will check out all of their equipment to make sure it is in proper working condition. For effective listening, you need to do the same. Make sure you can successfully complete the first step of the listening process—hearing. If your ear canals are full of wax, focusing on the later stages of the listening process is futile. First things first; make sure you can hear the messages you are trying to receive.
2. Eliminate physical noise. Get rid of outside distractions. Turn off any blaring radios or televisions. Put away your cell phone. Put aside any books or any other "playthings" you may have. Find a quiet, uncluttered room where you can more easily communicate with others.
3. Eliminate physiological noise. Get comfortable. Find a decent chair to sit in. If you are hungry or thirsty, eat a snack or get a drink of water. If you are hot or cold, adjust the heating or air conditioning, or put on or take off a jacket or sweater. Make sure there is good ventilation and plenty of oxygen in the room. If necessary, use the restroom. Attend to your body, and it will allow you to focus your mind.
4. Eliminate psychological noise. Clear your mind. Put aside distracting thoughts. Process any strong emotions you are experiencing. Avoid prejudging or rehearsing a response.
5. Focus your mind. The second step of the listening process is attending or focusing. Pay attention to the words and thoughts of those who are speaking. Realize that you need to listen not only because you want to understand what others are saying, but you also want to maintain good relationships with your communication partners. Paying attention to others sends the message that you think *they* are

important. An added bonus of focusing on the messages of others is that you can accurately receive these messages.

6. Observe carefully and delay judgment. The third step of the listening process is interpreting and understanding a message. Listen for understanding. Strive to fully understand what others are saying. Do not rush to attack others or to defend yourself. Do not evaluate the messages of others until you have made a good faith effort to fully comprehend these messages.
7. Observe both the verbal *and* nonverbal messages of others. Listen with your eyes as well as your ears. Be aware of the communication context in which a verbal message is embedded. Seek to reconcile and harmonize the verbal and nonverbal messages that you receive.
8. Provide nonverbal and verbal feedback. The fourth step of the listening process is responding. *Act* like you are listening. Nod your head. Look at the person speaking. Provide appropriate verbal responses. You can prompt the speaker to give more information, or you can ask clarifying questions. You can paraphrase a message to make sure you understand it, or you can provide a supportive response to encourage your communication partner.
9. Listen with your heart. Be sensitive to emotional and relational messages. If people are communicating strong emotions, do not ignore this element of their message. Acknowledge that they are angry, or ecstatic, or sad, and show empathy.
10. Remember what was said. The fifth step of the listening process is remembering. To pass the listening "test" you must be able to recall and retransmit the messages of others. If you struggle with memory, take notes. Write down the important messages of others so you can recite them when asked.

FIGURE 6.17

To become a better listener, you must focus your mind.

Summary

After reading this chapter on small group communication and small group communication climate, you have the concepts and tools to become an effective communicator and a supportive small group member.

You now have an understanding of the basic elements involved in a communication transaction, and you know several principles of effective communication. You know that communication competence is a combination of motivation, knowledge, and skill.

You also understand that different communication networks can exist in a small group, and you are now able to track the communication patterns in your small group using an Interaction Diagram.

You can now clearly distinguish verbal communication from nonverbal communication, and you understand the importance of nonverbal communication. You are now sensitive to the way your small group members use space, body position and body posture, hand gestures, facial expressions, eye contact, and paralanguage to communicate nonverbal messages.

You are equipped to become a good listener because you now know three general listening barriers, eight specific ineffective listening behaviors, the five steps of the listening process, and ten steps to take to become a better listener.

You know how to communicate clear verbal messages. In addition, you know how to use confirming verbal responses, and you know the disconfirming verbal responses you should avoid.

Finally, you are aware of the general defensive and supportive behaviors that can create either a defensive or a supportive small group climate. If you apply the information in this chapter to your small group, you should experience even richer, more enjoyable, small group interactions.

Glossary

Adaptors: Nonverbal behaviors that help people adapt or adjust to their environment.

Affect displays: Nonverbal cues that signal the emotional state of a communicator.

Ambush listening: An ineffective listening behavior that occurs when people listen to others primarily to gain "ammunition" which they can use to attack people.

Attending: The second step of the listening process: focusing on, and selecting, auditory and visual signals to be decoded and interpreted.

Channel: The medium that carries a message.

Communication: A transactional process whereby two or more communicators share meaning.

Communication climate: The atmosphere that exists in a small group. People can create defensive or supportive communication climates through their responses and communication behaviors.

Communication competence: The ability to communicate effectively in a given context.

Communication network: The patterns of communication that exist in a small group; how information typically flows from person to person during a small group discussion.

Communicator: Someone who either sends or receives a message.

Confirming responses: Responses to messages that create a supportive communication climate because they make people value themselves more. (See five types of confirming responses listed in this chapter.)

Decoding: The mental process of transforming messages received back into ideas and concepts.

Defensive communication climate: A small group atmosphere that discourages open communication due to the defensive behaviors of evaluation, control, strategy, neutrality, superiority, and certainty.

Defensive listening: An ineffective listening behavior that occurs when people assume that whatever others say somehow reflects negatively on themselves.

Disconfirming responses: Responses to messages that create a defensive communication climate because they make people value themselves less. (See five types of disconfirming responses listed in this chapter.)

Emblems: Nonverbal symbols that take the place of verbal symbols.

Encoding: The mental process of transforming ideas and feelings into symbols and then organizing these symbols into a message.

Feedback: Any response, verbal or nonverbal, that a receiver gives to a message.

Hearing: The first step of the listening process; receiving auditory or visual signals.

High-contact: People or cultures that prefer and are comfortable with a high degree of physical contact and touching.

High-context: People or cultures that focus not only on verbal messages sent through the auditory channel, but also on other messages sent simultaneously through paralanguage and the visual and tactile channels.

Illustrators: Nonverbal symbols that emphasize or reinforce a verbal message.

Information overload: An inability to process information when too much information is received at one time.

Insulated listening: An ineffective listening behavior that occurs when people tune out topics or ideas they do not like or find objectionable for some reason.

Low-contact: People or cultures that prefer a low degree of physical contact and that require personal space.

Low-context: People and cultures that focus primarily on verbal messages sent through the auditory channel.

Message: The content of a communication.

Noise: Anything that interferes with the transmission of a message.

Nonverbal communication: Any communication that occurs through means other than human language.

Nonvocal communication: Communication that occurs through means other than the human voice.

Paralanguage: Vocal, nonverbal communication elements such as pitch, rate, volume, and voice quality.

Phonetic level: The first level of language involving the sounds and letters that combine together to make words.

Posture: The way people hold their bodies as they stand or sit.

Pragmatic level: The fourth level of language involving the context of a communication.

Prejudging: An ineffective listening behavior that occurs when people determine ahead of time that a message will be problematic (boring, offensive, too complicated, too controversial, etc.).

Pseudo listening: An ineffective listening behavior that occurs when people act like they are listening when they are not receiving or attending to messages.

Regulators: Nonverbal cues that help control the flow of communication.

Rehearsing a response: An ineffective listening behavior that occurs when people rehearse responses to messages before they have fully received and decoded these messages.

Remembering: The fifth step of the listening process; recalling and retransmitting a message that has been received and decoded.

Responding: The fourth step of the listening process; giving verbal and nonverbal feedback to the sender of a message.

Selective listening: Ineffective listening behavior that occurs when people only listen to the topics or ideas that interest them.

Semantic level: The second level of language involving the meaning of words.

Stagehogging: An ineffective listening behavior that occurs when people interrupt others or dismiss what they are saying in order to present their own ideas or examples.

Supportive communication climate: A small group atmosphere that encourages open communication due to the supportive behaviors of description, problem orientation, spontaneity, empathy, equality, and provisionalism.

Syntactic level: The third level of language involving how words are put together into sentences.

Understanding: The third step of the listening process; decoding and interpreting the messages of others.

Verbal communication: Communication expressed in human language.

Vocal communication: Communication expressed through the human voice.

Works Cited or Consulted

Barnlund, D. (1970). A transactional model of communication. In Sereno, K.K., & Mortensen, C.D. (Eds.), *Foundations of communication theory* (pp. 83–102). New York: Harper. (*Barnlund's original research article presenting the transactional model of communication.*)

Ekman, Paul, & Friesen, V., Wallace. (1969). The repertoire of nonverbal behavior: Categories, origins, usage, and coding. *Semiotica*, 1 (1), 49–98. (*Paul Ekman and Wallace Friesen's original research article that set out five types of nonverbal behaviors.*)

Ekman, Paul, & Friesen, V., Wallace. (1984). *Unmasking the face: A guide to recognizing emotions from facial expressions.* Los Altos, CA: Malor Books. (*A popular book on reading facial expressions by Paul Ekman and Wallace Friesen.*)

Gibb, R., Jack. (1961) Defensive communication, *Journal of communication*, 11 (3), 141–148. (*Jack Gibb's original research article listing the six Gibb categories.*)

Hare, P., A. (1992) *Groups, teams, and social interaction: Theories and applications.* New York: Praeger. (*Paul Hare's book reviews many social science theories concerning social interaction in small groups, and it has examples of small group interaction diagrams used by researchers in the field.*)

Hoppe, H., Michael. (2006). *Active listening: Improve your ability to listen and lead.* Greensboro, North Carolina: Center For Creative Leadership. (*A practical guide to improving your active listening skills.*)

Katz, K., Lazer, D., Arrow, H., & Contractor, N. (2004). Network theory and small groups. *Small group research,* 35 (3), 307–322: Sage. (*A work by four scholars that reviews and summarizes how network theory has been applied to small group communication interactions.*)

Sieburg, E. (1969). *Dysfunctional communication and interpersonal responsiveness in small groups.* Doctoral dissertation, University of Denver, Denver, Colorado. (*Evelyn Sieburg's doctoral dissertation listing types of confirming and disconfirming responses.*)

Chapter 7:

Conflict in Groups

© Radoslaw Korga, 2013. Used under license from Shutterstock, Inc.

Chapter Objectives

- Define conflict and identify different types of conflict.
- Recognize and utilize different conflict management strategies and styles.
- Develop strategies for dealing with difficult people.

Types of Conflict

In a group, conflict may exist about the issues or procedures of the group. Substantive conflict occurs when group members are in conflict over the issues being debated in the group. Groups want a "heated" debate that flushes out all the ramifications of the groups' decision. Procedural conflict results from conflicts due to "how" to get the task completed. Some more formal groups rely upon parliamentary procedures to resolve procedural conflicts. In a courtroom, judges rule which procedure is a correct interpretation of the law. A third type of conflict results from difficulties between group members. Often, people conflicts can be extremely detrimental to the group. These perceived or real conflicts are discussed at length in the next section.

If, at the end of your small group communication course, your instructor asks you to discuss some of the conflicts that occurred in your small group during the semester, the incorrect response is, "We didn't really have any conflicts in our small group." This answer indicates that you do not understand the basic definition of **conflict**: *a conflict is a perceived incompatibility between two or more interdependent parties.* Using this definition, over the course of three months, a small group is likely to have dozens, even hundreds, of conflicts. Let's take a closer look at some of the terms in this definition:

FIGURE 7.1

A conflict is a perceived incompatibility between two or more interdependent parties.

"Perceived:" If two people or parties are unaware that an incompatibility exists, then there is no conflict. On the other hand, even if there is no actual incompatibility, just the perception of an incompatibility can create a conflict. For example, some family feuds or fallouts are the result of misunderstandings created by poor communication: one sibling may not speak to another sibling for months or even years because they misheard or misunderstood what the other person said.

"Incompatibility:" This is probably the most crucial term in the definition. An incompatibility can exist in goals, opinions, desires, or personalities. There is a very close relationship between the noun "conflict" (which is stressed in American English on the first syllable) and the verb "conflict" (which is stressed on the second syllable): a *con*flict (noun) exists when two goals, opinions, desires, or personalities con*flict* (verb). For example, some members may want a small group to meet only during the week, whereas other members may want the group to meet on the weekends. These incompatible desires create a conflict that must be resolved or managed.

"Interdependent:" The people or parties with incompatible goals, opinions, desires, or personalities must be in a relationship that requires them to rely on one another or work together with one another. Otherwise, the incompatible goals, opinions, desires, or personalities do not create a conflict. People with incompatible goals are not in a conflict unless they have to work together to reach these goals. People with incompatible opinions are not in a conflict unless they must share their thoughts with each other. People with incompatible desires are not in a conflict unless they must choose between these desires. People with incompatible personalities are not in a conflict unless they have to interact with each other.

Because small group members are interdependent, they will have many conflicts to manage or resolve. "Many conflicts," however, does not equate to "many violent altercations or unpleasant shouting matches." Some people deny that their small groups have any conflict because they associate conflict with shouting, abuse, or violence.

"Conflict" is a very general term that encompasses many other terms, terms such as "argument," "battle," "disagreement," "fight," and "war." The terms "battle" and "war" have negative connotations related to violence. If you were raised in a dysfunctional family or have seen people "fighting dirty," even the words "fight" or "argument" may have negative connotations.

Realize that battles, fights, and wars are all conflicts, but all conflicts are not necessarily battles, fights, or wars. Your small group can manage conflicts effectively without resorting to threats, abuse, or violence. A conflict is merely a perceived incompatibility between two or more interdependent parties.

The following five types of conflict that can occur in small groups are arranged in hierarchical order, from the least serious type of conflict to the most serious type of conflict. Knowing about these five types of conflict can help you analyze and evaluate the conflicts that may arise in your group.

FIGURE 7.2
A conflict is not necessarily a battle or a war.

Pseudo conflict: Pseudo conflict occurs when there is a perceived incompatibility between two or more people, but the perception is incorrect. Since pseudo conflicts are often the result of misunderstanding due to poor communication, they are fairly easy to resolve. Once a misunderstanding is cleared up through good communication, the perceived incompatibility disappears. For example, two group members who thought they disagreed will discover that they were actually making the same point or arguing for the same position.

Simple conflict: Simple conflict occurs when there is an actual incompatibility between two or more small group members. Just because a conflict is "simple" does not mean that it is necessarily easy to resolve. Some simple conflicts may by easy to resolve, but other simple conflicts may be impossible to resolve.

Serial conflict: Serial conflict is chronic conflict that occurs again and again. It is a more serious type of conflict because it can interfere with the effectiveness of a small group and it can negatively affect the group morale. However, sometimes serial conflict can be resolved when members try new conflict management strategies.

FIGURE 7.3

Group members involved in ego conflict personally attack one another.

Value conflict: Value conflict occurs when the incompatibility among group members involves their deep-seated values. Since people's values are deep-seated and hard to change, value conflict is difficult to resolve. Often, for the preservation of the group, members will have to "agree to disagree" about a conflict in values.

Ego conflict: Ego conflict occurs when two or more group members attack each other personally. What started as simple conflict can turn into ego conflict when members abandon discussion of the original incompatibility and focus instead on psychologically wounding one another with abusive names, put downs, and personal attacks. Ego conflict is almost always unproductive, can quickly spiral out of control, and can create long-term relationship damage, so we list it here as the most serious type of conflict.

FIVE TYPES OF CONFLICT
1. **Pseudo conflict**: Conflict that results from a misperception of incompatibility.
2. **Simple conflict**: A perceived incompatibility between two or more interdependent parties.
3. **Serial conflict**: Chronic conflict that occurs again and again.
4. **Value conflict:** Conflict based on deep-seated incompatible values.
5. **Ego conflict**: Conflict focused on personal attacks.

Five Conflict Management Strategies

Now that we have clearly defined conflict and pointed out the major types of conflict that may occur in a small group, we will now present to you some important strategies for dealing with conflict. In the 1970s, Kenneth Thomas and Ralph Kilmann identified five main conflict management strategies that they included in their TKI (Thomas-Kilmann Conflict Mode Instrument). This research tool has been widely used for the past thirty-five years.

According to Thomas and Kilmann, the five main strategies people use to manage conflict are: 1) avoiding, 2) accommodating, 3) compromising, 4) competing, and 5) collaborating. Thomas and Kilmann's categories have proven to be a very fruitful way to think about conflict and conflict management. The following chart is based upon these five categories.

We believe one of the most fruitful ways of dealing with conflict is learning to balance your concern for the principles involved in a conflict with your concern for the relationships that you have with the people involved in the conflict. If you thoughtfully analyze and evaluate both the principles and relationships involved in, and impacted by, a conflict, then you will be able to choose the appropriate conflict management strategy. We will describe each conflict management strategy in turn.

Avoiding strategy: People who use the avoiding strategy disengage from discussion when a conflict arises, or they attempt to change the topic under discussion. When pressed to address a conflict situation, they may physically disengage by leaving the room or by engaging in another activity. It is a passive conflict management strategy.

Since the conflict is completely avoided, the different goals, opinions, or desires of the parties involved are never adequately addressed, so both parties "lose." People who constantly use the avoiding strategy are sometimes labeled "ostriches" because when conflicts arise they seem to stick their heads in the sand and refuse to address the concerns of others.

However, there are times when the avoiding strategy is appropriate. When the principles involved in a conflict are not that important, and when you do not need to maintain a relationship with the person(s) involved in the conflict, then avoiding the conflict may be the best strategy. Or perhaps, you should avoid conflict when your physical safety is in jeopardy.

For example, suppose a small group member brings a relative or friend to a small group meeting. If this visitor expresses a strong opinion about how a small group project should proceed, the best response may be no response. There is no need to argue with this one-time visitor, especially if their strong opinion relates to a matter of little consequence.

Accommodating strategy: People using the accommodating strategy "give in" and let the other parties involved in a conflict have their way. They give up their own wishes or desires in order to accommodate the wishes or desires of others.

FIGURE 7.4

People who constantly use the accommodating strategy are sometimes labeled "doormats" because they always seem to let other people walk all over them. Since they always give in, excessive accommodators are not difficult to work with, but they may become unhappy people who think that others are constantly taking advantage of them.

However, the accommodating strategy may be a good response to a conflict. When the principles in a conflict are not that important but the relationships with the other parties involved in a conflict are important, then accommodating may be the best way to handle the conflict.

FIGURE 7.5

Excessive competitors find that every conflict is a fight that they must win and others must lose.

For example, suppose you are a member of a successful band or musical ensemble that needs to decide the song line-up for an upcoming concert gig. You may really like a certain song, but if the other members have very strong opinions about the songs they want to play, it may be best to accommodate their wishes. Your primary goal is to maintain the harmony in your group so you can continue to play music together. If you have no strong objections to the songs other members suggest, there is no reason you cannot accommodate them for one concert or performance. You do not always have to "win" when you are involved in a group decision. Accommodation can be a successful strategy if it is reciprocal. The group members take turns "giving in" so all feel treated fairly.

Competing Strategy: People using the competing strategy strongly advocate for their goals or opinions. They seek to gain the compliance of others involved in a conflict so that their own opinions prevail and their own goals are reached.

People who constantly use the competing strategy view every conflict as a competition that they must win. Excessively competitive people who insist that others always bend to their will may "win" most arguments, but they often lose out on meaningful relationships. Most people get tired of constantly giving in to them, so super-competitors often find themselves with few friends.

FIGURE 7.6

Compromise is best labeled a "partial win partial loss" situation because no one actually gets what they desired.

However, the competing strategy is sometimes warranted. When you do not need to maintain long-term relationships with the people involved in a conflict and you think that they are asking you to violate an important principle, then you should "stick to your guns" and battle for what you believe is right.

For example, suppose some students in another small group in one of your college classes were suggesting that students should use research in a class assignment without crediting the original sources. You should insist that such behavior is wrong, and you should refuse to participate in plagiarism. Even though you risk alienating these unethical students, you cannot afford to engage in a behavior that could result in your expulsion from the class or the college.

Compromising strategy: People using the compromising strategy give up a bit of what they actually desire, and they expect the other parties involved in a conflict situation to do likewise. All parties in the conflict are expected to yield a bit so that everyone gets at least some of what they desire.

Many people think that the compromising strategy is the best strategy for conflict management. Because, although there are no clear losers in a compromise, there are also no clear winners. No one involved in the compromise gets what they actually desired. Ultimately, a compromise may not be the best solution to the problem.

For example, suppose half the members of a small group want their team color to be blue and the other half prefers the color yellow. Both sides can compromise and settle on the color green, which is a mixture of the colors blue and yellow. Both sides in the conflict end up with a team color composed in part of the color they actually wanted, but neither side ends up with the team color they actually preferred.

When your concern for the principles and people involved in a conflict are moderate, the compromising strategy may be appropriate. However, there is one final conflict management strategy that can lead to a clear positive result.

Collaborating strategy: People using the collaborating strategy seek to negotiate a resolution to a conflict that provides both parties what they want. They ask the other people involved in a conflict to join them as partners seeking a mutually beneficial solution to a problem.

Since all the parties involved in a conflict work together to figure out how everyone can have their most important interests met, the best solution may be identified. Collaborators do not view the other parties involved in a conflict as opponents who will attack your bargaining position. Collaborators help you protect your interests and address your concerns to determine the best option for the group. All members of the group must be a part of the process or colloboration will fail. If some group members develop strategies secretly of other group members, colloboration is not a good option.

Since you need to work with your small group members in your small group communication class for an extended period of time, the collaborating strategy will often be the best strategy for resolving your small group conflicts. Your relationships with your small group members are important, so it will often pay to collaborate together to resolve conflicts and solve problems that arise.

FIGURE 7.7

Collaboration will often be the best strategy for your small group conflicts.

THE STRENGTH AND WEAKNESS OF THE CONFLICT STRATEGIES APPROACH

Learning to use the five different conflict management strategies can definitely enhance your communication competence. Competent communicators employ a wide variety of strategies and techniques in order to adjust to different communication situations. With definitions of conflict management style in mind, you can consider the importance of the principles and people involved in a conflict in order to choose and use the most appropriate response. When the principles involved in a conflict are of minor importance, sometimes avoidance or accommodation may be the best response. However, if a core principle is at stake in a conflict, it may be necessary to use the competing strategy in order to fight for this principle. On the other hand, if you want to sustain long-term relationships in a small group, you will often need to compromise or collaborate with others.

However, there is one major weakness to the conflict management strategies approach that we have just presented: it is very "Western" in that it privileges a direct approach to resolving conflict.

FIGURE 7.8

People in the East may handle conflict very differently than people in the West

Many people in Eastern cultures and Asian countries, however, avoid dealing with conflict directly precisely because they do have a high regard for group harmony and interpersonal relationships. In order to maintain group harmony, they will deny that a conflict exists.

Since people in our modern world have to work in culturally diverse small groups, we need to supplement the conflict management strategies approach with a discussion of conflict management styles that is sensitive to cultural differences and preferences. People around the world view and approach conflict differently, so we must acknowledge these differences.

In the early 2000s, Mitchell R. Hammer developed the following intercultural conflict management styles chart. The chart is used in Hammer's *Intercultural Conflict Style Inventory* published by Hammer Consulting Group (2003). It recognizes four different conflict management styles determined by two variables: first, whether a person prefers to address a conflict directly or indirectly; second, whether a person prefers to address a conflict with emotional restraint or with emotional expressiveness. Below the chart, we provide a brief explanation of each conflict management style, and then we offer some tips for dealing with conflict when people may be using these different styles.

CONFLICT MANAGEMENT STYLES CHART

	Emotional Restraint	Emotional Expressiveness
Direct	Discussion Style (Representative: U.S.)	Engagement Style (Representative: Italy)
Indirect	Accommodation Style (Representative: Japan)	Dynamic Style (Representative: Saudi Arabia)

FIGURE 7.9

Discussion Style: People who use the discussion style prefer to address conflict directly, but they avoid the open display of emotion. They want to "talk things out" in a "reasonable" manner. The discussion style of conflict management is the dominant style in England and the United States. Many British and American people value frank, direct discourse and cool, calm deliberation. They like to address problems head-on, but they may get uncomfortable if a conversation gets heated or emotionally charged.

Engagement Style: People who use the engagement style want to address conflict directly, but they also expect the people involved in a conflict to become emotionally engaged. A strong display of emotion, they believe, demonstrates that a person cares about the matter at hand. The engagement style of conflict management is the dominant style in Greece, Italy, and many Latin American countries. (It is also the dominant style of African-Americans in the United States.) Many Greeks, Italians, and Latin Americans value direct discourse that is animated and punctuated by strong emotional displays. They are willing to "get in your face" in order to make their point, and they expect you to be just as passionate when you express your viewpoint or position.

Accommodation Style: People who use the accommodation style do not like to address conflict directly, nor do they like strong displays of emotion. They prefer to address conflict indirectly in order to "save face," and they strive to maintain a calm, "inscrutable" demeanor that reveals little of their inward state, especially if they are angry or upset. The avoidance style of conflict management is the dominant style in Japan and many Southeast Asian countries. Many Japanese and Southeast Asians value verbal discourse that appears harmonious and they expect people to pay attention to subtle nonverbal signals which indicate disagreement and dissatisfaction. They often find it very difficult to express an opinion that contradicts the opinions of others in their group, and they also find it very difficult to display an emotion that they think may threaten the cohesiveness of their group.

Dynamic Style: People who use the dynamic style avoid the direct discussion of conflict, but they expect people to express strong emotions. They want to signal sincerity and commitment to their principles through the strong display of emotions, but their interest in strong relationships also causes them to avoid conflicts which may threaten these relationships. The dynamic style of conflict is the dominant style in Saudi Arabia and many other Arab countries. Many Saudis and other Arabs value animated, emotional verbal discourse and nonverbal displays, but they avoid "spelling out" the precise issues or concerns that they think may destabilize their political or social relationships. Instead, they often work through third-party intermediaries.

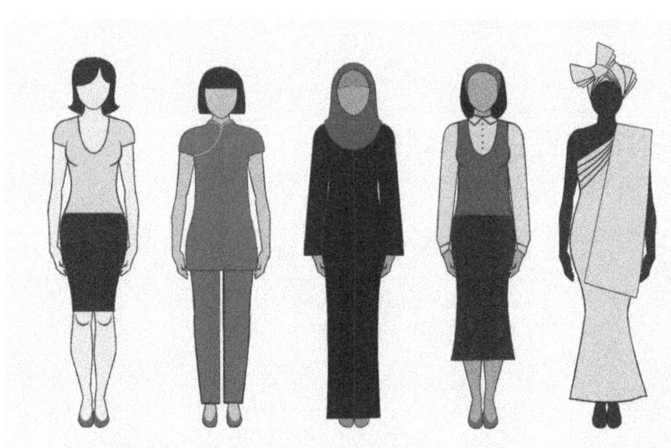

FIGURE 7.10
Conflict management styles, like clothing styles, differ around the world.

Now that you know about the four different conflict management styles, you can approach conflict in your small group with a more sophisticated understanding of people's different motives and preferences. Different people handle conflict differently. Everyone in your small group may not take the same approach to conflict that you take.

Here are some practical tips for working with people who have different conflict management styles:

- Educate the people in your small group about the different conflict management styles. When people know about these styles, they have a powerful tool for managing conflict more effectively.
- Do not stereotype people in your small group and automatically assume that they use the same conflict management style that is dominant in their national culture. There will always be deviations from a dominant style, so all four conflict management styles can be found in people from a particular country or ethnic group. You need to determine whether the people in your small group deviate from or conform to the dominant conflict management style of their country.
- Recognize that all four conflict management styles are valid. One of these styles is not "right" while the other styles are "wrong." Conflict management styles, like clothing styles, are a matter of preference.
- Identify the conflict management style you prefer, and share this preference with the people in your small group. They will have a better understanding of where you are coming from when a conflict arises.
- Identify the conflict management styles preferred by the other people in your small group so you can better understand their attitudes and behaviors when a conflict arises.
- Be especially sensitive to people who have a conflict management style most opposed to yours (in the quadrant of the conflict management styles chart that is diagonal to your quadrant). When people with opposing conflict management styles interact, there is greater potential for misunderstanding and confusion.

- Identify the negative thoughts and assumptions you tend to think and make when dealing with someone who has a different conflict management style. Recalibrate your thinking and recognize the strengths and benefits of their style.
- Stretch yourself and develop the ability to use all four conflict management styles. Just as you can use different conflict management strategies in different situations, you can also use these different conflict management styles for different interactions.

FIGURE 7.11

By presenting the concepts in the conflict management strategies, we believe we have sufficiently "complexified" the topic of conflict management. You should now have a fairly sophisticated understanding of how to handle conflicts.

The five conflict management strategies (avoiding, accommodating, competing, compromising, and collaborating) give you options for responding to a conflict based upon your analysis of the people and principles involved. The four conflict management styles (discussion style, engagement style, accommodation style, and dynamic style) give you options for handling conflict based upon people's preferences for a direct or indirect response, and an emotionally restrained or emotionally expressive response, to conflict.

The truth is, the people and cultures of the world can learn from one another. Those who prefer to directly address conflict can teach those who are afraid to directly address conflict that there is nothing inherently destructive in facing conflict "head on." When people approach the open discussion of conflict with good will and respect for one another, relationships can sometimes be strengthened, and conflicts can sometimes be effectively resolved.

On the other hand, people who prefer strong emotional communication can teach people who are uncomfortable with the expression of strong emotions that there is nothing inherently destructive in the communication of strong emotions. When people expect and allow one another to express their strong emotions, conflicts can be resolved in a way that actually draws people closer together.

MANAGING STRONG EMOTIONS (AFFECTIVE CONFLICT)

Conflict can generate strong emotions in people, emotions like frustration, anger, fear, and mistrust. Some people avoid conflict because they do not want to experience such emotions, nor do they want to "make" other people angry or upset.

When some people hit the "wall of conflict" they back off because people are "getting emotional." However, the "wall of conflict" can be transformed into the "door to deeper relationships" when people's emotions are expressed, acknowledged, and valued.

Emotional communication is one of the deepest levels of communication that exists. When strong emotions are expressed and acknowledged appropriately, this emotional communication is like glue—it helps to form strong relational bonds. Here are some tips for effective emotional communication during conflict situations:

- When very strong emotions are interfering with your ability to express yourself or listen to others, take a break. You can explain that you need some time to compose yourself and to process your strong emotions.
- Affirm your respect for, and relational commitment to, a person who communicates or displays strong emotion, especially if they prefer the discussion style or accommodation style of conflict management. They are likely to experience shame and regret when getting emotional. Assure them that they have done nothing wrong.
- Do not apologize for getting emotional or displaying strong emotions. An apology implies that you have done something wrong, and that others are doing something wrong, by displaying strong emotions.
- When dealing with people who are uncomfortable with strong emotional expression, "dial it down" and moderate your enthusiasm, especially if you prefer the dynamic style or engagement style of conflict management.
- "Own" your emotions. Take responsibility for them, and expect others to likewise do so. Do not blame others for your emotions. Do not use your strong emotions as a form of "emotional blackmail." Learn to say, "I am angry," and not, "You make me so angry." You have control over your thoughts and feelings. You can choose how you will perceive and respond to the behaviors of others—empower yourself and others to be in charge of their emotions.
- Explore the thoughts and perceptions that are creating your strong emotions. Emotions are outward signs of inward perceptions and thoughts. If others experience or express strong emotions, encourage them to examine and share why they are angry, or fearful, or upset.
- Determine if your strong emotions are justified and appropriate by identifying the perceptions and thoughts that are generating these emotions. If your perceptions and thoughts are accurate and true, then your strong emotions may be perfectly appropriate.
- Allow others to be emotional and to express their strong emotions appropriately. When you accept and respect other people's ability to express and communicate emotion, and when you reciprocate and share your feelings with others, you are forging deeper relationships with others and strengthening the cohesiveness of your small group.
- Do not allow yourself or others to "express" strong emotions inappropriately. Strong emotions are no excuse for demeaning or abusing other people. Name calling, personal attacks, and other "dirty tricks" should not be condoned or tolerated just because someone is angry or upset.

If you take these tips for effective emotional communication to heart, you will discover that even major conflict that generates strong emotions can be a positive experience. When you handle major conflict effectively by expressing your strong emotions appropriately, your small group conflicts can actually draw your members closer together instead of drive them farther apart.

FIGURE 7.12

Dealing with Difficult People

We will end this chapter by identifying ten particular types of "difficult people" that you may have to deal with in a small group. We give some general tips for dealing with difficult people. Next, we give a brief description of each type of difficult person, and we give some specific tips for dealing with that particular type of person.

IF YOU THINK YOU HAVE SEEN ONE OF THESE DIFFICULT PEOPLE:

- Do not be too quick to label someone as a "difficult" person. Be patient and forgiving. Sometimes people are just having a bad day, so do not rush to place any small group member on the "Ten Most *Not* Wanted People" list.
- Focus on people's strengths, rather than their weaknesses. Seek to treat each member of your group, even difficult people, with unconditional positive regard. Focus on, and draw attention to, the positive behaviors of each group member.
- If someone in your group really is being difficult, and if their behavior is out of character, look for power imbalances in your small group. Bad behavior is often a response to a perceived power imbalance. Make sure your group members are empowered to share opinions, make decisions, and fully participate in small group discussions and projects.
- Remember the five conflict management strategies and use each strategy when appropriate. Sometimes you can avoid or accommodate a difficult person. However, if the behavior of a difficult person is negatively affecting the group as a whole, you will need to have a confrontation with the person.
- If someone repeatedly shows a pattern of bad behavior, strategize with other group members about how to approach the difficult person. Elect someone to speak to the difficult person one-on-one in order to help them "save face."
- If a difficult person does not respond positively to a one-on-one intervention, then schedule a team meeting to discuss their behavior. First, objectively describe the difficult person's behavior. Be specific, and give concrete examples. Second, explain how that behavior is perceived and interpreted by other group members. Third, explain

the effect the inappropriate behavior has on the group and on other group members. Fourth, explain the consequences if the inappropriate behavior continues, and ask the difficult person to change their behavior.

- If a difficult person does not change their behavior after a team intervention, you could consult with someone outside your small group. For example, if you are in a small group communication course and have attempted to modify the inappropriate behavior of a difficult person without success, you may want to consult with your instructor about how to proceed.
- Sometimes people cannot be rehabilitated. You may need to ask a difficult person to leave your small group, or you may need to "work around" a difficult person that refuses to leave.
- Consider if any of your behaviors might cause your other small group members to label you a "difficult person." If you have been behaving inappropriately in your small group, apologize and modify your behavior. If you recognize yourself in the above "Most *Not* Wanted" list or in the descriptions that follow, check out the tips for changing inappropriate behaviors that come after the description of each type of difficult person.

The following ten most difficult people to work with in a small group are listed from least (number 10) to most (number 1) difficult:

FIGURE 7.13

The following "Top Ten" list is a list on which you do not want to appear.

Number 10: Conflict Avoiders (also called Ostriches): Conflict avoiders are often very pleasant, very helpful people, but their fear of conflict causes them to shut down, or to shut others down, whenever differences of opinion begin to surface. Do not confuse conflict avoiders with harmonizers, people who help small groups to manage conflict effectively. Harmonizers help to negotiate differences of opinion, whereas conflict avoiders prevent even the expression of the different opinions. They say things like, "Let's not argue about anything," and, "If you two are going to disagree, I am going to have to leave." Conflict avoiders may not intentionally harm your small group, but their fear of conflict prevents the group from exploring and evaluating the relative merits of different ideas and suggestions.

Tips for dealing with Conflict Avoiders:

- Educate conflict avoiders and help them to understand the necessity and benefits of healthy conflict which leads to better decision making and problem solving.
- Develop a group guideline that states that differences of opinion are allowed and even encouraged in your small group discussions.

- Develop a group guideline that states how differences of opinion will be handled. Healthy conflict and dialogue should be thoughtful and respectful.
- Ask a conflict avoider to play the part of "devil's advocate" during group discussions. Train them to look at a problem from different perspectives, and ask them to thoughtfully question the decisions of the group.

If you recognize yourself as a Conflict Avoider:

- Study the five conflict management strategies chart, and learn when it is appropriate to get out of the "avoiding" quadrant.
- Do not think of all conflict as unproductive or dangerous. Realize that conflict is unavoidable, necessary, and beneficial when managed effectively.

FIGURE 7.14
Healthy conflict leads to better decision making and problem solving.

Number 9: Isolates (also called Absentees): Isolates psychologically separate themselves from the rest of the group. They may sit apart from, or turn away from, their small group. They may "tune out" their small group and do their own thing (play on their cell phone, read a book, do homework for another class). When asked to participate or when directly addressed, extreme Isolates ignore their group and make no reply. Isolates often turn into Absentees that do not show up for team meetings or activities. Because they never bond with other small group members, Isolates often end up dropping out of the small group.

Tips for dealing with Isolates:

- Do not mistake introverts for Isolates. Some people, especially introverts, need time and courage to overcome their shyness. It takes greater effort for them to interact with other small group members.
- Seek to engage and involve the Isolate in small group discussions and activities.
- Provide non-threatening opportunities so the Isolate can socialize and bond with other small group members.
- Set a group guideline that everyone is expected to communicate and fully participate in small group discussions and activities.
- If an Isolate does not attend small group meetings, let them know that they were missed and that they are expected to attend all group functions.
- If an Isolate becomes a chronic Absentee, do not agonize over their decision to not participate. Sometimes you have to allow people to fail. Let them know that the group will have to move ahead without their participation.

If you recognize yourself as an Isolate:

- Make a conscious decision to focus on, and participate in, your small group. Sit with your group. Look at your other group members when they speak. Take part in the group discussions and activities.
- Try to develop interpersonal relationships with other small group members. You will find it much easier to participate when you feel connected to other people in the group.
- Bring a small treat or gift to share with your other group members. This simple act will signal that you want to make a positive contribution to the group.

FIGURE 7.15

Number 8: Stagehogs (also called Monopolizers): Stagehogs "hog the stage" during group discussions. Whereas Isolates do not communicate with their groups, Stagehogs make it difficult for anyone else in the group to get a word in edgewise. If someone in their group begins to share an opinion or experience, Stagehogs will interrupt and share their own opinions or experiences.

Stagehogs are self-centered, so they may be unaware of their behavior and how it affects others. When they realize that they have been monopolizing the small group time, they may feel guilty and apologize. However, if not held in check, self-centered Stagehogs will soon take center stage once again in the group discussion.

Tips for dealing with Stagehogs:

- Politely point out to the Stagehog that others would also appreciate an opportunity to share their thoughts and make useful contributions to the small group discussion.
- Set a group guideline that everyone is expected to share their ideas during small group discussions.
- Prepare an agenda for your small group meeting and set a time limit for each item to be discussed.
- Appoint a small group member to be "gatekeeper" during small group meetings. The gatekeeper's job is to keep the discussion "on topic" and to make sure that everyone has a chance to participate and share their ideas.

If you recognize yourself as a Stagehog:

- Express your concern about monopolizing the group discussion time, and request that the group use a timekeeper and gatekeeper during group meetings.
- Keep track of the meeting agenda and the time allotted for each agenda item. Allow yourself to use only so much of the allotted time.
- Every now and then, take a holiday from talking. Let your small group know that you would like to practice your listening skills.

FIGURE 7.16

Number 7: Diverters (also known as Jokers). Diverters constantly sidetrack the small group with "off-topic" comments, stories, or jokes. Humor and jokes can help relieve tension and develop relationships in a small group, but a group member who continually diverts the group from the task at hand with distracting jokes, comments, or questions is obstructing group progress. Diverters may initially be fun to have around, but if they constantly and consistently take the group in unproductive directions, their jokes and comments soon wear thin.

Tips for dealing with Diverters:

- As a group, decide what percentage of the group time should be on-track, task-focused time and what percentage of time should be used for socializing and relationship maintenance.
- Point out to the Diverter (and the group) when too much group time is off-track, and ask the Diverter to help keep the group focused on the task at hand.
- Set a meeting agenda with a list of topics to be covered and tasks to be completed, and set a time limit for each topic or task.
- Appoint an official "gatekeeper" to point out to the group when they are getting sidetracked.

If you recognize yourself as a Diverter:

- Express your desire to be a productive group member, and apologize for the continual distractions and off-track comments.
- Ask other group members to help you keep on track—it can become a new game to play!
- Sit where you can clearly see the gatekeeper during small group meetings.

FIGURE 7.17

Small groups should decide what percentage of group time should be on task and what percentage of group time should be used for socializing.

Number 6: Fanatics (also called Evangelists): Fanatics are a special type of Stagehog. They take up the small group time and focus the attention on one topic or concern that they single-mindedly pursue. Fanatics are very passionate about their object of devotion, but this passionate devotion to their cause is inappropriate when it causes them to take every small group discussion in the same direction. No matter what the small group is trying to discuss or accomplish, Fanatics or Evangelists will insist that the small group once again consider or focus upon their pet project or concern.

Tips for dealing with Fanatics:

- Acknowledge the importance of the topic or issue that concerns the Fanatic, but then point out that the small group has other concerns that need to be addressed.
- Give the Fanatic's topic or concern an official spot on the meeting agenda. Discuss this agenda item for an appropriate amount of time, and then move on to the other agenda items.
- If appropriate, design a small group project that addresses the Fanatic's concerns.
- If the Fanatic's pet project seems inappropriate for small group discussion or action, agree as a group to forego further discussion of this issue.

If you recognize yourself as a Fanatic:

- Realize that you can win more support for your ideas or concerns when you show an equal concern for the ideas and concerns of other small group members.
- Realize that you can actually cause people to reject your ideas or concerns, no matter how important they are, if you constantly beat the same drum.
- Find another venue to discuss your project or concern. Reserve your small group meeting time for small group business.

FIGURE 7.18

Number 5: Slackers (also known as Loafers): Slackers or Loafers do not do their assigned work. They may attend group meetings and participate in small group discussions, but they do not complete any individual work assignments or tasks, or they complete these tasks very poorly and with very little effort. The most difficult and destructive Slackers are the ones that claim they are doing their work, but then abandon or sabotage a small group when an important project or presentation is due. The day the project is due or the presentation is to take place, they do not show up, or they show up—unprepared—at the last minute.

Tips for dealing with a Slacker:

- Do *not* do the Slacker's work for them. If you have to work with this person for any length of time, you will always find yourself picking up their slack because they know you are willing to do so.
- Offer advice, help, and support for anyone who is struggling with their work.
- Set up a work chart for important group projects. Write down who is responsible for each task and the date this task needs to be completed. Make sure every member has a copy of this work chart.
- Communicate clearly, and in writing, the exact tasks that each team member needs to complete. Set due dates for both "rough draft" and "final product" work.
- Set a group guideline that if small group members do not complete their assigned tasks by the assigned due dates, they can be excluded from a group project or presentation.
- If you are concerned that a Slacker may not come through on a team project or presentation, have a back-up plan.

If you recognize yourself as a Slacker:

- Ask the group for clear due dates and for "checkpoints" along the way that will motivate you to make progress on your work.
- Set personal due dates that are a few days earlier than the official due dates for your work—this will give you a bit of a cushion if you run into problems.
- Schedule "work sessions" with other small group members to help you focus and get motivated.
- Give yourself a personal penalty if you miss a work deadline, and give yourself a small reward for every deadline you meet.

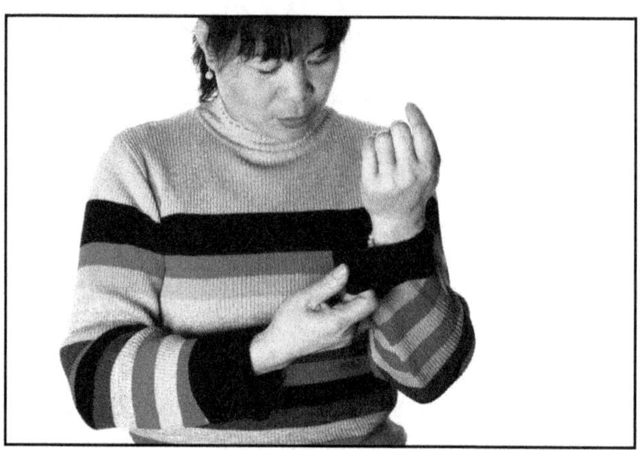

FIGURE 7.19

Number 4: Blockers (also called Cynics): Blockers or Cynics stand in the way of just about everything a small group tries to accomplish. They shout down any idea or proposal offered by their small group members, and they assert that whatever is proposed will not work or succeed. A Blocker with a seriously negative attitude can bring a small group's progress to a complete stop, but even a moderate amount of cynicism and "nay-saying" can do a lot of damage in a group. With a Blocker or Cynic on board, group members can lose all motivation to work together, and the task effectiveness of a group can plummet.

Tips for dealing with a Blocker:

- Ask the Blocker or Cynic if there is an underlying problem or concern that needs to be addressed. Make sure they feel empowered to help their small group succeed.
- Set a group guideline that whenever an idea or proposal is rejected or criticized, an alternate idea or proposal must be offered.
- Set a group guideline that sarcasm, pessimism, and cynicism should be avoided during group discussions.
- Ask the Blocker to become a "problem solver."

If you recognize yourself as a Blocker or Cynic:

- Realize that your negative attitude is harming both the task effectiveness of your small group and your relationships with other group members.
- Resolve to move your small group forward by changing your attitude and by actively encouraging your other small group members.
- Improve your mindset by reading a self-help book on positive thinking.
- Improve your mood by watching an uplifting comedy movie or television show.

FIGURE 7.20

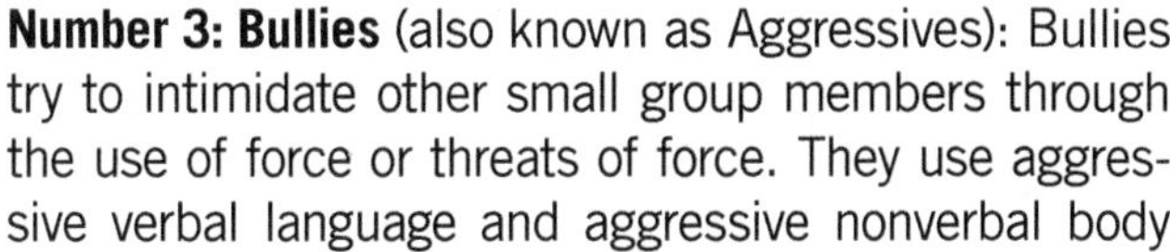

Number 3: Bullies (also known as Aggressives): Bullies try to intimidate other small group members through the use of force or threats of force. They use aggressive verbal language and aggressive nonverbal body language. Bullies seek to impose their will on other small group members through raised voices, intimidating postures and body language, and threatening verbal language.

Instead of arguing assertively for their ideas and positions with well-thought-out arguments and solid evidence, Bullies rely on brute force to get others to submit. Bullies can create a lot of fear in other group members, and their aggressive methods can prevent others from sharing their thoughts and feelings.

Tips for dealing with Bullies:

- Point out when a small group member is trapped in the "competing" quadrant of conflict management strategies, and ask them to use some of the other conflict management strategies (avoiding, accommodating, compromising, collaborating) when appropriate.
- Refuse to be bullied. Ask aggressive Bullies to lower their voices, modify their body language, and eliminate their threatening verbal language.
- Report any threats of violence or force. Let Bullies know that they will be held accountable for their behaviors.

If you recognize yourself as a Bully:

- Realize that you do not need to win every argument. Consider whether the issue or concern being discussed needs a "competing" response or whether your group might be better off if you collaborated or compromised with others. You might even need to accommodate to the desires of others, or you might need to avoid an argument altogether by keeping quiet.
- Think of your ideas and opinions as "gifts" which you give to your small group. When you give a gift to people, you cannot insist that they use it a certain way. Don't insist that other group members accept or agree to your ideas.

- Clearly understand the difference between aggressiveness and assertiveness. Stand up for yourself and your ideas, but do not get in people's faces when they disagree with you.
- Practice using a low voice volume, a friendly or neutral facial expression, and a non-threatening body posture.

FIGURE 7.21

Number 2: Passive-Aggressives (also known as Saboteurs): Note that Passive-Aggressives are number two on the "Most *Not* Wanted" list, which means they are considered to be even more dangerous than Aggressives or Bullies. Aggressives or Bullies are easy to recognize and identify because their obviously aggressive behavior draws our attention. Passive-Aggressives are harder to identify, and more dangerous, because they will smile to your face and then stab you in the back when you are not looking.

When confronted, Passive-Aggressives will deny that there is a problem or that they are dissatisfied in any way with their small group. They will then proceed to use negative "resistance" strategies to harm other small group members and to sabotage the work of the small group. Their use of deceit and denial makes it difficult to confront Passive-Aggressives.

Tips for dealing with Passive-Aggressives:

- Correct any power imbalances that may be causing a Passive-Aggressive to use negative resistance strategies.
- Point out and label the resistance strategies being used by the Passive-Aggressive person.
- Watch your back.

If you recognize yourself as a Passive-Aggressive:

- Seek to be assertive about your wants and needs.
- Own up to your concerns and fears about the behaviors of other group members, and be willing to discuss these concerns with your group.
- Practice engaging in productive, healthy conflict. Realize that differences of opinions can be openly negotiated and that power in a small group can be shared.
- Take a class or seminar in assertiveness training.

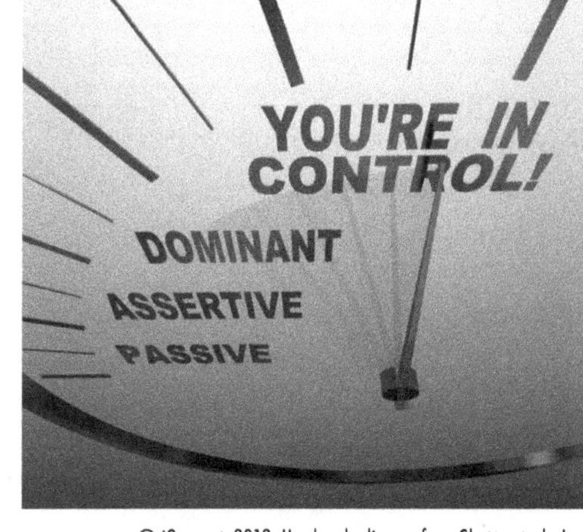

FIGURE 7.22

Passive-Aggressive people need assertiveness training

Number 1: Dangerous People: Although you want to have the default setting of "trust" when interacting with other human beings, realize that occasionally you may come into contact with truly dangerous people, people who are mentally unstable, violent, or criminal. When asked to work in a small group that includes strangers, you need to watch for behaviors or signs that indicate you may be dealing with a dangerous person. You will rarely encounter a dangerous person in a small group work or school setting, but such an encounter could happen.

Tips for dealing with Dangerous People:

- When beginning to work in a new small group, make sure your initial meetings are in a well-lighted, public place with lots of people nearby.
- Report threats of violence, criminal activity, and suspicious behavior to the appropriate authorities.
- Do not agree to keep a person's criminal activity secret—they can then make you an accomplice and threaten you with exposure.

If you recognize yourself as a Dangerous Person:

- Do not harm others. Realize that you reap what you sow.

FIGURE 7.23

Your default setting for interacting with others should be "trust."

Summary

After reading through this chapter, you are better equipped to use power and manage conflict effectively. You know five basic power resources you can use in your small group. You know the negative effects of power imbalances, and you know how empowerment can improve your small group.

You now know what conflict is, and you know that it is inevitable, necessary, and beneficial. You can distinguish between five different types of conflict. When conflicts arise in your small group, you now have five conflict management strategies and four conflict management styles you can use to try to resolve these conflicts. You also can now identify ten different types of difficult people, and you have specific strategies you can use to deal with these difficult people.

Glossary

Accommodating: Accommodating is one of the five conflict management strategies. The accommodating strategy is also called the "lose/win" strategy. A person using the accommodating strategy yields to, or accommodates, the other party involved in a conflict.

Accommodation style: One of the four conflict management styles. A person using the accommodation style prefers to address conflict indirectly and in an emotionally restrained manner.

Alliance: Alliance is a response to a power imbalance. People who feel that they do not have enough power may form alliances or factions with other people.

Avoiding: Avoiding is one of the five conflict management strategies. The avoiding strategy is also called the "lose/lose" strategy. A person using the avoiding strategy avoids dealing with a conflict, so both parties involved in a conflict "lose" because their needs, wants, goals, or opinions are never adequately discussed.

Collaborating: Collaborating is one of the five conflict management strategies. The collaborating strategy is also called the "win/win" strategy. A person using the collaborating strategy works with the other party involved in a conflict to find a solution or resolution that meets the needs of both parties.

Competing: Competing is one of the five conflict management strategies. The competing strategy is also called the "win/lose" strategy. A person using the competing strategy makes sure their wants or needs are met at the expense of the other party involved in a conflict.

Compromising: Compromising is one of the five conflict management strategies. The compromising strategy is also called the "partial win/partial lose" strategy. A person using the compromising strategy gives up some of what they want, and expects the other party involved in a conflict to also give up some of what they want.

Conflict: A conflict is a perceived incompatibility between two or more interdependent parties.

Defiance: Defiance is a response to a power imbalance. People who feel they do not have enough power may openly defy those in power.

Discussion style: One of the four conflict management styles. A person using the discussion style prefers to address conflict directly and in an emotionally restrained manner.

Dynamic style: One of the four conflict management styles. A person using the dynamic style prefers to address conflict indirectly and in an emotionally expressive manner.

Ego conflict: Ego conflict occurs when the parties involved in a conflict lose focus of an original incompatibility and focus instead on personal attacks.

Empowerment: A positive response to a power imbalance. A certain measure of power is given to everyone so no one thinks or feels that they are powerless.

Engagement style: One of the four conflict management styles. A person using the engagement style prefers to address conflict directly and in an emotionally expressive manner.

Expert power: One of the five basic power resources. A person with special knowledge or training has expert power.

Extrinsic rewards: Incentives such as money, gifts, or recognition that can be used to motivate people to accomplish tasks or reach goals.

Intrinsic motivation: The inner drive that people have to accomplish tasks or reach goals. Extrinsic rewards can reduce or eliminate intrinsic motivation.

Legitimate power: One of the five basic power resources. A person who is appointed or elected to a leadership position has legitimate power.

Personal power: One of the five basic power resources. A person with charisma, moral virtue, wisdom, and other positive personal attributes has personal power.

Power imbalances: Power imbalances occur when one or a few people hold(s) power and other parties feel powerless.

Pseudo conflict: An apparent conflict that results from an incorrect perception of incompatibility.

Punishment power: One of the five basic power resources. A person with the ability to impose penalties or punishments has punishment power.

Resistance: Resistance is a response to a power imbalance. People who feel that they do not have enough power may resist those who have more power.

Reward power: One of the five basic power resources. A person with the ability to provide favors or incentives to others has reward power.

Secondary tension: The tension created in a small group when conflicts and disagreements arise. Secondary tension is distinguished from primary tension, the awkwardness and nervousness that people feel when they first join a new group.

Serial conflict: Chronic conflict that reoccurs over and over again.

Simple conflict: An actual incompatibility between two or more interdependent parties.

Storming: The second stage of the small group process. After going through the first forming stage, small group members experience conflict as they begin to work together.

Value conflict: Conflict related to or focused on the different values held by two or more interdependent parties. Since values are deep-seated, value conflicts are often difficult to resolve.

Works Cited or Consulted

French, R.P., John, & Raven, Bertram. (1959). The bases of social power. In Cartwright, D. (Ed.), *Studies in social power* (pp. 150–167). Ann Arbor, MI: Institute for Social Research. (*The original research article that introduced the idea of five power resources.*)

Hammer, M.R., Bennett, M.J., & Wiseman, R. (2003). The intercultural development inventory: A measure of intercultural sensitivity, *International journal of intercultural relations, 27,* 421–443. (*The first version of the Intercultural Conflict Style Inventory which recognizes different cultural approaches to conflict.*)

Miller, G.R., & Steinberg, M. (1975). *Between people: A new analysis of interpersonal communication.* Chicago: Science Research Associates. (*Miller and Steinberg introduce the idea of pseudo conflict, simple conflict, and ego conflict in this book focusing on interpersonal communication.*)

Rothwell, J.D. (2013). Power in groups: A central dynamic. In *In mixed company: Communicating in small groups and teams* (8th ed.) (pp. 300–343). Wadsworth Cengage Learning. (*Rothwell devotes an entire chapter of his small group communication textbook to the dynamics of power in small groups.*)

Thomas, W., Kenneth, & Kilmann, H., Ralph. (n.d.). An overview of the Thomas-Kilmann conflict mode instrument (TKI). Retrieved March 24, 2016, from http://www.kilmanndiagnostics.com/overview-thomas-kolmann-conflict-mode-instrument-tki. (*Thomas and Kilmann provide a brief explanation of the five conflict management strategies that their diagnostic tool is designed to identify.*)

Chapter 8:

Decision-Making and Problem-Solving in Groups

© Phovoir, 2013. Used under license from Shutterstock, Inc.

Chapter Objectives

- Distinguish between decision-making and problem-solving.
- Understand the elements of poor quality decisions in small groups.
- Understand how to analyze and make high quality decisions in small groups.
- Employ standard problem-solving methods in small groups.

In Chapter 2, you learned that small groups go through a four-step process: 1) forming, 2) storming, 3) norming, and 4) performing. For a small group to function well, small group members must bond together (the forming stage), iron out differences (the storming stage), and negotiate the guidelines and norms by which they will operate (the norming stage).

However, the fourth step of the small group process—performing—is the primary goal of many small groups, especially decision-making and problem-solving groups. If you are a member of a decision-making or problem-solving group, in order to fulfill your group's primary function and finish well, you need to know how to make high quality decisions and how to solve problems effectively.

In this chapter you will learn 1) the difference between decision-making and problem-solving, 2) the elements of low-quality small group decisions, 3) the elements of high-quality small group decisions, and 4) how to employ the Standard Agenda, a six-step problem solving method.

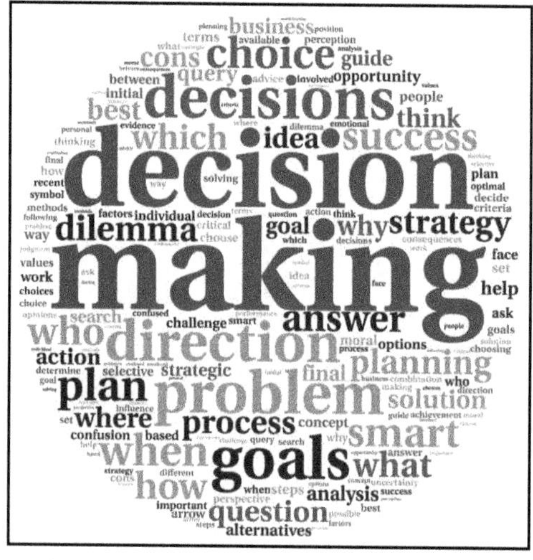

FIGURE 8.1

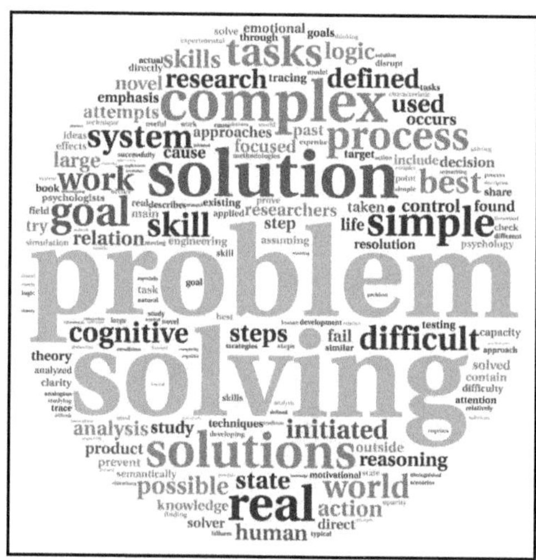

FIGURE 8.2

Decision-Making Groups versus Problem-Solving Groups

Although decision-making groups sometimes have to solve some problems, and although problem-solving groups have to make many decisions, there is a difference between these two types of small groups; small groups charged primarily with making decisions have a narrower scope of operation than small groups tasked with solving problems.

DECISION-MAKING SMALL GROUPS

The primary function of a decision-making group is usually to choose between a number of given alternatives or choices. Often a decision-making group is charged with making one or a few decisions, and after these decisions have been made, the small group is disbanded.

For example, a jury is a small group (usually of six to twelve people) charged with the responsibility of deciding the guilt or innocence of a person accused of a crime. A jury is given only a limited set of options for their decision—conviction, acquittal, conviction on a lesser charge, not proven, not able to decide, etc. Once the jury has rendered its verdict, the jury is usually dismissed.

Another short-lived decision-making group is a judging panel. The primary task of a judging panel is to rank the contestants or entries in a contest. There are usually a limited number of entries, and the charge of the judges is to decide first place, second place, third place, etc. Usually the judges have very specific rules and guidelines they must follow in making their decisions.

Similarly, the members of a hiring committee are charged with the task of deciding whom a company or organization should hire. There may be several steps in the hiring process—resumé evaluations, job skills tests, personal interviews—but the main task of the hiring committee is to recommend, or decide on, the new hire(s).

Some decision-making groups have longer life-spans. A student disciplinary committee may have the same members for an entire school year. A "standing" decision-making committee may have a semi-permanent place in a company or organization. Justices of the Supreme Court of the United States have life terms.

FIGURE 8.3
A jury

FIGURE 8.4
A judging panel

However, whether decision-making groups are short-term or long-lived, the charge of these groups, and the tasks they are allowed to carry out, is limited. Small groups organized and recognized as decision-making groups cannot undertake problem-solving tasks outside their decision-making charge. Juries are not allowed to propose new ways for law courts to operate. Contest judges (in their role as judges) do not get to design new contest events or formats. Hiring committees do not provide solutions for funding new hires. Even Supreme Court Justices, with all their decision-making power, do not get to propose or create new laws. Their job is to decide how to interpret laws, and that is the extent of their power. They are not members of a problem-solving group.

FIGURE 8.5

PROBLEM-SOLVING SMALL GROUPS

Groups charged with solving problems have a much more complex task than decision-making groups. Problem-solving groups have many decisions to make on the way to developing, suggesting, and/or implementing solutions for various problems: What method or methods should be used to solve a problem? How is a problem to be defined? Will the scope of a problem be limited or enlarged? What are the criteria to be used to judge the possible solutions to a problem? How should these criteria be measured? How should these criteria be ranked? How many possible solutions should be generated? How will the solutions be evaluated and selected? Should one solution be selected, or should several? How should the solution(s) be implemented? Who should implement the solution(s)? How will the implemented solution(s) be evaluated? When should the implemented solution(s) be evaluated? These are just some of the many questions that need to be answered and decisions that need to be made when people work together in problem-solving groups.

FIGURE 8.6

There are many questions to be answered, and many decisions to be made, in the problem-solving process.

Some problem-solving groups have to work very quickly. A fire crew has to quickly identify the extent of a fire, determine the best way to fight the fire, and deploy rapidly in order to minimize the loss of life and property. A S.W.A.T. team has to quickly identify and isolate a criminal threat, develop a plan to neutralize this threat, and swiftly execute this plan.

Other problem-solving groups take weeks, months, or even years to work through the many steps of the problem-solving process. An engineering team may need weeks or months to design a device. A legislative committee may take a year to hammer out the details of a law designed to address a thorny social problem. A group of medical researchers may take years to discover the cure for a disease.

FIGURE 8.7

Some problems need to be solved quickly.

FIGURE 8.8

Some problems take a long time to solve.

Whether problem-solving groups work swiftly or slowly and methodically, the problem-solving process is more complex than the simpler decision-making process; consequently, the problem-solving process requires a larger skill set and oftentimes special training.

Although jury members are expected to examine and evaluate evidence and use their intellects to decide the guilt or innocence of an accused person, citizens usually receive no special training before they sit on a jury. Members of problem-solving groups (like firefighters and S.W.A.T. team members), on the other hand, receive many hours of training. Engineers and medical researchers, likewise, are trained in the scientific method. They learn how to identify and analyze problems, and they learn how to generate, evaluate, and test possible solutions.

One special skill or ability that is needed in problem-solving groups, and that is not needed in decision-making groups, is creativity. Jurors and contest judges are not expected to get creative; they are expected to follow the jury instructions and the judging guidelines faithfully in order to yield a just and fair decision. People in problem-solving groups, on the other hand, are encouraged to be creative when brainstorming possible solutions to a problem. Like jurors and judges, they need to be able to analyze and evaluate evidence, but, unlike jurors and judges, they need to be able to "think outside the box" in order to generate new ideas and novel solutions to old problems.

Problem-solving groups often have more authority than decision-making groups. Oftentimes, once a decision-making group announces its decision(s), the job of this group is done. The jury verdict is read. The contest winners are announced. The hiring recommendations are given. The decision-making group disbands, and others are responsible for dealing with these decisions.

However, some problem-solving groups do much more than just recommend a solution to a problem. Some problem-solving groups are given the authority and responsibility for implementing the solutions that they propose. Like fire crews and S.W.A.T. teams, some small groups in business, industry, politics, and education are expected to actually implement their proposed solutions.

Differences in Decision-Making and Problem-Solving Groups

Decision-Making Groups	Problem-Solving Groups
Have a limited decision-making charge.	Have a complex problem-solving task.
Often receive no special training.	Often receive special training.
Use a narrower skill set.	Need creative problem-solving skills.
Often have no authority or responsibility after making and announcing a decision.	Sometimes have the authority and responsibility for implementing a solution.

DECISION-MAKING AND PROBLEM-SOLVING GROUPS

Now that we have distinguished small groups which are primarily decision-making groups from small groups which are primarily problem-solving groups, it is important to note that there are some small groups which are expected to carry out both functions. Some small groups are expected to make important decisions *and* solve problems as they arise.

Many small groups and committees in business and education are charged both with making decisions and with solving problems related to a designated subject or area. Pooling the group

FIGURE 8.9

Some small groups have the twin charge of both making decisions and solving problems.

members knowledge and expertise, the group strategizes how to solve problems, and then develops the best strategies they can devise to solve these problems.

If you are asked to serve on a committee or task force or a small group team, make sure you understand the committee charge, the task force goals, or the team purpose. Are you a work group, a decision-making group, or a problem-solving group? Is your small group limited to one of these functions, or does it have more than one charge? If you are charged with making decisions and solving problems, and if you want to carry out this twin charge well, read on to discover the elements of high-quality (and low-quality) small group decisions and the six steps you can take to solve problems effectively.

The Elements of Poor-Quality Small Group Decisions

Chapter 1 ended with a list of advantages of working in a small group, and the very first advantage listed was that "human beings often make better decisions and solve problems more effectively when they work together in small groups."

People do not always make better decisions when they work together in small groups.

There are several elements or factors that can result in low-quality small group decisions: 1) too much evidence or information (information overload), 2) insufficient evidence or information (information underload), 3) insufficient deliberation time, 4) influence from outside parties, 5) hidden agendas, 6) poor communication, 7) poor or faulty reasoning, 8) too much conflict, 9) too little conflict (groupthink), and 10) poor decision-making processes. If you are aware of the elements or factors that can result in low-quality decisions, hopefully you can eliminate or avoid these factors and situations when you are working with others to make decisions. Let's take a closer look at each of these ten elements.

TEN ELEMENTS OF LOW-QUALITY SMALL GROUP DECISIONS
1. Too much evidence or information (information overload)
2. Insufficient evidence or information (information underload)
3. Insufficient deliberation time
4. Influence from outside parties
5. Hidden agendas
6. Poor communication
7. Poor or faulty reasoning
8. Too much conflict
9. Too little conflict (groupthink)
10. Poor decision-making processes

TOO MUCH EVIDENCE OR INFORMATION (Information Overload)

Sometimes small groups trying to make decisions are overwhelmed by the amount of evidence or information they have to sort through. A jury for a major trial may have hundreds of witnesses to listen to, dozens of pieces of evidence to consider, and many pages of trial transcripts to sort through. Members of a hiring committee may need to consider hundreds of applicants who have submitted letters of interest, resumés, reference letters, college transcripts, etc.

FIGURE 8.10

If you need to gather some evidence in order to make a small group decision, it is easy to be overwhelmed with information in the computer age. One internet search can yield millions of "hits." You need to scan through many pages of possible articles and websites that you could access in order to gain more information about the topic or issue under consideration, and then you need to decide which articles and websites you will actually access and mentally process.

INSUFFICIENT EVIDENCE OR INFORMATION (Information Underload)

Although it is difficult to sift through and process a large amount of information, evidence gathering and information processing is an important part of the decision-making process. We would be appalled if a jury or a hiring committee gave their verdict or made their decision without considering the evidence or information that was provided to them.

"Information underload" occurs when a small group makes a decision without taking the time or making the effort to gather the necessary information or to evaluate the evidence provided. Small groups can pool the knowledge of their group members together, but sometimes groups need outside information and knowledge that cannot be provided by any group member.

INSUFFICIENT DELIBERATION TIME

Small group discussion and deliberation takes time. If a group is rushed into making a decision, or if a group makes a decision too quickly, the deliberation process is short-circuited. You have personally experienced the effect that being rushed has on your decision-making capability if you have ever been pressured by a salesperson to decide quickly about a purchase. Your poor decision to purchase an item that you didn't really need at a price you couldn't really afford was the result of being pressured to decide on-the-spot about the purchase.

FIGURE 8.11

Sometimes small groups are pressured by outside parties to arrive at a decision, but sometimes small groups just do not take the time they need to make a high-quality decision. Although they may have plenty of time to look at evidence, share their individual opinions, and come to a group consensus, they may not use their time wisely, or they may decide to "get it over with" and come to a decision prematurely. Insufficient deliberation time will lead to a low-quality decision.

INFLUENCE FROM OUTSIDE PARTIES

If a small group has been given the responsibility for making a decision, then people and parties outside the small group decision-making process should have no influence on, or say in, the decision. That is why juries are sequestered during deliberations and why members of hiring committees are required to sign confidentiality agreements.

If it is suspected that someone has influenced a jury member, a charge of "jury tampering" can be leveled, and the entire decision-making process of a jury can be tainted and invalidated. If it is discovered that a contest judge has received a bribe or a favor from one of the contestants, the judge may be removed from the judging panel.

You may not be a jury member or a contest judge, but if you are a member of a small group that needs to make a decision, be careful about discussing your small group deliberations with an outside person. That person, intentionally or unintentionally, may influence the way you perceive and participate in the small group discussions. Since an outside person has not fully participated in the small group deliberation process, his or her influence can lead to a lower-quality small group decision.

HIDDEN AGENDAS

Influence from outside parties can negatively affect the quality of a small group decision, but sometimes there are influences *within* a small group itself that can lead to lower-quality decisions—one of these influences within a small group is **hidden agendas** held by small group members.

A "hidden agenda" is a personal desire or goal held by a group member that may run counter to the goals of a group. In decision-making groups, one of the primary group goals is usually to make the best decisions possible. However, small group members may have personal hidden agendas that conflict with this goal of making high-quality decisions.

For example, a small group member may want to make another group member look bad or foolish, so they will tend to disagree with or ridicule any ideas or opinions offered by the other group member. Another small group member may be a covert sexist or racist, so they will support any decision which they think benefits their sex or race. Obviously, hidden agendas can lead to low-quality small group decisions, especially if the person with the hidden agenda has high group status or persuasive power.

POOR COMMUNICATION

Several different kinds of poor communication can lower the quality of small group decisions: 1) particular small group members may be withholding important messages and not sharing their opinions, and 2) group members may be having difficulties sending and receiving messages. We will discuss these two.

First, even if there is a good flow of information and ideas in your small group as a whole, if even one member withholds important information or opinions, a lower-quality decision could result.

This poor communication may result in lower-quality group decisions.

Second, small group members may be attempting to send and receive messages during small group deliberations, but a variety of factors can interfere with the transmission, reception, and interpretation of these messages. Even if members are committed to the goal of making high-quality decisions, if information is being lost, distorted, or misunderstood during the group discussion and deliberation, low-quality decisions are the inevitable result.

FIGURE 8.12

POOR OR FAULTY REASONING

The conclusions to be drawn from information are not self-evident. Information and evidence has to be analyzed, evaluated, and interpreted. Even good information and solid evidence can lead to low-quality small group decisions if small group members analyze and evaluate this information incorrectly due to poor or faulty reasoning. Let's look at several types of reasoning errors that can occur in small groups.

TOO MUCH CONFLICT

Too much conflict in a group, especially ego conflict, can result in low-quality small group decisions. Small group members need to share different ideas, thoughts, and perspectives, and sometimes these ideas, thoughts, and perspectives will conflict. The group will then have to manage these conflicts and negotiate how to reconcile or handle these different ideas and opinions. However, when group members are constantly and forcefully disagreeing with each other over even the most minor points, the healthy conflict needed to negotiate perceived incompatibilities has turned into unhealthy conflict that decreases the decision-making effectiveness of the group.

Small group members who constantly disagree with each other as a matter of principle are not helping move the small group discussion and deliberation forward; instead, they are interfering with, and sometimes even preventing, the productive group discussion that needs to occur if ideas and opinions are to be adequately developed and tested. If group members are involved in ego conflict and resort to personal attacks, they also create a defensive communication climate that makes it difficult for anyone to freely express their ideas.

FIGURE 8.13

Too much conflict, especially negative ego conflict, can also lead to the generation of strong emotions in different small group members—anger, frustration, disgust, fear, etc. These strong emotions can cloud the thinking of group members and make it difficult to concentrate on the issues and concerns related to the decisions that have to be made. When the ego conflict fireworks finally fizzle, low-quality decisions are often the result.

TOO LITTLE CONFLICT (Groupthink)

Surprisingly, group decision making often suffers from *too little conflict.* When group members agree with one another too much, they are not performing important error-correction and decision-making functions. Ideas need to be challenged, defended, clarified, and corrected in order to be as strong as possible. Different ideas, opinions, and perspectives need to be offered by group members in order to compare and test the merits of each.

The term "groupthink" sounds like it could be a positive group activity akin to creative "brainstorming," but groupthink is far from positive. Sociologist Irving Janis blames groupthink for some of the worst disasters that have occurred in history, including Pearl Harbor, Watergate, the escalation of the Vietnam War, and the explosion of the space shuttle *Challenger.* When groupthink kicks in, individual members are actively discouraged from expressing opinions that run counter to the group.

FIGURE 8.14

The conditions which create groupthink are excessive group cohesiveness and the desire to present a united front. The main symptoms of group think are arrogance, closed-mindedness, and the absence of any dissenting opinions. Not all instances of groupthink exhibit all of these symptoms, but approximately one-quarter of the small groups in my small group communication courses self-report at the end of the semester that they had too little conflict in their small groups. In an effort to "be nice" and not "rock the boat," students report that they often agreed with the first idea or suggestion offered by a group member. An agreement that is gained too easily, without any dissent or true discussion, yields low-quality decisions.

POOR DECISION-MAKING PROCESSES

The final element we will mention that leads to low-quality small group decisions is poor decision-making processes. Instead of working together as a small group to make the best decision possible, sometimes small groups use poor decision-making processes such as 1) making a totally random choice, 2) asking an outside expert or authority to make the decision, 3) averaging individual member's rankings or ratings, 4) making a minority decision, or 5) making a majority decision. Let's consider each of these decision-making processes.

1) Making a random choice. Sometimes groups get so frustrated with the decision-making process, or they are so afraid of taking any responsibility for making a decision, that they use a completely random method for making a decision such as flipping a coin, rolling a pair of dice, or playing the game "Rock, Paper, Scissors." Using a random method like this is not really "small group decision-making." A random method may be fine for matters of little importance, but small group members should not abandon their individual and corporate responsibility for making wise decisions on matters of importance.

FIGURE 8.15
Rock, Paper, Scissors is a poor small group decision-making process.

2) Asking an outside expert or authority to make the decision. If members of a small group think that they are underqualified to make a decision, or if they are unwilling to make a decision, they may ask a recognized expert or authority to make the decision for them. Although asking an outside expert or authority to make a decision for a small group may result in a good decision that is superior to the random method, a small group is still not using the power of small group communication to yield a high-quality decision. A small group can consult an expert, but then they should incorporate this expert knowledge and opinion into their own small group deliberations.

3) Averaging individual member's rankings or ratings. This decision-making method can be used when multiple decisions have to be made. For example, judges of a contest or members of a hiring committee could rate or rank all the candidates, and then they could combine these ratings or rankings to mathematically determine who should be placed first, second, third, etc. Although this mathematical method is a good place to begin a small group deliberation (to discover where the individual members initially stand) it should not be the end point of the deliberation. Otherwise, once again, the small group is bypassing the important small group discussion that needs to occur for a high-quality decision to emerge.

4) Making a minority decision. Sometimes a small group lets one or a few members make the decision for the group. Perhaps one member has high status, so the other members defer to this person with social or political power. Perhaps two or three members of a small group are very vocal and demanding, so other group members give in and let them have their way. Whatever the case may be, a minority decision is not based on the full participation of all the group members, and, in the long run, it will likely lead to dissatisfaction in the majority of the group members that acquiesced in the decision.

5) Making a majority decision. Although a majority vote works well in a democracy with many citizens, it does not work as well in a small group. If there are five members in a group, a "majority decision" could be made by a three-to-two vote. Three members may be happy with this outcome, but what about the other two members? Like a minority decision, a majority decision in a small group can lead to dissatisfaction and lack of "buy in" for small group decisions. Furthermore, when "majority vote" is invoked before a small group discussion has fully unfolded, the deliberative process is once again short-circuited. You may need to fall back on a "majority vote" if your small group cannot come to an agreement, but making a majority decision should not be your first move.

If even a majority vote has drawbacks for small groups making decisions, what decision-making process should small groups use? We will end the next section with the alternative to these five poor small group decision-making processes—the method of making "consensus" decisions.

POOR DECISION-MAKING PROCESSES FOR SMALL GROUPS
1. Using a random decision-making method.
2. Asking an outside expert or authority to make the decision for the group.
3. Averaging individual member's rankings and ratings.
4. Making a minority decision.
5. Making a majority decision.

The Elements of High-Quality Small Group Decisions

Now that we have revealed to you many of the elements and factors that can lead to low-quality small group decisions, we will take the positive approach and tell you the elements and factors that lead to high-quality small group decisions. If you want "Grade A," high-quality decisions to emerge from your small group discussions and deliberations, then make sure the following ten elements are present.

FIGURE 8.16

Aim for high quality small group decisions

TEN ELEMENTS OF HIGH-QUALITY SMALL GROUP DECISIONS
1. The right people are in the room, and they know why they are there.
2. Adequate time has been set aside for the decision-making process.
3. Members set aside preconceptions and biases.
4. Open, frank, discussion is encouraged—even the discussion of dissenting opinions.
5. All the necessary information and evidence is made available.
6. Members share their analysis and evaluation of the information.
7. Members support their assertions with adequate evidence and sound reasoning.
8. All options and alternatives are explored.
9. Conflict is managed appropriately.
10. Members aim for a consensus decision.

THE RIGHT PEOPLE ARE IN THE ROOM, AND THEY KNOW WHY THEY ARE THERE

When a small group needs to make an important decision, every member of the group should be present and should fully participate in the small group deliberations. Sometimes groups will establish a quorum for a meeting. A "quorum" is the minimum number of members that need to be present in order to have a discussion and to make group decisions. However, the *optimum* number of members to have present is not the minimum number of members, but the maximum; all decision-makers should participate in the small group decision-making process.

In addition to all the decision-makers, small groups will sometimes need to speak to and hear from people outside the group. In order to make a high-quality decision, small groups may need to consult "expert witnesses," or they may need to have an outside person explain and interpret some technical data.

However, when it is time to begin small group discussion and deliberation, it is usually best to dismiss anyone from the room that is not directly involved in the decision-making process. After experts and other witnesses have been consulted, they should usually be asked to leave the room so the small group can carry out its discussion without outside influences. If your small group is not required (usually by law) to hold an "open" meeting, a closed meeting will allow for uninhibited small group discussion that will hopefully yield a high-quality decision.

In addition to having the right people in the room, it is important that small group members know why they are there. They should know who has invested them with their decision-making authority, they should know their decision-making charge, and they should know what will happen once the group has made the necessary decision(s). Knowing that they are charged with the task of making decisions (and that they have been given legitimate authority to make these decisions) should motivate group members to strive to make the best decisions possible. Knowing what will happen after the decision-making process concludes clarifies where the small group charge ends.

ADEQUATE TIME HAS BEEN SET ASIDE FOR THE DECISION-MAKING PROCESS

When small groups need to make decisions, they can schedule one or several decision-making sessions. For major decisions, small groups could schedule four different meetings: the first

FIGURE 8.17

meeting could be devoted to gathering information and evidence, the second meeting could be devoted to analyzing and evaluating the information and evidence gathered, the third meeting could be devoted to brainstorming possible alternatives or choices, and the fourth meeting could be devoted to evaluating and selecting the best alternative(s).

If a decision needs to be made at one group meeting, you should announce the amount of time set aside for making the decision. Some groups use meeting agendas which list each agenda item, designate whether it is a "decision" item, and specify how much time is set aside for each item. With this information given up front, all group members can help keep the group discussion focused and on track. When necessary, and if it is appropriate, a group can extend the time set aside for making a decision.

Sometimes it is best to postpone a group decision, especially if it is an important decision and group members think that the process is being rushed. However, if the decision-making process has fully unfolded with good participation from all group members, there is no need to postpone the decision. Sometimes difficult decisions need to be made, and if adequate time has been set aside for the decision-making process, then the group can confidently assert that they have done their best to make a high-quality decision.

MEMBERS SET ASIDE PRECONCEPTIONS AND BIASES

Group members need to set aside preconceptions and biases in order to approach the decision-making task with an open mind. When people's minds are open, they can process all the available information and they can examine the evidence fairly. If you are on a judging panel charged with yielding impartial, fair decisions, you need to set aside any thoughts or feelings you have about any of the contestants (prior knowledge, stereotypes, prejudices, etc.), and you need to judge each contestant based on his or her current performance.

Concern about unfair bias results in judges instructing jury members that they should assume an accused person is "innocent until proven guilty." This assumption actually gives the accused the benefit of the doubt. Instead of assuming that a person is guilty of a crime, jury members are expected to find evidence that proves "beyond a reasonable doubt" that a person is guilty.

Similarly, when making decisions in a small group, group members should not assume they know what decision is "right" or "wrong." Instead, they should approach the decision-making task with an open mind, and they should look for solid evidence that leads them to conclude that a certain decision is warranted/wise or unwarranted/unwise.

OPEN, FRANK DISCUSSION IS ENCOURAGED (Even the Discussion of Dissenting Opinions)

In order for a high-quality decision to emerge, open, frank discussion must occur. Status differences need to be de-emphasized so every member feels comfortable speaking his or her mind. "Yes" people who typically agree with high-status members must be put on notice. Members should be empowered to speak and to share their thoughts, opinions, concerns, and reservations.

Although the final goal of the small group decision-making process is to reach a consensus decision, during the small group discussion and deliberation there should be the expectation of honest disagreement and healthy conflict. In order for the best ideas to emerge, ideas must be questioned and tested. Bad ideas need to be weeded out and discarded. Good ideas need to be elaborated, clarified, and strengthened. Through the process of small group deliberation, the fittest ideas will survive, and a high-quality decision will result.

FIGURE 8.18

Some small groups "normalize" and ensure disagreement by appointing a devil's advocate. A person appointed to play the role of "devil's advocate" is charged with presenting alternate viewpoints and dissenting opinions during a small group discussion. The role of devil's advocate is designed to decrease the possibility of groupthink. To ensure that everyone doesn't jump on the same bandwagon, the devil's advocate presents alternate possibilities and choices to the group to make sure that all angles have been considered and all options have been explored.

ALL THE NECESSARY INFORMATION AND EVIDENCE IS MADE AVAILABLE

In order to make a high-quality decision, small group members need access to all the pertinent information. This information should be provided to all the group members either before or at the decision-making session. If the information is provided at the decision-making session, members need to be given enough time to process this information and to examine the evidence before moving on to their group discussion and deliberation.

Necessary information and evidence may include research articles, books, recorded interviews with experts and others, opinion polls, surveys, and past small group meeting minutes. In addition to this type of information, small group members also need to be able to access any decision-making instructions or decision-making criteria that have been given to the group. It is very helpful if the meeting chair or another group member places the decision to be made in context by providing a brief narrative of why the small group is charged with making this decision. After this brief narrative explaining *why* the group is making the decision, reminders of *how* the group is to proceed (a review of any decision-making instructions and criteria) will help keep the group on track.

FIGURE 8.19

When you want to make a high-quality decision, provide only the *necessary* information to the group. Watch out for "information overload." Sometimes defense lawyers try to overwhelm a jury with a flood of information—instead of helping the jury reach a just decision, these defense attorneys are using a questionable tactic that seems designed to obscure the important facts of a case. Too much information confuses rather than clarifies an issue. Provide the necessary information a small group needs to make a high-quality decision, and no more.

MEMBERS SHARE THEIR ANALYSIS AND EVALUATION OF THE INFORMATION

Small group members must share their analysis and evaluation of the information and evidence available in order to sort out the "garbage" information and evidence. Computer programmers created the acronym GIGO—"garbage in/garbage out"—to point out that the quality of information makes a difference. Bad information can lead to bad decisions, and high-quality information can lead to high-quality decisions.

There are several criteria you can use to evaluate the quality of information and evidence: information should be 1) credible, 2) current, 3) relevant, 4) representative, and 5) sufficient. Credible information is balanced and unbiased. Current information is up-to-date. Relevant information is pertinent and to-the-point. Representative information accurately represents the majority of situations being discussed or considered. Sufficient information allows for valid generalizations and conclusions to be drawn.

FIVE CRITERIA FOR EVALUATING INFORMATION OR EVIDENCE
1. **Credibility:** How credible or trustworthy is the information?
2. **Currency:** How current or up-to-date is the information?
3. **Relevance:** How relevant or applicable is the information?
4. **Representativeness:** How representative or common is the information?
5. **Sufficiency:** How sufficient or profuse is the information?

Members need to work together to determine what information and evidence is important. When individuals share their analysis and evaluation of the available information and evidence with others, an important quality-control process kicks in—many eyes, ears, and minds working together to examine and evaluate evidence results in more accurate observations and more powerful insights. When the meaning and merits of the available information and evidence are discussed, the group as a whole can correct errors in analyzing and evaluating information.

MEMBERS SUPPORT THEIR ASSERTIONS WITH ADEQUATE EVIDENCE AND SOUND REASONING

In order to make high-quality decisions, small groups must strive to make decisions that are based on solid evidence and sound reasoning. When you make an assertion in a small group discussion, you should be prepared to provide evidence and support for this assertion, and you should expect the other members of your small group to do likewise. A basic principle of sound reasoning is that assertions need support.

For high-quality decisions, small groups must make valid inferences based on solid, "quality" evidence. After pointing out what the best available information or evidence seems to indicate, group members should then offer reasonable conclusions based on this evidence. Group members may draw specific conclusions from general principles (deductive reasoning), or they may draw general conclusions from specific evidence and examples (inductive reasoning). If they are reasoning inductively, group members should use qualifying terms like "some," "most," "sometimes," and "often" in order to limit the scope of their assertions, and they should think carefully before using absolute terms like "always," "never," "everyone," and "no one" in order to avoid inaccurate statements or invalid hasty generalizations.

When considering causes and effects, group members using sound reasoning do not assume causal connections without appropriate evidence or reasoning. Causal connections must be established with evidence and/or argumentation. Sound reasoning also requires group members to consider if there might be multiple causes of a problem, or several possible consequences for a course of action.

ALL OPTIONS AND ALTERNATIVES ARE EXPLORED

In order to make the best decision possible, small groups must consider and explore all their possible options. It is not enough to consider three possible choices when a fourth choice is possible, and it is not enough to consider four possible choices when a fifth choice is possible. All the "live," reasonable (but not always obvious) options must be considered.

When getting ready to make a decision, small group members should ask the following questions in order to fully explore the options and alternatives that are available.

- What alternatives are available? How many choices do we need to consider?
- What are the advantages and disadvantages of each possible decision?
- What are the moral implications of each possible decision?
- What are the probable short-term and long-term consequences of each possible decision?

FIGURE 8.20

CONFLICT IS MANAGED APPROPRIATELY

In order to make good decisions, small group members must manage conflict appropriately. Pseudo conflict should be eliminated through effective communication. Ego conflict and personal attacks should be avoided. However, lots of healthy "simple" conflict should occur during small group deliberations. For high-quality decisions to emerge, group members must disagree with and challenge one another. The goal of effective small group decision-making is not to avoid necessary, beneficial conflict, but to encourage and manage this conflict.

In Chapter 7 of this textbook, we presented five conflict management strategies that are appropriate in different situations. When small groups are making decisions that directly affect their group, then the conflict management strategies that will be most appropriate are accommodation, compromise, and collaboration. In order to maintain group harmony and cohesiveness, sometimes small group members will accommodate the wishes and desires of other group members on minor matters. In order to maintain long-term satisfaction and "buy in" for important small group decisions directly affecting the group, often compromise and collaboration will be the most appropriate strategies because everyone needs to work together to try to create a "win/win" situation for all group members.

However, when an outside party is asking a small group to make an important decision, oftentimes competition will be the appropriate conflict management strategy. Juries, judging panels, and hiring committees often do not have the option of collaborating together to reach a decision that will please everyone. Instead, people serving on these types of decision-making bodies must advocate for the decision which they think is best, and then the small group must decide which decision is the "winner" through intelligent small group deliberation.

MEMBERS AIM FOR A CONSENSUS DECISION

At the end of the previous section (on the elements of low-quality decisions), we promised to present the most effective process for making a decision, and we labeled this process "consensus." A **consensus decision** is a decision which all the group members support. Consensus does not necessarily mean total agreement on every single point related to a decision, but it does mean that every single group member agrees to support the final decision made by the group.

A consensus decision is very different from groupthink. When a consensus has been reached, members have not been pressured into agreeing with the group through personal attacks, bandwagon appeals, or other types of psychological manipulation. For a true consensus to be reached, the concerns of dissenting members must be heard, addressed, and answered. These dissenting members must then be willing to change their minds and agree with the majority opinion of the group.

FIGURE 8.21
Consensus yields high quality decisions and high group member satisfaction

It takes time and effort to reach a consensus decision, but this method of deliberation usually yields high-quality decisions. In the American legal system, juries are expected to reach "unanimous" or consensus decisions for their verdicts because this is the decision-making method deemed most likely to yield the best result. However, aiming for consensus does not always mean that consensus can be reached. Sometimes a "hung" jury occurs and a mistrial is declared.

Like juries, many other small groups cannot always reach consensus decisions—that is why the final element of high-quality small group decisions is that members *aim* for a consensus decision. Even if a consensus cannot be reached, just aiming for unanimity will yield a higher-quality decision. Investing the time and effort into building a consensus improves the quality of a decision even when full consensus cannot be reached.

If you are in a small group that has to make decisions, ask your small group to aim for consensus decisions. Not only will your group make higher-quality decisions, but your attempts at consensus will also yield greater satisfaction with the decision, more "buy in" for the decision, and long-term acceptance of the decision. When a consensus decision cannot be reached, a small group should then aim for a "supermajority," or 2/3 majority vote.

The Standard Agenda (A Six Step Problem-Solving Method)

When we distinguished decision-making groups from problem-solving groups earlier in this chapter, we noted that problem solving is a more complex activity than simple decision making. There are many decisions that need to be made on the way to solving a problem. In the early twentieth century, American philosopher and educator John Dewey helped standardize the problem-solving process. In his 1910 book *How We Think*, Dewey coined the term "reflective thinking," and the reflective thinking that he described was broken down into several steps.

The problem-solving steps that Dewey described for individual problem solvers were repeated, expanded, and applied to the small group problem-solving process in the 1920s and 1930s. So many people have referred to and used these problem-solving steps in the last few decades that they are now part of The Standard Agenda, a well-recognized prescriptive approach to problem solving.

Although there are many different approaches that small groups can take when attempting to solve a problem, we will now present the six step problem-solving method enshrined in many critical thinking and small group textbooks as The Standard Agenda: 1) identify and define the problem, 2) analyze the problem, 3) brainstorm possible solutions, 4) decide on criteria for judging the solutions, 5) evaluate and select the solutions, and 6) implement the solutions. We will give you practical advice for completing each of these steps.

THE STANDARD AGENDA FOR SMALL GROUP PROBLEM SOLVING
1. Identify and define the problem
2. Analyze the problem
3. Brainstorm possible solutions
4. Decide on criteria for judging the solutions
5. Evaluate and select the solution(s)
6. Implement the solution(s)

STEP 1: IDENTIFY AND DEFINE THE PROBLEM

"Houston, we have a problem." This line from the 1995 movie *Apollo 13* immortalizes the words of an Apollo 13 crewmember after an oxygen tank exploded and damaged his spacecraft. This tag line is now spoken by many people around the world whenever a serious problem is recognized in any situation. However, to complete the first step in The Standard Agenda, you need to do more than recognize or admit that a problem exists; the first step to take in solving a problem is to clearly identify and define the exact problem that needs to be solved.

One way to clearly identify a problem that needs to be solved is to frame it as a policy question. There are four types of questions that you can ask: 1) questions of definition, 2) questions of fact, 3) questions of value, and 4) questions of policy. Questions of definition, fact, and value can lead to small group discussion and decision-making, but they will not lead to full-blown problem solving. In order to clearly identify a problem that needs to be solved, state it as a policy question.

FOUR TYPES OF QUESTIONS
1. Questions of definition: What is *x*?
2. Questions of fact: Does *x* exist? Does *x* cause *y*?
3. Questions of value: Is *x* good or bad? Is *x* better than *y*?
4. Questions of policy: Should we or should we not do *x*? Should we do *x* or *y*?

For example, if you want to tackle the problem of poor student performance at the college level, you can ask the policy question, *"How can we increase student success?"* *"What is student success?"* is an important question of definition. *"What factors lead to student success?"* is an important question of fact. *"Why is student success important?"* is an important question of value. All three of these questions are important, but none of these three questions requires us to come up with a solution. However, when we ask the question *"How can we increase student success?"* we are asking a policy question that requires us to propose solutions.

FIGURE 8.22

Once you have worded a problem as a policy question, you need to define the important concepts or terms in the question. You do not need to "nitpick" the definition of every single word in a question of policy, but you do need to gain agreement on the critical concepts and most essential terms used in the description of a problem. Definitions are foundational—they undergird all your statements of fact, value, or policy. Clear thinking begins with effective definitions. You can't solve a problem until you pin down exactly what is the problem. You can't decide on an effective solution until you know exactly what are your goals and objectives.

FIGURE 8.23

First, you need to decide the scope of the question. Are you trying to solve a problem on a personal level, at the local level, at the national level, or at the world-wide level? For example, do you want to come up with a solution to air pollution that you can personally implement, or that your city can implement, or that the United States of America can implement, or that all the people and nations of the world can implement?

Second, you need to decide to what degree you need to solve the problem. Do you want to reduce a problem? Substantially reduce a problem? Eliminate a problem for some time? Eradicate a problem forever? For example, is it reasonable to seek a solution that would totally eliminate crime or eradicate crime forever, or should you seek to reduce, or substantially reduce, crime?

Third, you need to decide if you will "distribute out" parts of a problem in order to focus on one particular area of a problem. For example, when addressing the problem of marijuana and its prohibition or legalization, you need to decide if your focus will be on marijuana used for industrial purposes, or marijuana used for medical purposes, or marijuana used for recreational purposes. You and your small group could decide that the real issue to be addressed is the use of marijuana for recreational purposes, so that would become the focus of your research, discussion, and deliberation.

However, when you are deciding on which part of a problem you need to focus, make sure you do not distribute out the most essential or difficult part of a problem or issue; otherwise, you will end up with a "straw man" argument that is easy to win but that does not really get to the heart of a problem or issue. For example, if your small group was trying to come up with a pro-abortion legislative plan, you would need to focus on more than just medically necessary, first-trimester abortions. This narrow focus would make it easy for your group to argue the necessity of abortion in these instances, but you would be side-stepping the more controversial, more problematic abortion issues like elective abortions and partial-birth abortions.

When discussing an issue or solving a problem, you and your small group must clearly identify the exact issues you are trying to address and the precise problems you are trying to solve. You do this by assigning specific, clear meanings to the words that you use. Remember, meanings are not in words—words are only symbols that people must decode and interpret.

For example, if your goal is to increase student success at the college level, you must clearly define the exact nature of student success. Is student success completing a course? Mastering a subject? Attaining a certain skill level? Passing a test? Receiving a degree? Getting a job? Becoming a productive citizen? If you do not clearly know what your goal or objective is, how can you design a solution to help you reach this goal or objective?

Another example that emphasizes the importance of definitions is the topic of "world hunger." When tackling the problem of world hunger, what exactly is the problem that needs to be solved? Hunger is not really the heart of the problem—hunger is a natural biological mechanism designed to inform human beings that they need to eat food. The "problem" of world hunger is not hunger, but the inability of human beings to feed themselves when they are hungry. The problem is actually something like "scarcity of food" or "unequal food distribution."

Coming up with good definitions for the terms in your problem statement or policy question takes effort. Do not mindlessly grab the first definition of a word that you find in a dictionary. Words have multiple meanings, so you and your small group must choose useful, reasonable definitions for the important concepts and terms related to your target problem. Work together to select definitions that are reasonable and acceptable to your group members. If you need to speak to people outside your small group, make sure these people outside your group would also understand and accept your definition or description of a problem.

STEP 2: ANALYZE THE PROBLEM

Once a problem has been clearly identified, it then needs to be carefully analyzed. Some people find it difficult to clearly distinguish the first two steps of The Standard Agenda, but there is a difference between identifying a problem and analyzing a problem. Identifying a problem is a narrower initial task that involves posing a policy question and/or defining important concepts or terms related to the problem. Analyzing a problem is a broader, more substantial task that involves much more research, analysis, and thought.

We should note that small groups often give the identification of the problem (step one) and the analysis of the problem (step two) a brief nod. It is essential that you fully complete these first two steps. Small groups are sometimes guilty of "jumping to solutions;" the desire to solve a problem, or to quickly solve a problem, can short-circuit the problem-solving process. However, you need to *understand* a problem before you can solve it effectively.

In step two of the standard problem-solving process, you need to gather the important information you need to know in order to fully understand a problem. There are two main things you need to know: 1) what are the effects of the problem? and 2) what are the causes of the problem?

Knowing the effects of a problem reveals the extent and degree of the problem. What are the short-term and long-term effects of a problem? How many people are affected by the problem? How long have the effects of the problem been experienced? When you know the answers to these questions, you can convince people that a problem needs to be addressed.

A problem is a problem because it leads to negative effects or consequences. A problem is a serious problem because it has serious negative effects or consequences. There are the immediate consequences of a problem (often called the "symptoms"), and there are sometimes far-reaching effects of a problem. Sometimes problems have "ripple effects" which harm or negatively impact many people or things.

For example, poverty is a problem with far-reaching effects. You have a better chance of convincing people that poverty, or the unequal distribution of wealth, needs to be addressed when you can point out that poverty often leads to hunger, sickness, disease, stunted physical and mental growth, lack of education, dependency, crime, and social unrest. If evidence can be gathered that establishes the link between poverty and these other negative situations or effects, you will have more than a persuasive tool—you will have a clearer understanding of poverty and its consequences.

FIGURE 8.24

An analysis of poverty should include an analysis of its short-term and long-term effects.

In addition to analyzing the effects of a problem, it is also important to analyze the causes of a problem. Analyzing the causes of a problem is crucial for finding a long-term solution to the problem. Good doctors do more than treat the symptoms of an illness or disease—they try to find a cure by identifying the "root" cause of the medical condition. When the "root" of a problem is addressed, a problem can often be completely eliminated. Medical researchers work to determine the cause of a disease in order to discover and produce long-term cures.

For example, when long sea voyages became common in the seventeenth and eighteenth centuries, ship doctors and navy personnel attempted to treat the terrible scourge of "scurvy," a gruesome life-threatening disease that afflicted almost all ship passengers after an extended stay at sea. Many different solutions were proposed, based on many different possible causes. Some people thought that scurvy was the result of sea air, so they proposed "land therapy." Some people thought that scurvy was caused by poor sanitation, so they proposed regular baths as a cure. When the true cause of scurvy—vitamin C deficiency—was identified in the nineteenth century, scurvy was finally eradicated.

In the 1980s and 1990s, when doctors and medical researchers named a certain medical condition "AIDS," people did not understand why a cure was not quickly found. After all, if the disease of AIDS was clearly identified, why couldn't a cure be found? Understanding what the term AIDS means—acquired immune deficiency syndrome—helps us to understand why a cure was not immediately forthcoming. All the term "AIDS" reveals is that a person has something wrong with their immune system; this term does not give any indication of what the cause of this immune deficiency might be. Medical researchers have been working for two decades to isolate and fully understand the cause of AIDS.

Without an understanding of the causes of a problem, your small group may only come up with "Band-Aid" solutions; solutions which treat the effects of a problem but do not really solve or eliminate a problem. For example, if you were on a committee at work that asked you to tackle the problem of low employee morale, to come up with a truly effective, long-term solution you would need to analyze the causes of the low morale: is this low employee morale caused by low wages, a hostile working environment, ethical violations, lack of recognition, unfair labor practices, or something else? Without knowing the answer to this question, you cannot implement a long-term solution. You could throw a company party to boost morale, but that would only be a "Band-Aid" solution.

We will now present to you four different methods for analyzing a problem: 1) the journalist's six questions, 2) the fishbone diagram, 3) a Pareto chart, and 4) a force-field analysis.

Analytical Method One: The Journalist's Six Questions

In order to quickly develop a news story, journalists are trained to answer six basic questions: 1) Who? 2) What? 3) When? 4) Where? 5) Why? and 6) How? These six questions can also be used by problem solvers to quickly gain an understanding of the basics of a problem. Who is involved in the problem? What is the cause of the problem? What are the effects of the problem? When does the problem occur? Where does the problem occur? Why does the problem occur? How does the problem manifest itself?

Before your small group meets to discuss a problem and its possible solution, you can ask group members to write down their answers to the journalist's six questions. When your small group meets, members can then share their answers to begin your discussion and analysis of the problem.

THE JOURNALIST'S SIX QUESTIONS
Who?
What?
When?
Where?
Why?
How?

Analytical Method Two: The Fishbone Diagram

Japanese quality management consultant Kaoru Ishikawa developed the Fishbone Diagram to help people analyze the possible causes of a particular known effect. Placing the known effect at the "head" of the Fishbone Diagram, you then draw bones radiating off of the spine of your Fishbone Diagram and you label the possible causes of the effect under consideration.

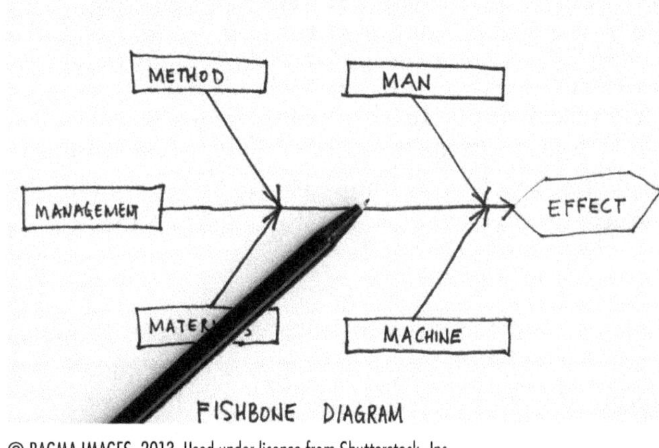

FIGURE 8.25

Ishikawa suggests that people should consider the "Four Ms:" 1) Manpower (people problems), 2) Machines (technology), 3) Materials (supply problems), and 4) Methods (process problems). As you consider these common causes, you can add more bones to your diagram as needed.

Analytical Method Three: A Pareto Chart

In the 1940s, American quality management consultant Joseph M. Juran popularized the work of Italian economist Vilfredo Pareto who, a generation earlier, had noted that 80% of the land in Italy was owned by 20% of the population. Juran applied the Pareto Principle in many different areas, including problem solving. Now we often assert that 80% of a problem comes from 20% of the incidents, or that 80% of the effects of a problem come from 20% of the causes.

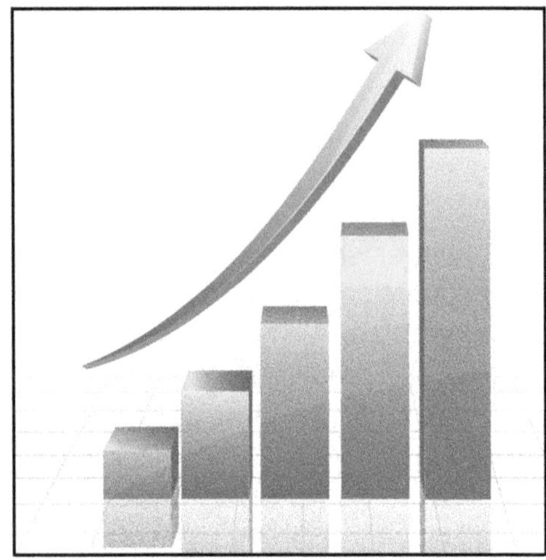

FIGURE 8.26

A Pareto Chart can give you a better understanding of the causes contributing to a problem, and it can help you focus on the most important causes that you need to address. A Pareto Chart is a simple bar chart that lists all the known causes of a problem and visualizes how much each cause contributes to the problem. If a cause is responsible for 60% of a problem, a bar is drawn which reaches to the 60th percentile; if a cause is responsible for 20% of the problem, a bar is drawn which reaches to the 20th percentile; and so on. . . . A Pareto Chart is an excellent tool for getting your small group members to think about multiple causes and their influence on a problem.

Analytical Method Four: A Force-Field Analysis

German social psychologist Kurt Lewin developed the concept of a force-field analysis in the 1930s and 1940s. He was one of the first to study group dynamics, and he asked people to consider the driving and restraining forces that work both on an individual and in a group. These driving and restraining forces can be represented in a Force-Field Diagram.

FIGURE 8.27

A Force-Field Diagram is similar to a "pro and con" T-Chart. At the top of your Force-Field Diagram, you draw an arrow to the right and you label this arrow with the goal or objective you want to reach. You then draw a vertical line down the middle of your chart, and you draw arrows from the left side of the diagram to this center line representing the driving or helping forces which are propelling you toward your goal, and you draw arrows from the right side of the diagram to the center line representing the restraining or hindering forces that are keeping you from your goal.

A Force-Field Diagram is a useful tool to identify and label the positive and negative forces that are at work in a problem situation. This diagram can also make your small group aware of the obstacles that must be overcome in order for a problem to be solved.

STEP 3: BRAINSTORMING POSSIBLE SOLUTIONS

We Americans are so familiar with "brainstorming" processes and procedures that we take them for granted, but they were virtually unknown before advertising executive and creativity coach Alex Osborn published several books in the 1940s and 1950s that explained and popularized the concept of brainstorming.

Osborn's term for the output of effective brainstorming is "ideative efficacy." In order to generate high-quality ideas, Osborn claims, you need to generate a lot of ideas. His focus is on quantity, and one of his tag lines is "Quantity breeds quality." In order to stimulate idea generation, you need to reduce social inhibitions. If people think their ideas will be judged or criticized, they will not want to share their thoughts. Therefore, people in a brainstorming session are instructed to defer judgment and withhold criticism of all ideas that are being suggested.

To increase overall group creativity, Osborn also suggests that you welcome unusual ideas. In brainstorming sessions, you can encourage people to "think outside the box," and you can recognize the most unique ideas that are suggested. Sometimes these unique ideas can be modified or combined with other ideas in order to create novel solutions to a problem. Here is some practical advice for holding a brainstorming session in a small group when you are trying to generate solutions to a problem.

BRAINSTORMING SOLUTIONS IN A SMALL GROUP DISCUSSION SESSION
1. Inform group members that your discussion goal is to generate a large quantity of possible solutions.
2. Instruct group members to delay judgment of the suggested solutions during the brainstorming session.
3. Ask for everyone to suggest solutions, and to suggest as many solutions as possible.
4. Encourage members to "piggyback" on the suggestions of others. They can combine or modify other suggested solutions to generate new solutions.
5. Allow some time for thought. It is okay to have a few moments of silence as small group members generate ideas.
6. Allow a sufficient amount of time for the brainstorming session. Announce the time set aside for brainstorming, and keep group members focused on the brainstorming task.
7. Have a group member record the ideas generated, and display these ideas on a board or large sheet of paper that everyone can see.

In addition to the traditional brainstorming process, there are other procedures you can use to maximize group creativity. You can try rolestorming and ask members to brainstorm solutions while playing different roles (victim, advocate, citizen, policymaker, etc.). You can try reverse brainstorming and ask members to brainstorm solutions that would make the problem worse instead of better. You can try the random word technique and ask a group member to periodically read from a list of random words during the brainstorming session to keep ideas flowing.

Besides these procedures which are designed to enhance traditional brainstorming in a small group setting, there are other brainstorming techniques which make more substantial modifications to traditional brainstorming. These techniques are 1) the Nominal Group Technique, 2) the Affinity Technique, 3) the Delphi Technique. Let's consider each technique and the advantages it has over traditional brainstorming.

Nominal Group Technique: The Nominal Group Technique is also called "silent brainstorming." Instead of sharing their ideas verbally with the small group, group members are asked to write down their ideas on paper before sharing them with the small group. It is called the "nominal group" technique because group members are not really working together—each member is generating ideas on their own, and then sharing these ideas with the group.

There is one strong advantage of the Nominal Group Technique: group members do not have to worry about their ideas or suggestions being evaluated or criticized as they are being generated. In traditional brainstorming, although members are instructed to defer judgment of ideas, they may inadvertently send an evaluative message verbally or nonverbally. The Nominal Group Technique can also be less threatening and more comfortable for shy people that do not like to speak in front of a group.

The Affinity Technique: The Affinity Technique requires Post-It Notes. It is a variation of the Nominal Group Technique. Group members are asked to write their ideas down on Post-It Notes, and these ideas are then posted on a wall. Group members can then rearrange the Post-It Notes and organize similar ideas together. The ideas that have an affinity with each other are grouped together on one section of the wall.

There are several advantages of the Affinity Technique. Like the Nominal Group Technique, it allows members to brainstorm ideas individually before sharing them with the group. However the Affinity Technique also gets people up and moving, it allows members to think about the connections between the ideas that are generated, and it demands the physical participation of all group members.

FIGURE 8.28

The Affinity Technique uses Post-It Notes to group similar ideas together.

The Delphi Technique: The Delphi Technique is named after the Greek oracle at Delphi. Like the oracle at Delphi, one group member coordinates all the brainstorming by communicating separately with all the group members. The Delphi Technique is also called "absentee brainstorming" because people do not even have to be in the same room to use this technique. The brainstorming leader can ask members to send in their ideas, and then the leader can summarize and share these ideas with the group at large.

Like the Nominal Group Technique and the Affinity Technique, the Delphi Technique lets individual members generate their ideas without fear of criticism or judgment. However, the Delphi Technique also provides a higher level of anonymity once the ideas are shared with the group (the leader does not have to reveal who generated the ideas), and the Delphi Technique can also be carried out without a face-to-face small group meeting.

THREE ALTERNATIVES TO TRADITIONAL SMALL GROUP BRAINSTORMING

1. **The Nominal Group Technique:** Group members write down their ideas before sharing them with the small group.
2. **The Affinity Technique:** Group members write down their ideas on Post-It Notes and place the notes on a wall. Similar ideas are then grouped together.
3. **The Delphi Technique:** A brainstorming leader communicates separately with each group member. The members share their ideas with the leader, and then the leader summarizes and shares these ideas with the small group.

STEP 4: DECIDE ON CRITERIA FOR JUDGING THE SOLUTIONS

This step, deciding on criteria for judging possible solutions, is the not-so-standard step of The Standard Agenda. Sometimes this step is not listed as an independent step—sometimes it is folded into step two (analyzing the problem), which places it *before* brainstorming solutions, and sometimes it is folded into step five (evaluating and selecting solutions), which places it *after* brainstorming solutions.

Realize that steps three and four of the six-step problem-solving method that we are describing are reversible: you can brainstorm solutions first (step three), and then you can decide on the judging criteria you will use to evaluate these solutions (step four), or you can decide on the judging criteria (step four) before brainstorming solutions (step three).

If the criteria for judging solutions are provided by others outside your small group, it makes sense to pay attention to these judging criteria before generating possible solutions. For example, if you are a group of engineers trying to design a structure or gizmo, you need to know if there are any "design specifications" that you must fulfill. There is no reason to brainstorm structures or gizmos that do not meet the required design specifications.

However, if your small group is deciding its own judging criteria for possible solutions, it makes sense to delay a discussion of judging criteria until after you have completed the brainstorming step. If you want to generate many possible solutions, and if you want group members to delay judgment and criticism of these possible solutions, then brainstorm solutions first, and then decide how you will evaluate and judge these solutions.

Sooner or later, however, your small group will need to discuss what a good solution looks like. Think of your solutions like contestants in a beauty contest. If you were judging a beauty contest, you would need to know what judging criteria you were expected to use to select the winner of the contest: are you primarily looking for and rewarding physical beauty? Intelligence? Talent? Poise and charm? Similarly, if you are a small group member, you need to know what judging criteria you are using to evaluate and select a solution to a problem: are you primarily interested in a low-cost solution? A long-term solution? An easy-to-implement solution?

FIGURE 8.29

Here is another comparison. Think of your solutions like applicants for a job. If you were on a hiring committee, you would need to know what the company or organization was looking for in a new hire: does the company need a person with new ideas? A person who will follow the rules? A person who can get along well with others? Similarly, if you are trying to evaluate possible solutions, you need to know what criteria you are using to judge these solutions: do you need a solution that has a low impact on the environment? A solution that is acceptable to people? A solution that is elegant and aesthetically pleasing?

Some Criteria for Evaluating Solutions

acceptability	efficiency	portability
cost	quality	serviceability
effectiveness	manufacturability	usability

In addition to the nine general judging criteria listed above, your small group can consider the importance of the following questions. Is the solution ethical? Can the solution be implemented easily? Do you need a short-term or a long-term solution? Do you need an obvious solution or a low-profile solution? Should the solution use technology? Do you want an innovative solution or a tried-and-true solution? When your group answers these kinds of questions, group members will know how to evaluate possible solutions in order to select the "best" solution.

Weighting criteria: In addition to deciding on what judging criteria to use for evaluating solutions, your small group must also decide which judging criteria are most important: which judging criteria should be given the most weight? You can have small group members rate or rank the judging criteria in order to decide which criteria are the most crucial. For example, after rating or ranking judging criteria, your group may decide that the most important criteria for a solution is cost (you need a low-cost solution), and the second most important criteria is acceptability (you need a solution that people will readily accept).

STEP 5: EVALUATING AND SELECTING THE SOLUTION(S)

Once your small group has agreed upon the judging criteria, you can evaluate the solutions and choose the best solution or solutions to a problem. If you have generated many possible solutions, you can use the judging criteria to eliminate all the solutions that do not minimally meet the solution judging criteria. Through this process of elimination, you can narrow down a large list of possible solutions to a manageable number of solutions to be evaluated and discussed.

FIGURE 8.30

A simple "pro/con" T-chart can help you discuss the advantages and disadvantages of a possible solution to a problem.

If your small group has narrowed down a large list of solutions to around twenty possible solutions, you could have members rate each of these twenty solutions to determine which solutions are strongest. For example, you could have each member rate each solution on a scale of 1 to 5, with 1 being a low score and 5 being a high score. When all of these ratings are compiled together, the solutions with the lowest scores can be considered and eliminated, if appropriate. The solutions with the highest scores are good candidates for much discussion and deliberation.

If your small group has narrowed solutions down to around five or six possibilities, instead of rating each solution (on a scale of 1 to 5), you may want to have the members rank each solution (first place, second place, third place, etc.). When the rankings are compiled together, your group should know which solution is preferred above all other solutions.

If your group decides to rate or rank solutions, however, these ratings and rankings should only be the *beginning* of your small group deliberations. Your small group needs to consider the advantages and disadvantages of each solution. A tool you can use to help you accomplish this task is a **T-chart** that lists the pros and cons of each solution. Place the solution description at the top of the chart, draw a line down the middle of the chart, and list the pros or advantages on one side of this line and the cons or disadvantages on the other side of the line.

Multiple solutions: Once your small group has evaluated solutions, you may decide that more than one solution should be chosen or selected. A problem may need to be addressed on several different fronts. For example, if you have identified three major causes of a problem, you may want to propose three solutions, with each proposed solution addressing a different cause. Or your group may select a solution that will get immediate results *and* another solution that will yield long-term benefits. Or your group may propose one solution that is easy to implement and another solution that is harder to implement. Complex problems may need complex solutions.

Modifying judging criteria: After evaluating different solutions, your small group may decide that a solution that doesn't quite meet the judging criteria has serious merit. At this point, your group might want to discuss changing or modifying the judging criteria. Of course, this modification is not an option if the judging criteria are given to the group by an outside entity (like engineering design specifications). However, if your small group has decided on its own judging criteria, there is nothing preventing your group from modifying these criteria after further thought and reflection.

STEP 6: IMPLEMENT THE SOLUTION(S)

Too often, the problem-solving process is derailed after step five—a committee or a small group works diligently to propose an effective solution to a problem, but no one is actually given the authority or responsibility for implementing the solution. A committee report is filed or a small group presents its findings, but no one in the company or organization is tasked with carrying out the proposal. For effective problem solving, an implementation plan has to be developed and carried out. There are two tools you can use to develop an implementation plan: 1) you can develop a flow chart, and 2) you can develop an action chart.

Flow charts: Flow charts help to visual how a process is supposed to unfold. When developing an implementation plan, you can create a flow chart that illustrates the steps that need to be accomplished in order for a solution to be implemented. Flow charts clarify the steps of a process, and they help people see what options are available if a task cannot be accomplished.

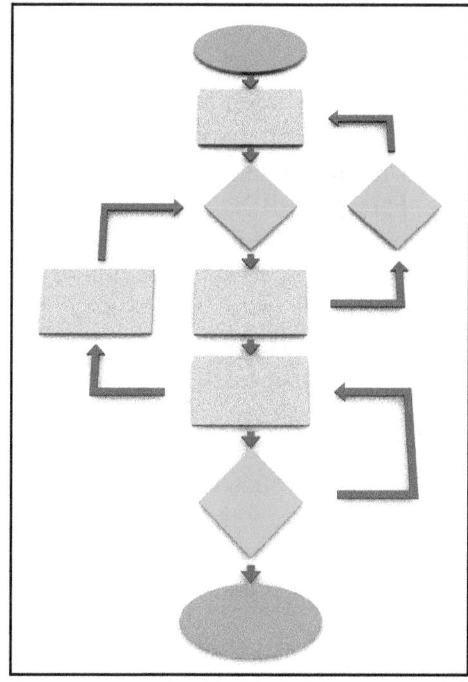

FIGURE 8.31

Flow charts clarify the steps of a process and reveal options available to accomplish a task.

Action charts: Action charts list all the tasks that need to get done, who is responsible for accomplishing each task, and when the task needs to be accomplished. If you grew up in a family that posted a "chore chart" on the refrigerator, you are already familiar with action charts. Action charts are especially useful for implementing solutions because they assign responsibility to particular individuals or groups for carrying out tasks, and they set deadlines for when these tasks need to be accomplished.

If your small group is responsible for implementing a solution, you can draw up an action chart that specifies what tasks need to be accomplished to implement the solution, when they need to be accomplished, and who is responsible for each task. On a large sheet of paper, list on the left side all the tasks that need to be accomplished. At the top of the paper, list the person or persons responsible for each task and when the task needs to be accomplished. You can then check off a box on your action chart when each task is completed.

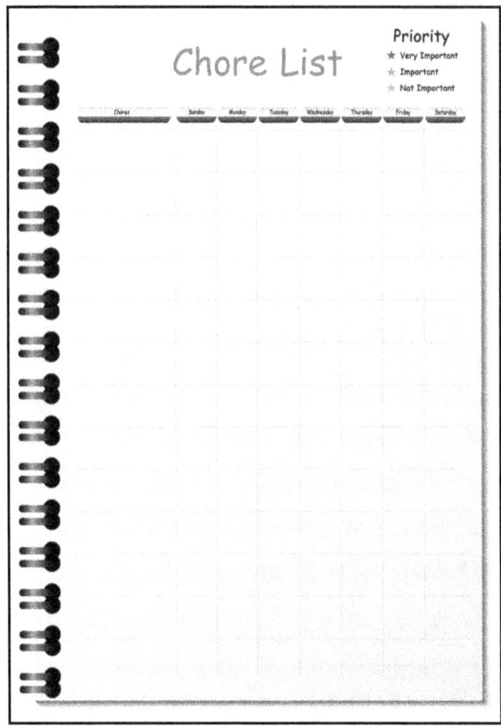

FIGURE 8.32

Another reason that step six (the implementation of a solution) may not occur is that people are resistant to change. If your small group develops a solution to a problem, you need to consider who will resist the implementation of this solution. You may want to take another look at any Force-Field Diagrams you have constructed. Since Force-Field Diagrams list the restraining or hindering forces that prevent people from reaching a goal, they can help you determine who is most likely to resist or hinder the implementation of your proposed solution.

In order to implement a solution smoothly, you should try to reduce resistance to change as much as possible. First, consider the degree and rate of any changes you are suggesting in your implementation plan. You can reduce resistance to change if you make small changes over a long period of time, rather than large changes in a short period of time. Second, involve the people affected by your proposed solution in the planning and decision-making process. Let them play a part in deciding how the solution will be implemented. Third, be open to revisions and modifications of your implementation plan. You can announce that a "trial period" will be started in order to "beta test" your implementation plan.

Make sure you build into your implementation plan guidelines for evaluating how well the solution is working. Just as you need to specify who is responsible for implementing a solution, you also need to specify who is responsible for evaluating how well an implemented solution is working, or if a solution is working at all. Sometimes a solution is ineffective, and sometimes a solution can actually make a problem worse instead of better. If you do not have a plan for evaluating the effectiveness of your proposed solution, you will never know if your small group successfully solved the original problem.

Practical Advice for Using the Standard Agenda

The Standard Agenda we have just described can be used as a guide for small group problem solving. Your group members can go through the six steps outlined in The Standard Agenda to tackle problems inside and outside your small group. Here are some specific tips for using The Standard Agenda:

- Realize that there are other ways to go about solving problems than following The Standard Agenda. If group members want to try another problem-solving method, be open to other approaches.
- Do not be too rigid when following The Standard Agenda. Small groups often jump around when they work through the problem-solving steps, so sometimes you may need to backtrack to an earlier step if you realize this step was neglected.
- Remember not to "jump to solutions." Take the time to clearly identify and understand a problem before considering possible solutions.
- Do not expect your small group members to be familiar with The Standard Agenda. You may need to explain the steps of The Standard Agenda to group members, and you may need to review these steps during the problem-solving process.
- Use the charts and diagrams suggested in this textbook section. We have described these problem-solving tools because they can help you work through the problem-solving steps.
- Problem solving is a complex intellectual process that requires sustained attention. Keep your small group focused and shepherd them through all six steps if you want to implement an effective solution.
- Emotion management is also an important part of small group problem solving. As you work through the six steps of The Standard Agenda, you must maintain a positive attitude. Along the way, you may get tired, confused, annoyed, or frustrated. To manage these emotions appropriately, keep your final goal in mind.

FIGURE 8.33

Summary

Now that you have completed reading this chapter, you are better equipped to make decisions and solve problems. You now know the difference between a decision-making group and a problem-solving group. You understand the elements that create low-quality small group decisions, and you understand the elements that create high-quality small group decisions. Finally, you are now able to use the six steps of The Standard Agenda as a guide for solving problems.

Once your small group has made a difficult decision or come up with a plan to solve a problem, you may need to explain your decision or present your plan to people outside your small group. Chapter 9 (Small Group Presentations) will give you the tools you need to share your small group work with others.

Glossary

Action chart: A tool used to specify tasks to be completed, when these tasks must be completed, and who is responsible for completing the tasks.

Affinity technique: A variation of brainstorming that requires small group members to write their ideas on Post-It Notes. Similar ideas can then be grouped together.

Bandwagon fallacy: An error in reasoning. One argues that something should be done because "everyone is doing it" or that something is right because "everyone thinks it is right."

Brainstorming: A process for generating many ideas.

Confirmation bias: An error in reasoning. One discounts or ignores information that disconfirms a belief and focuses only on information that confirms a belief.

Consensus decision: A decision supported by every member of a group. Small groups should often aim for a consensus decision.

Criteria: Also called judging criteria. The qualities or elements a small group decides on in order to judge or evaluate ideas or solutions.

Currency: A criteria used to judge information or evidence. Information should be current or up-to-date.

Credibility: A criteria used to judge information or evidence. Information should be credible or trustworthy.

Decision-making group: A group charged primarily with making a decision. Examples of decision-making groups are judging panels, juries, and hiring committees.

Deductive reasoning: A primary form of valid reasoning. One draws specific conclusions from general principles.

Delphi technique: A variation of brainstorming. Also called "absentee brainstorming." Group members share their ideas with a group leader who then summarizes and shares these ideas with the group.

Devil's advocate: A small group role designed to combat groupthink. A group member assigned the role of devil's advocate is given the responsibility of voicing dissenting opinions and alternate viewpoints.

False dichotomy: An error in reasoning. Also called the "either/or fallacy." One assumes that only two choices or options are available when other alternatives exist.

Fishbone diagram: A tool used to analyze the causes of a problem or effect.

Flow chart: A tool used to visualize the steps of a process.

Force-field diagram: A tool used to analyze the helping forces and hindering forces that promote or prevent the reaching of a goal or objective.

Groupthink: A negative condition that exists when small group members are too eager to reach agreement. Groupthink discourages disagreement and leads to bad decisions.

Hasty generalization: An error in reasoning. A specific type of inferential error. One draws a general conclusion from one or a few specific instances or examples.

Hidden agendas: An element that can lead to low-quality small group decisions. Hidden agendas are unspoken, private or personal goals that conflict with the goals of a small group.

Inductive reasoning: A valid form of reasoning. One draws a general conclusion from a sufficient number of specific examples.

Inferential error: An error in reasoning. One makes an assumption or inference based on insufficient or faulty information.

Information overload: An element that can lead to low-quality small group decisions. Group members are given so much information they cannot process this information effectively.

Information underload: An element that can lead to low-quality small group decisions. Group members do not have, or do not pay attention to, the necessary information or evidence they need to make a decision.

Journalist's six questions: Six basic questions that can be posed and answered to analyze a problem—who, what, when, where, why, and how.

Majority decision: A decision supported by over half the members of a small group. Majority decision is not the best method of decision-making for small groups because some members of the group are not satisfied with the decision.

Minority decision: A decision made and supported by only one or a few small group members. Minority decision is not the best method of decision-making for small groups because most members of the group are not satisfied with the decision.

Nominal group technique: A variation of brainstorming. Group members write down their ideas before sharing these ideas with their small group.

Pareto chart: A tool used to analyze the causes of a problem. The causes of a problem are placed on a bar graph, and the percentage contribution of each cause is noted.

Problem-solving group: A group charged primarily with solving problems. Problem-solving groups have a more complex task to complete than simple decision-making groups.

Questions of definition: One of four types of questions, and the most basic type. Question related to how a term or concept should be defined.

Questions of fact: One of four types of questions. Questions related to matters of existence.

Questions of policy: One of four types of questions, and the most complex type. Questions related to whether a policy should or should not be put into effect.

Questions of value: One of four types of questions. Questions related to whether something is good or bad, better or worse, right or wrong.

Quorum: The minimum number of group members required to carry on business and make decisions. If a quorum is set by a small group, then members cannot make official small group decisions when this minimum number of members is not present at a small group meeting.

Random word technique: A technique used to enhance traditional brainstorming. During a brainstorming session, a small group member periodically reads out random words to stimulate the creative flow of ideas.

Relevance: A criteria used to judge information or evidence. Information must be relevant—it must directly relate to the topic being considered or discussed.

Representativeness: A criteria used to judge information or evidence. Information must be representative—it must represent what is common or usual.

Reverse brainstorming: A technique used to enhance traditional brainstorming. Group members are asked to generate solutions that will make a problem worse instead of better.

Rolestorming: A technique used to enhance traditional brainstorming. Group members place themselves in different roles (victims, advocates, citizens, policymakers, etc.) while they generate ideas or solutions.

Sufficiency: A criteria used to judge information or evidence. Information must be sufficient—there must be sufficient information or evidence to warrant drawing a conclusion.

T-chart: A tool used to analyze the pros and cons or advantages and disadvantages of an idea or solution.

The Standard Agenda: A well-established, six step problem-solving method: 1) identify and define the problem, 2) analyze the problem, 3) brainstorm solutions, 4) decide on criteria to judge the solutions, 5) evaluate and select the solution(s), and 6) implement the solution(s).

Works Cited or Consulted

Damer, T., Edward. (2012) *Attacking faulty reasoning: A practical guide to fallacy-free arguments* (7th ed.). Boston, MA: Wadsworth Cengage Learning. (*An entire textbook devoted to weeding out fallacious arguments from your thinking and communication.*)

Dewey, John. (1910). *How we think.* Boston: D.C. Heath & Co. (*A book from the early 20th century that helped to standardize the steps of problem solving.*)

Ishikawa, Kaoru. (1968). *Guide to quality control.* Tokyo, Japan: JUSE. (*In this Japanese management book, Kaoru Ishikawa brings the fishbone diagram into the problem-solving world.*)

Janis, L., Irving. (1982) *Groupthink: Psychological studies of policy decisions and fiascos* (2nd ed.). Boston, MA: Wadsworth Cengage Learning. (*Irving analyzes how groupthink played a role in The Bay of Pigs, the Koren War, Pearl Harbor, and the Vietnam War. He also shows how people avoided groupthink during The Cuban Missile Crisis and the making of the Marshall Plan.*)

Juran, M., Joseph, & De Feo, A., Joseph. (2010). *Juran's quality handbook: The complete guide to performance excellence* (6th ed.). New York: McGraw Hill. (*A thousand-page compendium of quality management tools, including Juran's Pareto Chart.*)

Lewin, Kurt. (1951). *Field theory in social science.* New York: HarperCollins.' (*An early version of Kurt Lewin's Force Field theory.*)

Osborne, Alex. *Applied imagination: Principles and procedures of creative thinking.* New York: Scribner. (*In this classic book, Alex Osborne popularizes the idea of creative brainstorming.*)

Skorepa, Michael. (2011). *Decision making: A behavioral economic approach.* Great Britain: Palgrave MacMillan. (*A thick book with over 300 pages devoted to the science of decision making. Michael Skorepa clearly distinguishes decision making from problem solving.*)

Chapter 9:

Critical Thinking & Argumentation in Groups

Chapter Objectives

- Understand the value of argumentation in groups.
- Learn how to present and refute arguments using the Toulmin Model.
- Identify fallacies of reasoning.

In the last chapter, we identified the components of decision-making and problem-solving. To make good decisions and effectively solve problems, group members must present and analyze compelling arguments. This chapter identifies the relationship of critical thinking to effective solutions through the value of argumentation to groups. In addition, the chapter outlines how to present and refute arguments using the Toulmin Model. It wraps up by identifying faulty or fallacies of reasoning.

"We had an argument." When we say these words in American culture, it has a negative connotation. Most of us think of a very undesirable event that has just occurred. This is unfortunate. Arguments are vital to your group's success. If you can present a good argument, your group members may be persuaded. In a court room, you hope your lawyer can present compelling arguments to persuade the jury. The next section discusses the importance of presenting and refuting arguments to assist in making good decisions in your group.

The Importance of Arguments in Groups

The last chapter identified several poor decision-making processes including groupthink, too little or too much conflict, and poor communication. Having positive argumentation in groups helps eliminate these problems and leads to better decision-making.

So let's throw away our negative thoughts about arguments to discuss why arguments are important in groups.

First, arguments help promote an understanding of your position on the issue. At minimum, your group members will understand your point of view. This even works in our interpersonal relationships. If you tell your loved one how you feel, at least they will understand though they may not change!

Second, since group members need to effectively analyze group members' ideas, critical thinking is employed. To come to the best decisions, group members need to be able to challenge arguments by examining the evidence, the logic, the reasoning, and assumptions of the argument. Think about serving on a jury. As a jury member, you will need to assess all of the evidence presented in the trial. In addition, you will test the logic and determine if the reasoning is sound. Finally, you need to look at yourself. Are you making a decision based on your assumptions regarding the defendant? Do you possess stereotypes of "criminals?" By critically thinking, your group will produce more effective decisions and solutions to problems.

Third, poor communication or too little communication can often lead to group think. Thus, if your group engages in presenting and analyzing arguments, the chance of group think will be reduced. The critical analysis of the issue will insure that group think will not occur because the evidence, logic, reasoning, and assumptions were argued.

Finally, it makes sense that effective arguments will increase the chance that better decisions will be made in groups.

Clearly presenting and refuting arguments in groups leads to better outcomes. The next step is to identify how to present and refute an argument.

*What is an argument? Stephen Toulmin offered perhaps the best contemporary answer with the development of his model. Toulmin was a philosopher, logician, and educator. His interest in argumentation was practical and his model reflects his interest in constructing a descriptive model of how people actually argue. Toulmin first proposed his model in the 1958 publication, *The Uses of Argument*. The book has been reprinted fifteen times and remains in print. While he is distinguished in other academic areas, Toulmin's model of argumentation is uniformly considered his most influential work.

The Components of the Toulmin Model

Toulmin's model identifies six components of an argument: claim, data, warrant, backing, rebuttal, and qualifier. Only the first three parts, the claim, data, and warrant, are required components of every argument. The second set of three, the backing, rebuttal, and qualifier, are optional.

The Mandatory Components

CLAIM

The claim is the conclusion, the end purpose and end point of the argument. The claim is the point that the argument seeks to establish. It describes what the arguer wants to show is true.

DATA

The data is the evidence used to support the argument. It is the argument's foundation and the basis upon which the argument rests. Data is also the beginning of the argument because it lays the groundwork for the process of argumentation.

WARRANT

The warrant is the argument's reasoning. It serves as a connective bridge, linking the data (evidence) to the claim (conclusion). Consider the following example, first in paragraph form:

> We shouldn't sign a treaty with Libya. Libya has broken every single treaty it's signed for the last 50 years. If you can't trust a country to keep its word, you shouldn't be signing treaties with it.

Within this argument, the claim is stated first. The speaker is expressing the view that we ought not sign a treaty with Libya. Then, the evidence is offered second. The data of this argument is the evidence detailing Libya's 50-year history of breaking its treaties. The argument concludes with the warrant connecting the data to the claim.

The claim, data, and warrant are found in every argument, according to Toulmin. However, these three components may be explicit or implicit. If the component is explicit, it is actually voiced or said. If the component is implicit, then it is unsaid but understood due to the cultural or social framework surrounding the argument. According to Toulmin, it is possible to not state a claim but still make an argument. Similarly, it is possible to not say the warrant or the data and still have an argument.

The Optional Components

The Libya argument example does not contain backing, rebuttal, or qualifier. These three items are absent because they are not required for every argument. However, Toulmin observed that they occurred frequently enough in real debates to include within his model as optional components.

BACKING

First of all, the backing of an argument is the support for the warrant. Backing explains the qualifications or credentials of the warrant. It helps to explain why the warrant is credible. In many cases, the quality of the evidence presented is self-evident or the credibility of the data goes unchallenged. In those cases, backing is not necessary.

Backing is not automatically accepted within an argument. It is possible to have a warrant challenged, to provide backing and to have that backing challenged. The questioning of a debater's source is a common practice and merely stating that the source was published by the *New York Times* or discussed on Fox News does not automatically confer validity to the warrant. If the backing is questioned, the arguer may feel the need to provide additional evidence, or backing, to validate the initial backing.

In the example above, the arguer may have been challenged about the data. A listener might have found it difficult to believe that Libya had not honored a single treaty over a 50-year period. If that objection had occurred, then the argument could have been extended to include backing. The arguer could have explained the source of that information. If pressed for further backing, the arguer could provide additional backing about why that source has sufficient credentials to warrant belief.

REBUTTAL

The second optional component of an argument identified by Toulmin is the rebuttal. The rebuttal acknowledges that there may be some legitimate limitations or restrictions that can be applied to the argument's claim. As a result, the rebuttal acknowledges those restrictions.

In the Libya example, the arguer may recognize that there are some legitimate restrictions applicable to the argument's claim. If those exist, then the claim could be qualified by the inclusion of a rebuttal. For example, the claim statement could be changed to, "We shouldn't sign a treaty with Libya, unless the country replaces its prime minister."

QUALIFIER

The sixth and final component of an argument is the qualifier. Qualifiers express the degree of certainty, or modal qualification, that the arguer feels about the claim. Common qualifiers include "probably," "certainly," "necessarily," "presumably," and "impossible." Not every qualifier has the same meaning and some are more rhetorically powerful. Consider the following variations on the Libya example:

> Claim without qualifier: We shouldn't sign a treaty with Libya.
>
> Qualifier 1: We probably shouldn't sign a treaty with Libya.
>
> Qualifier 2: We certainly shouldn't sign a treaty with Libya.

Certainly is a more powerful statement of certainty than probably, so the second statement with a qualifier is more forceful than the first. However, the original claim statement without the inclusion qualifier appears more forceful than either statement containing a qualifier. Certainly, the qualifier is optional.

Rebuttals and qualifiers are linked. The inclusion of a rebuttal can create a need to also include a qualifier. After all, rebuttals acknowledge that there may be a legitimate shortcoming or limitation of the claim. Therefore, the claim cannot be concluded with absolute certainty. Similarly, the presence of a qualifier suggests that a legitimate rebuttal does exist. Therefore, when evaluating claims, it is not uncommon to find both a rebuttal and a qualifier within the claim. Within the example, such a claim would look like: We certainly shouldn't sign a treaty with Libya, unless the country replaces its prime minister.

Analyzing Arguments using Toulmin's Model

Toulmin's model may be used to identify the components of an argument and construct visual representations that are useful for analysis. The general diagram of an argument containing just the three mandatory components would look like:

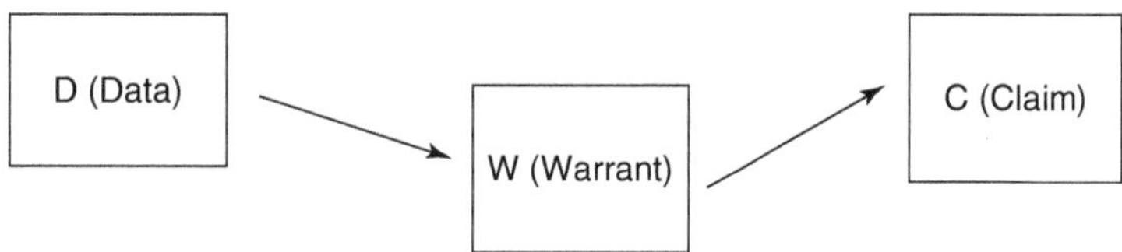

When given a specific argument, you can fill in this basic diagram in order to identify the existing components of the argument.Consider again the following argument:

> We shouldn't sign a peace treaty with Libya. Libya has broken every single treaty it signed for the last 50 years. If you can't trust a country to keep its word, you shouldn't be signing treaties with it.

From the previous discussion, we already know that this argument contains only the three mandatory components, the data, warrant, and claim. The argument can be drawn to show that the warrant is connecting the data to the claim.

The Toulmin model's visual representation of this argument would look like:

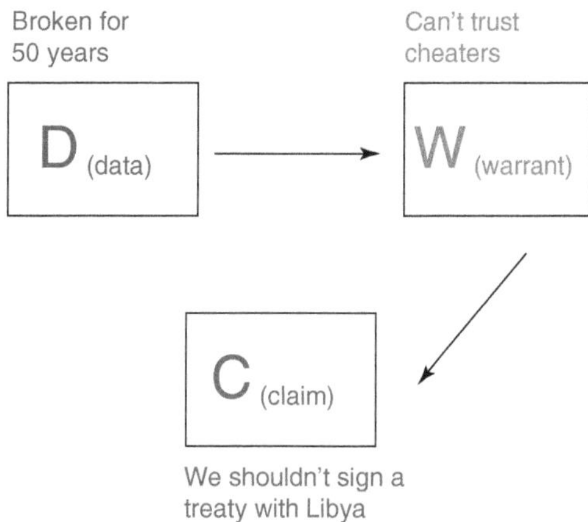

This diagram is relatively simple because the argument contains only the three required components of an argument. Suppose the argument was revised to include the three optional components of an argument:

> We shouldn't sign a peace treaty with Libya. Libya has broken every single treaty it signed for the last 50 years. The Council for Foreign Relations just released a study, and they are very dead-on in all the country studies that they've done so far, that indicates that Libya has cheated on every treaty for the last 50 years, and you can't trust cheating cheaters in the international realm.

In order to construct a Toulmin model diagram, you should begin by identifying the three mandatory components of the argument. After all, you know that every argument must contain a claim, data, and warrant.

> Main Claim: We shouldn't sign a peace treaty with Libya.
>
> Data: Libya has broken every single treaty it's signed for the last 50 years.
>
> Warrant: You can't trust cheating cheaters in the international realm

Once the three mandatory components are identified, you should then look at the rest of the arguments to determine their status.

Additional statements:

1. Council for Foreign Relations just released a study
2. They are very dead-on in all their country studies

These two additional points are not mandatory. They can be omitted and the argument would still be complete. So, you know that the two statements are either backing, qualifier, or rebuttal. You must then use your understanding of these terms to study how they function within the argument to determine their relationship to the data, claim, or warrant.

The complete Toulmin model diagram would look like:

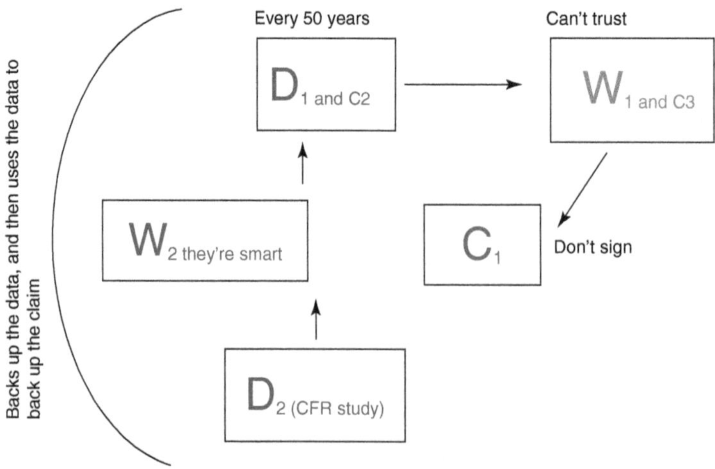

Within this example, both "Council for Foreign Relations just released a study" and "They are very dead-on in all their country studies" are backing up the data.*

*From *Contemporary Argumentation and Rhetoric* by Michael Korcok and Andrea Thorson. Copyright © 2016 by Kendall Hunt Publishing Company. Reprinted by permission.

Presenting an Argument:

1. State the Claim
2. Provide the Data
3. Explain the Warrant

In addition to presenting an argument, a group member needs to know how to refute the argument. The following is a simple process of refutation:

1. Listen carefully to your opponent's argument. Often by listening you will be able to identify poor evidence, logic, reasoning, and/or contradictions.
2. Identify your opponent's claim.
3. Preview your objections to your opponent's claim—tell the group why you don't agree with the argument.
4. Assess Reasoning—point out fallacies of reasoning.
5. Assess Evidence—point out poor or flawed evidence or evidence that does not support the argument.

By learning how to prevent and refute an argument, group members will enjoy the benefits of positive arguments influencing group outcomes.

Fallacies of Reasoning

In the process of refutation, it is necessary to examine the reasoning in arguments. Unfortunately, not all reasoning is logical. In this section, we will identify some common fallacies of reasoning.

*Ad Hominem Attacks

An **ad hominem** fallacy occurs when an arguer attacks someone personally rather than the argument itself. Argumentation should always be directed at the logic and reasoning, not at the people progressing them, straying from this ideal results in a personal attack fallacy. Think of all the "name calling" in American politics. These who engage in name calling usually do not possess effective arguments.

Appeal to Tradition

An **appeal to tradition** fallacy occurs when it is argued that because something has been done in the past, is older, historical, or tradition it is therefore better or the best. This type of reasoning is problematic because age alone does not determine the legitimacy of something. Because people like their traditions they are likely to use this fallacy. We tend to stick with things we know because they are comfortable, safe, and predictable. But the idea that just because something is older or done more often in the past is inherently right is wrong and illogical.

Appeals to Authority and False Authority

We have all encountered this argument. Just recently I was told that I must not support the new healthcare initiative because, "Kim Kardashian says its going to cost a lot of money out of our pockets and let poor people have free insurance while the rest of us have to pay for it ourselves." This is an example of an argument based on a false authority. Who is Kim Kardashian? She is a reality TV star who rose to fame after a scandalous sex video went viral. Is this the definition of a credible authority on national healthcare reform? The answer is clearly a "no."

When we rely on the quotes and reasoning of others to substantiate our own arguments we must be critical of their character and expertise. If they are experts and credible in the field they are discussing they are not usable in argumentation. Similarly, just because someone has "Ph.D." after their name doesn't inherently make them credible either. There are many different credentials and each is relevant only depending on the topic at hand. For instance, let's say the authors of this book were asked to discuss a recent trend in argumentation and rhetoric and our evaluation of it. Given that the area is an area of our expertise, we would be considered credible experts. However, if we were asked to discuss the validity of the most recent physics theory, we would not be credible authorities on the subject.

Another way the appeal to authority fallacy is used is when someone is considered a credible expert in the field being discussed, but their perspective is offered as evidence that the claim is true instead of recognized as the opinion of one expert, which may not be representative of the entire field of experts. In other words, when citing or quoting an expert who agrees with your claim, make sure your entire claim doesn't rest solely on the opinion of that one person, or you may be committing a fallacy of authority.

Bandwagon

Out of all the fallacies, the bandwagon fallacy causes the most irritation, and yet, can be highly successful on unsuspecting audiences. You will want to avoid this fallacy and all fallacies during your argumentation process because it reflects poorly on your credibility, calls your ethics into consideration, and just looks bad. Now, the bandwagon fallacy is simple, it asserts that because everyone else is doing it so should you. The bandwagon fallacy appeals to your sense of conformity, your desire to be similar, and the idea that we should be "keeping up." You will have seen this fallacy in action when your child comes to you begging for an iPad because, "everyone else in my class has an iPad!" There are actually a few types of bandwagon fallacies, but they all basically argue the same way, which is by purposely constructing an argument that appeals to the audience's desire to fit in or been seen as "normal."

Slippery Slope

The next most common fallacy is called the "slippery slope." The slippery slope fallacy you have seen from the time you were small. You might have seen it in your local anti-drug campaigns, during parental reasoning, or while discussing politics. The slippery slope argument is basically what it sounds like, it asserts that if you take one tiny step in a certain direction you will fall head first in a downward tumble and that you will not be able to stop that momentum until you have hit the bottom of the hill.

The "fear tactic" is often used in conjunction with the slippery slope fallacy. Frequently, arguers will assert that one small choice will just domino into a catastrophe and that catastrophe will be something to greatly fear or avoid. The key to not committing this fallacy is to make sure you have enough evidence to support the claim that If A, then B, if B then C, and if C then D, and that nothing will be able to stop that result. In short, the key to having a consequence argument not be a slippery slope fallacy is to ensure your data supports the claim totally.

Red Herring

A red herring fallacy occurs when something irrelevant is presented in an attempt to divert the audience's attention from the actual issue at hand. This person will often make an argument that is basically unrelated to the topic, but just slightly connected in an attempt to get you thinking about that new (often emotion-evoking) issue and thus forget to argue the point at hand. They are primarily changing the topic.

False Analogy also known as "Weak Analogy"

Analogies, as you have learned, are excellent forms of argumentation at times, but like any other argument they run the risk of becoming fallacious. The way to keep yourself from creating a false analogy is to be critical of your analogy. Make sure the things you are comparing are only different in very irrelevant ways.

False Cause or "Post hoc, ergo propter hoc"

In Latin, the false cause fallacy means, "after this, therefore because of this." Although that may sound confusing it is actually quite simple. What false cause fallacy means is that false cause fallacy occurs when an arguer asserts that because one event followed another even the first event caused the second event. You can see why this is weak. Of course, there are occasions where one thing did cause another to occur right after, but more often, the cause of a given effect is not always due to what ever happened just before it.

This is a dangerous fallacy because it can be convincing to an audience who can see and understand the relationship between the two events, but has not really thought it through. Causality is difficult to demonstrate and control, so most often it is difficult to prove a cause and much easier to prove a correlation.

Hasty Generalization

This is probably the most used fallacy in interpersonal, small group, and college argumentation classes. The hasty generalization fallacy is just as it sounds, it is a generalization that an arguer makes hastily (with little consideration). In direct terms, hasty generalizations are inferences drawn from insufficient data.

Summary

In this chapter, we have discussed why arguments are a good practice in groups. We identified how to present and refute an argument in addition to examining eight fallacies of reasoning.

British philosopher and logician Stephen Toulmin created a six-part model of argumentation based upon his empiric observation of real-life arguments. Based upon his observations, Toulmin identified three required components found in every argument. The claim is the conclusion of the argument and the point that the argument is attempting to show as true. The data is the evidence that serves as the foundation of the argument. The warrant is the reasoning of the argument that connects the claim to the data.

Toulmin's model also recognizes the existence of three optional components. First, the backing is the qualifications or credentials of the warrant. Backing is not automatically accepted within an argument and it is possible to provide backing for backing to satisfy the skepticism of an arguer. Second, the rebuttal acknowledges that there may be some legitimate limitations or restrictions that can be applied to the argument's claim. Finally, the qualifier expresses the degree of certainty, or modal qualification, that the arguer feels about the claim. If the speaker is not totally certain that the claim is true, then the statement of the claim will likely contain a qualifier such as "probably" or "likely."

In addition, Toulmin acknowledged the existence of explicit and implicit components of an argument. Explicit components are spoken by the arguer. Implicit components are unspoken. However, the surrounding cultural environment permits the acknowledgement of the unstated part of the argument.

The Toulmin model can be used to analyze arguments. Knowledge of the parts of the Toulmin model permits the individual to identify and map the components of any argument.

Inductive fallacies move from the general to produce an inaccurate conclusion. They are also known as faulty generalizations. Common inductive fallacies are cherry picking, hasty generalization, false analogy, confirmation bias and the slippery slope.

Glossary

Analogy: A type of inductive reasoning that looks at one or two examples to determine a conclusion about another case or example.

Antecedent: The component of a causality argument that is responsible for causing the observed effect upon the consequent.

Backing: Within the Toulmin model, the qualifications or credentials of the warrant and an optional component of an argument.

Causality: The type of inductive reasoning that contends that one thing produces/creates/causes another.

Cherry Picking: A type of inductive fallacy that focuses solely upon a limited number of cases to prove a point, while ignoring the larger number of cases that contradict that point. Synonymous with the fallacy of incomplete evidence.

Claim: Within the Toulmin model, the conclusion of the argument and a mandatory component of every argument.

Confirmation Bias: A form of cherry picking which describes how individuals will tend to focus upon data that supports their pre-existing beliefs.

Consequent: The effect generated by the antecedent within a causality claim.

Counterfactual: A counter to a fact claim and a useful tool for evaluating causality arguments.

Data: Within the Toulmin model, the evidence and foundation for the argument and a mandatory component of every argument.

Dicto Simpliciter: Hasty Generalization—drawing a definite conclusion using only a small sample, rather than utilizing statistics that are more descriptive and appropriate for the typical situation. The Fallacy of Composition.

Explicit: The stated parts of an argument.

False Analogy: A flawed analogy.

False cause: this fallacy occurs when an arguer asserts that because one event followed another even the first event cause the second event.

Faulty Generalizations: Synonym for inductive fallacies. An inaccurate argument that moves from the specific to the general.

Generalization: The most common form of inductive reasoning. Generalization takes the form of identifying multiple examples and then coming to a general conclusion based upon those examples.

Implicit: The unstated parts of an argument that are still acknowledged due to the surrounding cultural or social framework.

Inductive Fallacies: Arguments which move from the specific to the general in an erroneous manner. Also known as faulty generalizations.

Inductive Reasoning: Reasoning that involves premises that support the truth of the conclusion, but do not make it entirely certain.

Metaphor: A specialized type of analogy that compares two unrelated objects in order to point to a shared characteristic or sameness.

Post hoc ergo propter hoc: An inductive fallacy, after the fact therefore because of the fact.

Probability: The field of study which measures the likelihood of an event.

Qualifier: Within the Toulmin model, the qualifier expresses the degree of certainty, or modal qualification, that the arguer feels about the claim. Examples include the words "certainly," "probably," "never," and "definitely".

Rebuttal: Within the Toulmin model, the acknowledgement that there may be legitimate limitations placed upon the argument's claim and an optional component of an argument.

Slippery Slope: An inductive fallacy that inappropriately assigns causation for major events to a relatively minor event.

Syllogism: According to Aristotle, an argument containing a major premise, a minor premise, and a conclusion.

Tenor: In a metaphor, the subject of the metaphor's conclusion.

The Scientific Method: The specific steps used by scientific researchers to gather, critique and revise new knowledge.

Vehicle: In a metaphor, the subject whose characteristic is borrowed in order to describe the tenor.*

Warrant: Within the Toulmin model, the reasoning of the argument and a mandatory component of every argument.

Works Cited or Consulted

Toulmin, S.E. (1958). *The uses of argument*. Cambridge University Press.

Chapter 10:

Small Groups in the Real World – A Practical Approach

Chapter Objectives

- Learn how to select members for a small group.
- Learn some strategies you can use to help small group members get over their initial nervousness and anxiety.
- Learn how to establish clear lines of communication.
- Learn how to set up group expectations through the use of group guidelines.
- Learn how to develop a small group identity that will increase group cohesiveness.
- Learn how to schedule, conduct, and report out on small group meetings.
- Learn ten things <u>not</u> to do in your small group.

This chapter is designed to help you get started in a new small group. You will receive practical advice and "how to" tips that will help you develop a cohesive, effective work group.

Throughout this text, we have completed a journey that now takes us to the implementation of what we have learned. We have defined small group communication, investigated the types of groups in our society, learned why people join groups and how they develop. In addition, we now know how group members develop their norms and roles based on leadership and diversity. We have discovered how verbal and nonverbal communication and listening affect our group's performance. Finally, we identified how to deal with conflict and how to build effective arguments. It is now time to put it all into practice.

Forming a Small Group

When you were in grade school, junior high, or high school, were you ever given the task of choosing your teammates for a pick-up game of baseball? You may remember picking the best ballplayers available, or you may remember choosing your friends for your team even though they were not that good at playing baseball. In either case, the burden of selecting team members rested on your shoulders.

FIGURE 10.1
Choosing team members is an important task

Selecting the members of a small group is an important responsibility. If you are responsible for selecting the members of a small group, strive to create a diverse group that includes people of different ages, ethnicities, social classes, and sexes. You should also exploit the skills and abilities of your individual members by creating a small group composed of people with different skills and abilities that will complement one another.

Just as a manager or coach tries to assemble a sports team that has strong players at every position, your goal should be to create a diverse small group that can draw upon the different perspectives, personalities, life experiences, skills, and abilities of its group members.

In your small group communication course, there is a good chance that you will be placed in a small group by your instructor, and you will most likely not get to choose your other small group members. You may even be purposely separated from your friends or people that you know well.

Small group instructors have discovered that self-selected groups are among the least effective groups. Even randomly formed small groups, on average, outperform self-selected small groups. Why are self-selected groups often so ineffective? Because "birds of a feather flock together." When asked to form their own small groups, people tend to gravitate towards people like themselves. They create groups with a high degree of homogeneity instead of **heterogeneous groups** with diverse membership.

Furthermore, when allowed to choose their own small group members, people often choose friends, family members, and close acquaintances, regardless of the appropriateness of those choices. Like kids who pick their best friends to be on their pick-up baseball team (no matter how poorly they play baseball), adults also tend to choose friends and family members for small group work without considering whether this choice based on familiarity is actually creating an effective team.

If you are placed in a small group with people you have just met, realize that your instructor may want you to learn how to bond together with strangers in a small group setting. If you work with people you do not already know, you can learn how to form working relationships with your different small group members, and you can learn how to develop and maintain these relationships.

However, when you are in a small group that includes friends, family members, or close acquaintances, you may have difficulty bonding with other group members. At best, your well-established relationships give you less incentive to bond with other group members. At worst, these well-established relationships can interfere with, and even prevent, other relationships.

In addition to *whom* you select for a small group, consider *how many* people you will select. Aim for a good group size. More is not necessarily merrier. As you learned in Chapter 1, as group membership increases arithmetically, small group relationship complexity increases exponentially. You do not want too large a group.

The optimal size for many small group settings is five to seven members, but sometimes the need for representative membership on a committee or in a work group requires more members. A good rule of thumb is to make the group large enough to include the necessary members, but as small as possible to cut down on communication and relationship complexities. Remember that the maximum practical size for small group work is around twelve or thirteen people.

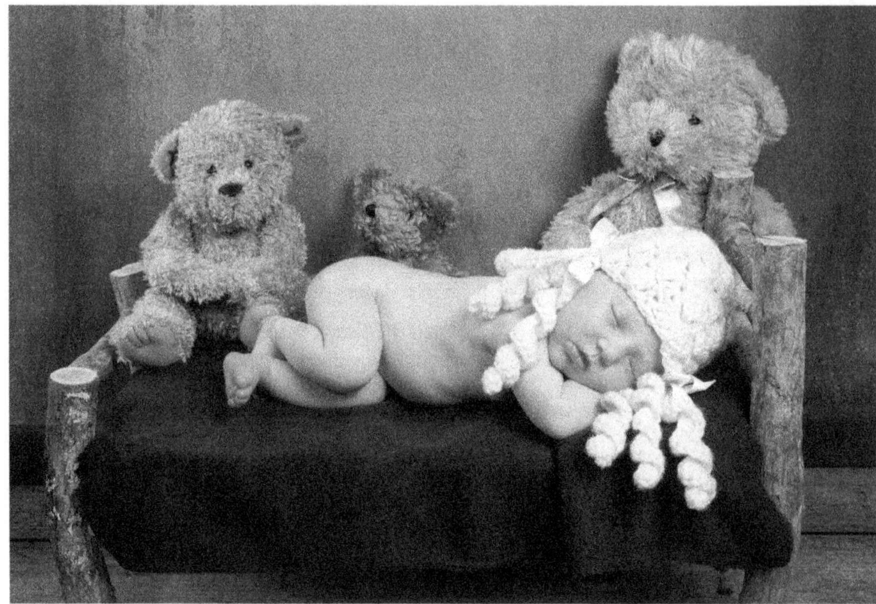

FIGURE 10.2

Like Goldilocks, you must work to form a group that is just the right size.

Setting Your Small Group Members at Ease ("What Have We Gotten Ourselves Into?")

When people first join or are placed in a small group, it is natural for them to be nervous. The anxiety and awkwardness that most people feel when they join a new group has been labeled "primary tension." Almost everyone experiences primary tension in a new small group situation, but there are practical steps you can take to reduce this tension.

First, recognize and acknowledge primary tension when first meeting with a new small group. Acknowledge that group members are experiencing some anxiety and awkwardness, and point out that this is normal.

Second, ask "icebreaker" questions or have a warm-up activity the first time your small group meets. The main purpose of these questions and activities is to "break the ice" and to let people get to know one another. In Chapter 2, you will learn that small groups go through some standard stages of group development and that the first stage is the "forming" stage. Your small group cannot effectively pass through the other stages of development without first taking time to form interpersonal relationships.

FIGURE 10.3

Third, encourage appropriate self-disclosure. Self-disclosure is the act of sharing important information about yourself with others. When you share personal information with others, you demonstrate a willingness to engage with and trust other people. Self-disclosure is a powerful tool for developing interpersonal relationships. When others see that you are willing to trust them with personal information, they often self-disclose in return, giving you the opportunity to demonstrate that you are also trustworthy. As appropriate self-disclosures are made and reciprocated in a small group, a foundation of trust and openness is laid for future small group work and discussions.

Fourth, design and suggest some low-risk, non-threatening initial activities and tasks for your small group. These low-risk activities and tasks are more likely to engage and involve all your group members, and as your small group experiences some initial success, members will gain confidence and develop a shared history of group cooperation and effective task completion.

PRACTICAL STEPS TO REDUCE PRIMARY TENSION
1. Recognize and acknowledge primary tension when first meeting with a new group.
2. Ask icebreaker questions or have warm up activities.
3. Encourage appropriate self-disclosure.
4. Design and suggest some low-risk, non-threatening activities and tasks.

ICEBREAKER QUESTIONS:

1. What is one of the worst or one of the best small group experiences you have had? What made it such a bad or good experience?
2. Imagine you are a weather reporter: what is the weather forecast for our small group? What kind of climate do you hope or expect to experience? Why?
3. If our small group was a movie, what kind of movie would you want it to be? Why?

ICEBREAKER ACTIVITIES:

1. Have your small group compose a "small group fairytale." Ask one member to begin with "Once upon a time . . . " and have each member add a sentence as you go around the circle. Make sure that the last person to add a sentence ends with, " . . . and they lived happily ever after."
2. Have members pretend they are interviewing for a spot on your small group team. Have them share why they should be hired, and then "hire" them on the spot for your group. Let the group congratulate and welcome each member.
3. Have members break into pairs and ask them to "interview" each other for a few minutes. Let each person introduce their conversation partner to the small group.

INITIAL LOW-RISK GROUP TASKS

1. Have each member share contact information and contact instructions.
2. Discuss and confirm the charge or purpose of your small group.
3. Plan a simple "getting to know each other function" and have each member sign up to bring a food dish or drink.

Establishing Clear Lines of Communication

When a small group first forms, members should share their contact information. Sharing contact information is a fairly low-risk self-disclosure activity that can help build group trust, so it is an important initial group task. A group "secretary" can gather contact information and print an official contact sheet with member names and contact information.

Sharing contact information can also be an icebreaker activity. At the first group meeting, you can ask small group members to introduce themselves and specify the way they prefer to be contacted by other group members. Group members may share telephone numbers, email addresses, etc. If group members are reluctant to share contact information, explain that it is crucial for members to have a way to contact one another and allow members to add specific instructions for when and how they wish to be contacted.

For example, some members may prefer text messages. Some members may prefer that you leave a voicemail message. Some members may not want you to contact them after a certain time in the evening or before a certain time in the morning. When these preferences are shared, members should feel more comfortable about sharing contact information and about contacting each other.

FIGURE 10.4

Sharing contact information is crucial for clear communication in a small group.

In addition to *how* to contact people, your small group needs to decide who should contact whom. If members must miss a group meeting, whom should they contact? Should they contact one member, or everyone in the group? Your group may decide to appoint a central contact person whom everyone can contact. This central contact person can relay messages to the group as needed.

You may also want to set up an email list so one person can contact all other members with the press of one button. See Chapter 10 to learn more about how you can use technology to help your small group members communicate and work together.

Establishing Group Guidelines

Many small groups never establish explicit behavioral guidelines. Instead, members "feel their way along," and over the course of several weeks or months they learn the unstated, implicit rules by which their group operates. After several issues have arisen and after several minor or major confrontations have occurred, people learn what is and is not acceptable in their group.

However, you can avoid misunderstandings and you can speed up the group formation process by asking your small group to openly discuss and decide upon some **group guidelines**. Formal group rules or guidelines help individual members understand what is expected of them. If every member participates in the establishment of these guidelines, and if the group works to get "buy in" for these behavioral expectations, then your group should be able to function smoothly.

FIGURE 10.5

On the other hand, if your small group has difficult group members and things do not go smoothly in your small group, your formal group guidelines can help you clearly identify and address any behavioral problems that arise.

Aim for around a dozen group guidelines. Too few guidelines, and you have not adequately clarified behavioral expectations. Too many guidelines, and group members cannot remember or keep track of them all. You can have a member type up your small group guidelines and then formally indicate approval of these guidelines by having members "sign off" on them by placing their signatures on the official guideline sheet. A copy of these guidelines can be distributed to every group member.

FIGURE 10.6

Contrary to what some people might think, rules and guidelines do not necessarily create a constricting environment. If your small group guidelines are created through a collaborative, cooperative effort, members should be able to relax and feel comfortable working in their small group because they know what is expected and they are in accord with these expectations.

Here are some general tips for creating small group guidelines:

- A group guideline discussion should occur fairly early in the small group formation process so members can commit (or not commit) to the group based on an accurate knowledge of group expectations.
- Although a group guideline discussion should occur fairly early in the small group formation process, it should not come too early. Since there may be disagreement about proposed guidelines, a group guideline discussion is not an appropriate ice-breaker activity.
- Emphasize that group members need to speak up if they disagree with or have reservations about a proposed guideline. You want to get "buy in" for all of your small group guidelines.
- You can periodically review group guidelines to remind members of behavioral expectations. A guideline can be clarified and adjusted if all group members agree that it is ambiguous or problematic.

Here are some basic questions small groups should answer as they consider possible group guidelines:

- How often shall we meet?
- Where will we meet, and for how long?
- How many meetings can a member miss and still function effectively in the group?
- How many members must be present at a meeting for the group to carry on business?
- What should members do if they must miss a meeting?
- How will we make group decisions?
- What climate or atmosphere do we want to create in our group?
- What percentage of time should we be "on task" getting work done, and what percentage of time should the group be socializing and maintaining relationships?

Here are some sample guidelines that most small groups find acceptable and workable:

- Attend all group meetings.
- Come to meetings on time, and stay for the entire meeting.
- Complete all assigned work on time.
- If you must miss a meeting, or if you must come late to a meeting, contact the group ahead of time so they can plan accordingly.
- Share your ideas and opinions with your group. Your input is necessary and valuable.
- Treat others with respect, even when you disagree with them.
- Group decisions will be made by consensus. When a consensus cannot be reached, the group will rely on majority vote.
- Consistent deviations from these guidelines should be addressed at a group meeting.

Developing a Small Group Identity

In Chapter 1, you learned that many teams are small groups, but not all small groups are teams. Teams are usually more cohesive than small groups in general. An elevating goal for your small group is to aim at becoming a cohesive team. To create a cohesive team, you need every member to stop thinking "me" and start thinking "we." You need to create a small group identity that becomes a part of every member.

FIGURE 10.7

A small group identity can help members think "we" instead of "me."

When people identify with a small group, they "belong" to this group because it has become an important part of who they are. To create a cohesive small group with a strong identity, you can develop 1) a team name, 2) a team mascot or symbol, 3) a team motto, and 4) a team Mission Statement.

A TEAM NAME

Names play an important role in identity development. We individualistic Americans emphasize and value first names. When we call someone by their first or given name, we are recognizing their unique personhood. However, people in collectivistic cultures emphasize and stress family names because they value being part of a family, tribe, or collective. If you want people in a small group to identify with and value their group, give the group a name.

Creating a group name can be a formal or informal process. If you are part of a short-term work crew, you can casually nickname your small group and see if the moniker sticks. If you are forming a small group that will work together for months or years, the group may want to go through a more formal process of brainstorming and selecting a group name. For example, musicians who wish to form a band or ensemble will usually take the naming of their band or music group quite seriously, devoting much time and effort to sift through many possible names until they have found the "perfect" name for their group.

If you are asked to give input into the group naming process, suggest a name (or names) that will inspire and motivate your group members to work together and achieve excellence. Avoid names with negative connotations. For example, names like "The Slackers," "The Stoners," and "Team Goof-off" may be funny, but they do not create a good public image for your small group and they do not reinforce the positive behaviors you want to encourage in a small group.

FIGURE 10.8

Many musicians take the naming of their band very seriously.

If you are developing a name for a small group that may increase or decrease in size, avoid names with numbers like "The Fantastic Four" or "The Magnificent Seven." These names, if they do not match the number of people in your small group, will draw attention to the fact that you have gained or lost members.

You may want to look for similarities or commonalities among your small group members and then create a group name which captures this unifying characteristic. Or you may want to create a name that helps your team strive for a noble goal or take part in a worthy cause. Whatever name you choose, make sure that all your group members are on board. You want the name to unite, not divide, your group members.

FIGURE 10.9

A team mascot can help to form a team identity that unifies your small group members.

A TEAM SYMBOL OR MASCOT

In addition to a team name or nickname, many small groups also create a team symbol or **mascot** to visually represent their team. Visual symbols can continually communicate a nonverbal, nonvocal message about your small group. Every time members see the team symbol or mascot, they are reminded that they are a part of a small group with a particular identity.

Create a small group symbol or mascot carefully. Like a team name or nickname, a team symbol or mascot should generate "positive vibes" in your small group. Avoid symbols or mascots that have negative connotations, could be misinterpreted, or that others may find offensive. For example, even if you could give a positive spin to a Nazi Swastika, this symbol should be avoided. You should also avoid team mascots that appear to trivialize any people groups.

Your team symbol or mascot could reinforce your positive team name, or it could represent a positive characteristic or goal of your small group. For example, you could represent your team with a "lightning bolt" symbol because you want to indicate that your team is powerful. Or you could adopt a frog as your team mascot because you want to communicate to others that your team is "hopping" to get good work done.

Although symbols and mascots may contain humorous elements or be represented in cartoon images, you should take them very seriously. Companies invest thousands of dollars and hundreds of hours into developing company symbols because they know that they are creating a "brand" that will form their company identity and public image. When you see an "apple" symbol, you think of a particular computer company, don't you? When you see a talking gecko, you think of a certain auto insurance company, right?

Your small group symbol or mascot can represent your small group to others, and it can direct the minds of your individual members to identify with the larger team to which they belong.

A TEAM MOTTO

In addition to a team name and a team symbol or mascot, you can also create a team motto. A motto is a short phrase or saying that members of a team, company, or organization can recite out loud when they want to energize or unify others.

For example, students, faculty, and staff at Bakersfield College in Bakersfield, California are unified by the college nickname "Renegades" and the college mascot, a knight on horseback. If you want to encourage college pride or energize the students and staff of Bakersfield College, you can also shout out the college motto, "Go, Gades!"

Although mottos are popular with, and expected from, college cheerleaders and cheer teams, you can become a "cheerleader" for you small group by developing and formalizing a motto for your small group team. If you get "buy in" for this motto from all your group members, you have another tool for strengthening your small group identity.

FIGURE 10.10
A motto can unify and inspire a group of people.

A TEAM MISSION STATEMENT

In addition to names, symbols, mascots, and mottos, companies and organizations often develop mission statements that set forth the purposes, procedures, and values of the organization or group. They also may draft vision statements that typically set forth several elevating goals that they can strive to achieve.

Mission and vision statements are normally two to four sentences long. They are carefully crafted, concise statements that are easy to memorize and internalize. Mission statements should be clear and accurate. Vision statements should be clear, positive, and inspirational.

Some companies and organizations combine their mission and vision statements together. This combined statement is often called by the more general term "mission statement." Mission statements are often printed and published in company flyers or posted in organization buildings.

Mission statements help to focus the minds and guide the behaviors of all the employees or members of an organization. If members internalize the organizational mission statement, this statement can synchronize their efforts and create shared beliefs, values, and attitudes.

Companies and organizations typically revise their mission statements every three to five years to keep them fresh. They take this task very seriously because they know that a mission statement helps to create a company or organizational culture that has a powerful influence on all the people in the organization.

Mission statements are not just for large companies or organizations. In the self-help and personal growth field, individuals are encouraged to craft personal mission statements that can help them improve their self-image and achieve their dreams. Similarly, you can work together with your small group members to draft a mission statement that delineates the purposes of your small group and sets forth the elevating group goals your small group team will strive to reach.

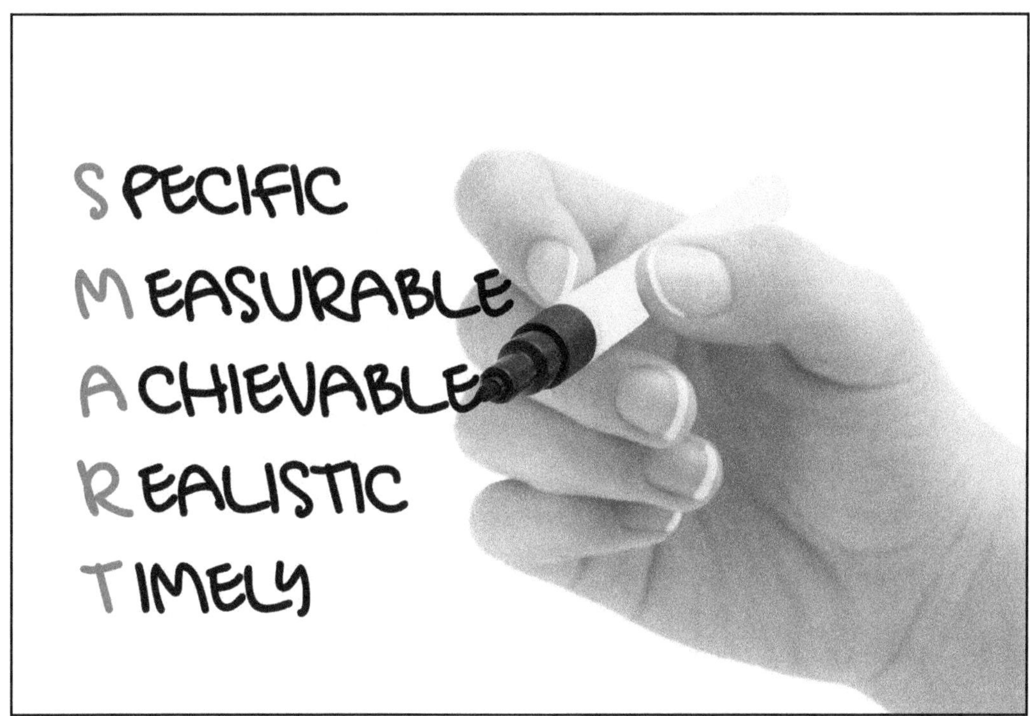

FIGURE 10.11

To develop an effective small group mission statement, make sure the goals set forth in the mission statement can pass the S.M.A.R.T. test: the group goals should be specific, measurable, attainable, realistic, and time-bound. Consider each of these criteria:

Specific: You have a much better chance of accomplishing specific goals. Do not make your group goals too general. For example, "Be a good team" sounds positive, but this very general goal can mean many different things to different people.

Measurable: Make sure your group can determine when they have reached a particular goal or measure how close they have come to reaching a goal. Otherwise, the goal has very little practical value.

Attainable: You want to have elevating goals that will stretch your team. On the one hand, do not set a group goal that aims too low (e.g., "Have every small group member pass our small group communication class."). On the other hand, do not aim too high and set goals that are unattainable (e.g., "Have every small group member be recognized as top student in our small group communication class.").

Realistic: A realistic goal is a goal that all group members are willing and able to work towards. Surprisingly, sometimes high goals that stretch a small group are more realistic than low goals because high goals can motivate and inspire your group members.

Time-bound: If you do not set a time limit for a group goal, the goal could always be "out there on the horizon." However, when you set a time limit for a goal, your motivation to reach the goal can actually increase as the time limit approaches. Make sure any group goals you set are reachable in the time that is available to your small group.

Below are some possible goals for a group in a small group communication course. Determine which of these goals passes the S.M.A.R.T. test.

Goal #1: *Become excellent small group communicators and public speakers.*

Goal #2: *Have some fun.*

Goal #3: *Make high-quality decisions and solve problems effectively by encouraging full group participation.*

Goal #4: *Become a cohesive, unified small group team that functions effectively.*

Goal #5: *Produce high-quality work efficiently while maintaining effective small group relationships.*

Goal #6: *Improve our communication skills and our grades.*

Goal #7: *Create a positive group climate that fosters open communication and harmonious group relationships.*

Goal #8: *Become effective critical thinkers who test all ideas and consider multiple perspectives.*

Goal #9: *Accomplish all small group tasks on time.*

Goal #10: *Crush the competition and win the majority of small group challenges.*

If your small group develops a mission statement that sets forth several S.M.A.R.T. goals, you will have yet another tool for creating a group identity that will help in unifying your group. Your small group can work as a team to reach these elevating goals, and your group members can feel good about their efforts as these goals are approached or attained.

Scheduling, Conducting, and Debriefing from Meetings

To get off to a good start with your small group, you need to schedule and hold some effective group meetings. Many people avoid serving on committees or working in small groups because they do not want to sit in unnecessary, unproductive meetings. If you can kick off your small group work with some productive meetings that accomplish important tasks, your group members will lose their reluctance to make your small group a part of their lives.

FIGURE 10.12

People should not have to sit in boring, unproductive meetings.

CHOOSING A MEETING TIME AND PLACE

When you ask your small group members when they can meet, be prepared for scheduling difficulties. In small group communication courses, students consistently rank "scheduling meetings" as their top area of conflict. Modern Americans lead busy lives, so it often takes work to find or make a time when every group member can meet with the group. However, "I can't meet with the group" is not an acceptable assertion for anyone to make when you are negotiating and setting some meeting times. Everyone must make a commitment to meet with their small group.

One method for scheduling a meeting is to suggest a convenient time when most of your members might be available. For example, if you are all in the same small group communication class, you can try to schedule an outside-of-class meeting time immediately before or after this common class.

Another method for determining a meeting time is to ask each member to fill out a schedule which lists the times of the week when they definitely can*not* meet. These schedules can then be compared to determine a common time when all members' schedules are open for a group meeting. For example, if everyone marks down that they are not available during the mornings, afternoons, and evenings of every weekday, you know that you need to schedule weekend meetings.

If your group needs to meet over a period of several months, you should schedule a regular meeting time that all members know they can attend. Once this regular meeting time is on everyone's calendar, you can always cancel a regularly scheduled meeting time if there is no pressing group business which must be addressed. It is much easier to cancel a regularly scheduled meeting than it is to schedule a last-minute meeting that everyone can attend.

FIGURE 10.13

If only one member is unavailable for a group meeting time, you can schedule the meeting and make arrangements to get the absent member caught up. However, this should be a rare occurrence. You need to work together and problem-solve so that all members can usually attend the group meetings. If members cannot or will not attend meetings, they need to understand that their group will have to move forward and make decisions without their participation and input.

If several members cannot attend a face-to-face group meeting, use technology to hold a "virtual" meeting. Your group may be able to meet with the aid of their phones, their video links, or their computer keyboards. (See Chapter 12 on using technology.)

In addition to a meeting time, put some thought into an appropriate meeting place. For your first few meetings, choose a public space like your college library or cafeteria. Never agree to meet with strangers in an isolated setting, and never ask others to put themselves in such a situation.

Once your small group members have developed relationships and some level of trust, you might be able to schedule some meetings at the homes of group members. However, make sure that you choose a meeting place that is free from excess noise and clutter and other distractions. You want your group members to be able to focus on the task at hand.

FIGURE 10.14

Avoid a meeting place with distractions.

For effective small group discussion and interaction, you need a meeting place with a central table that members can gather around. You also need good lighting, comfortable (but not too comfortable) seating, and the ability to control the room environment. Small group members will have difficulty focusing if they are freezing or overheating.

DEVELOPING A MEETING AGENDA

To hold a productive meeting and to use your small group time wisely, you need to develop a meeting **agenda**. An agenda is a printed or written-out list of topics to be covered and/or tasks to be completed at a meeting. In addition to specifying *what* is to be covered or completed at a meeting, an agenda can also specify *how much time* is to be devoted to each agenda item.

When a meeting agenda is prepared and then passed out to all group members, everyone knows exactly what is to be accomplished at a meeting, and they know how the group is to go about accomplishing these tasks.

FIGURE 10.15
An agenda can keep a group on track.

A small group can ask one member (designated the meeting "chair") to prepare an agenda, or several members can work together to develop an agenda. If you are part of an informal small group with no clearly designated meeting chair, you can volunteer to prepare a meeting agenda. Volunteering to prepare an agenda is one step you can take to emerge as an informal small group leader.

CONDUCTING AN EFFECTIVE MEETING

When members show up for a meeting, you can assign members different meeting tasks or roles. You can designate members as meeting chair, timekeeper, gatekeeper, and secretary. The meeting chair guides the group through the meeting agenda. The timekeeper keeps track of the time spent on each agenda item and informs the group when it is time to move on to the next item. The gatekeeper makes sure that group members stay "on topic" and is given the authority to ask people to keep focused on the issue at hand. The secretary takes written notes that summarize how the group handled each agenda item.

If you are in an informal, short-term small group, you can play all of these meeting roles yourself without ever labeling or explaining them to other group members. If you are in a more formal, long-term small group, you can introduce your group members to these standard meeting roles. You can place the title of these roles at the top of a meeting agenda, and at the beginning of a meeting you can assign members to play these roles.

STANDARD MEETING ROLES
Chair: Guides the group through the meeting agenda
Timekeeper: Keeps track of the time spent on each agenda item
Gatekeeper: Keeps people "on topic"
Secretary: Takes written notes of the decisions made and tasks accomplished

FIGURE 10.16

Meeting roles can help a small group meeting run smoothly.

Meeting roles can be rotated or reassigned at each group meeting, or your group may decide to have particular members play the same meeting roles over the course of several meetings. Here are some specific tips for each meeting role.

Meeting Chair: Guide your small group through the prepared agenda with enthusiasm. A good meeting is a balance between order and energy. The meeting agenda provides your group a structure to follow (order), but you and your small group members need to provide the enthusiasm (energy).

If you want to be an excellent meeting chair, observe effective orchestra conductors during a live performance. They do not bring the orchestra performance to a stop when a note is missed or "glitches" happen. Instead, they spur the musicians on to work together to execute the best performance possible.

Similarly, when you conduct small group meetings, do not get hung up on minor meeting glitches. Keep focused on the overall goals of the group meeting, enthusiastically strive to reach these goals, and your group members will thank you afterwards for conducting a lively meeting.

FIGURE 10.17

Seek to conduct a lively group meeting.

Timekeeper: You are responsible for helping your small group use its time wisely, so make sure your group members are aware of the time allotted for the entire meeting and for each agenda item. Work with your small group to determine how time extensions, if any, are to be allowed. Once the allotted time for an agenda item has expired, who decides whether to extend the time for that item? Some groups give that authority to the meeting chair, while other groups require a majority vote of all the members present.

Do not be overly strict when timing a meeting. You are the timekeeper, not the time sheriff! Do not, for example, interrupt a group member and make them stop mid-sentence because the time for an agenda item has expired. If you use a timer with a buzzer or alarm, members will know that time has expired without you having to say a word.

If you do not have a timer with a buzzer, you will have to speak up when the group has used up the allotted time for an agenda item. Wait until the member speaking has concluded his or her remarks, and then announce that time has expired. The chair or group can then decide how to proceed.

FIGURE 10.18

A timekeeper can help move a meeting along

Gatekeeper: Your job is to help the meeting chair make sure that no one "hijacks" a group meeting by introducing issues that are not on the meeting agenda or by monopolizing all the group discussion time. If someone is introducing new business, or if the group has gotten completely sidetracked, you need to draw attention to the specific agenda item that the group is supposed to be addressing. If one member has spoken at length, you can thank them for their input and ask other members to also share their thoughts and opinions.

Gatekeepers, like timekeepers, need to avoid being overly strict. If you are gatekeeper, you can help keep group members on track, but you do not need to prevent them from ever making a joke or a side comment. An important element of small group work is relationship development and maintenance. Group members need to get to know one another and they need to strengthen their relationships by sharing personal information.

Help your small group balance their relationship development with their task completion. Allow some room for off-track comments that play an important role in creating a comfortable, warm group climate, but do not allow members to continually side-track the small group with extended off-topic discussions.

FIGURE 10.19

Secretary: Much of the work completed in a small group meeting can be lost if no one keeps track of it. Your job is to keep a record of the important items discussed and the important decisions made. You do not need to write down every word spoken. Aim for a concise, accurately written report that can be shared with, and referenced by, the other group members.

CONCLUDING A SMALL GROUP MEETING

Toward the end of a meeting, note which agenda items have not been covered, and decide if another meeting needs to be scheduled to get this work done. If another meeting is required, move the uncovered agenda items to the new agenda for the next meeting. If some work needs to be completed before the next group meeting, assign this work to individual members and make sure the assignments are recorded by the meeting secretary.

When a meeting concludes, the meeting secretary can send out written (or typed) notes of the meeting (called the meeting minutes). These meeting minutes can be archived for future reference, and they can be reviewed at the beginning of the next group meeting to re-orient group members and remind them of what was accomplished and decided at the last group meeting.

Now that you know the basics of scheduling, conducting, and following up on group meetings, you should be able to hold meetings that make your small group work a pleasure.

10 Things *Not* To Do As a Small Group Member

1. Do not place your individual interests and goals above the interests and goals of your small group. In order to become a bona-fide member, you must make a commitment to your small group.
2. Do not underestimate yourself or other group members. Systems Theory (which you learned about in Chapter 4) reveals that every member of a group is important. You each have things to contribute to your small group.
3. Do not isolate yourself or close yourself off from your team members. Communicate! Chapter 6 will give you lots of tips and hints about effective small group communication.
4. Do not let your fears about small group work stop you. Trust is the foundation of healthy human relationships, so take the risk of trusting the people in your small group. If they prove unworthy of your trust, you have still done the right thing by giving them a chance.
5. Do not compete or fight for the "leader" role in your small group. In Chapter 7 you will learn that small group leadership is often shared, and there are many different important roles you and other members can play in your small group.
6. Do not refuse to meet with your small group. Almost everyone is busy and has lots of responsibilities. Be willing to adjust your schedule in order to meet with your group.
7. Do not create a defensive communication climate by being overly critical. (You learned more about defensive and supportive communication climates in Chapter 6.) Avoid pessimism, cynicism, and sarcasm in your small group.
8. Do not hold back voicing your opinions or ideas because you are afraid they will be rejected. Your opinions and ideas are just as valid as those of others. Your team needs to hear what you have to say.
9. Do not squash different or divergent ideas. Chapter 8 taught you that small groups get the best results when different perspectives are shared and explored.
10. Do not overlook the part that technology can play in your small group. Many small groups in the modern world are meeting virtually. Chapter 12 will give you some ideas on how you can use technology to enhance your small group experience.

Summary

After reading through this chapter, you are prepared to get a productive start in your small group this semester. You know how to choose the members for a small group team, and you know why a diverse small group is important. You know how to get over the initial nervousness of meeting with your small group for the first time. You know how to set up clear lines of communication with your small group members, and you know how to set behavioral expectations with group guidelines. You know how to create a small group identity by creating a team name, a team symbol or mascot, a team motto, and a team mission statement. You know how to schedule, conduct, and follow up on group meetings.

Glossary

Agenda: An official schedule of the topics to be covered at a meeting. An agenda may also include the amount of time to be devoted to each agenda item.

Gatekeeper: A person who is chosen to keep a meeting on track and to make sure that no one dominates the meeting time.

Group guidelines: Formal written rules or guidelines which set forth the behavioral expectations for members of a group.

Heterogeneous groups: Groups composed of different types and kinds of people.

Homogeneous groups: Groups composed of people who are very similar.

Mascot: An individual or character that represents a group or organization.

Meeting chair: A person chosen or appointed to conduct a meeting.

Minutes: Notes taken to record the important points and decisions made during a meeting. The minutes are often typed up and distributed after a meeting is over.

Mission statement: A two-to-four-sentence formal statement which sets forth the purposes, procedures, and values of a group or organization. Some mission statements also include the elevating goals of the group or organization.

Motto: A short phrase or expression used to instruct, inspire, or unify the members of a group or organization.

Primary tension: The anxiety and awkwardness that most people feel when they join a new group.

Secretary: A person appointed to take notes and keep the minutes of a meeting.

Self-disclosure: The act of sharing personal information with others. Self-disclosure can be used to establish trust and develop interpersonal relationships.

Static evaluation: The application of the same evaluative label to a person regardless of his or her future behaviors.

Timekeeper: A person appointed to keep track of time during a meeting and to announce when time for an agenda item has expired.

Vision statement: A two-to-four-sentence formal statement which sets forth the elevating goals and future aspirations of a group or organization.

Works Cited or Consulted

Abrahams, Jeffrey. (2004). *The mission statement book: 301 corporate mission statements from America's top companies.* Berkeley, CA: Ten Speed Press. (*A thick compendium of mission statements from American corporations.*)

Booth-Butterfield, M., Booth-Butterfield, S., & Koester, J. (1988). The function of uncertainty reduction in alleviating primary tension in small groups. *Communication Research Reports* 5 (2), 146–153. (*Research article exploring how primary tension can be alleviated in small groups.*)

Derlaga, Valerian J., and John H. Berg. (1987) *Self-Disclosure: Theory, research, and therapy.* New York: Springer Science & Business Media. (*A thick anthology of scholarly articles on self-disclosure.*)

Eckel, C., Catherine, & Grossman, J., Philip. (2005). Managing diversity by creating team identity. *Journal of Economic Behavior & Organization,* 58, 371–392. (*Research study that verifies a strong team identity can curb shirking and free-riding behavior.*)

Hinds, J., Pamela, Carley, M., Kathleen, Krackhardt, David, & Woley, Doug. (2000). Choosing work group members: balancing similarity, competence, and familiarity. *Organizational Behavior and Human Decision Processes,* 81 (2), 226–251. (*A very detailed research article using data from 33 small group projects over a four year period. Concludes that people strive for predictability when choosing future work group members.*)

Streibel, Barbara J. (2002). *The manager's guide to effective meetings.* New York: McGraw-Hill. (*A practical, hands-on guide in the Briefcase Books series that teaches meeting chairs how to keep a meeting focused and productive, including virtual meetings.*)

West, Edie. (1999). *The big book of icebreakers: Quick, fun activities for energizing meetings and workshops.* New York: McGraw-Hill Education. (*Excellent source for a plethora of icebreaker activities to reduce primary tension.*)

Chapter 11:

Making Presentations in Groups

Chapter Objectives

- Know the basic parts of a speech, including the function of the introduction, body and conclusion.
- Research and outline a speech and prepare delivery note cards.
- Create and use effective visual aids.
- Manage speech anxiety.
- Know the formats of group presentations.

After many of your small group discussions, you will be asked to report to the class the viewpoints expressed in, and the conclusions reached by, your small group. During the semester, your small group may be asked to complete a major research or service project, and then your group members may be expected to share the results of this research or service project in a public presentation. When your small group disbands at the end of the semester, you and group members may be asked to divulge your small group experience in "case study" oral reports.

Similarly, when you are asked to be part of a project team or work group on the job, your communication tasks will most likely extend beyond the small group communication that occurs among your group members. In addition to communicating in your small group, you will be expected to communicate with people outside your small group, and sometimes this communication will involve public speaking.

FIGURE 11.1

You need public speaking skills to report out your small group work to others.

In order for your small group to finish well, you and your group members need good public speaking skills that will allow you to present your small group work to others. You can get some good work accomplished if you work together as a cohesive team, and if you learn how to speak effectively in public, your small group work can also benefit many other people.

This chapter is designed to give you the knowledge and skills you need to become an effective public speaker. First, you will learn the basic elements of a speech, including the basic parts of a speech and the basic tasks of a speech introduction, a speech body, and a speech conclusion. Second, you will learn some crucial public speaking skills, including how to gather and use research, how to outline a speech, how to make delivery note cards and presentation aids, and how to manage your public speaking anxiety. Third, you will learn about some types of public speaking related to small groups, including speaking as a small group spokesperson, participating in a small group "tag team" presentation, and participating in a small group panel, symposium, or forum.

The Basics of a Speech

If you take a college course in public speaking, you will probably use a textbook that is several hundred pages long because there is a large body of knowledge related to public speaking that has been developed over the past 2,500 years. The art of oratory has a long and distinguished history, and many different people have contributed to the field of rhetoric and public address.

However, in this textbook chapter, our goal is to give you the most basic, essential information you need to give a decent speech. In this chapter you will not learn everything there is to know about public speaking (like the dozens of organizational patterns you can use to structure a speech body, or the hundreds of stylistic devices you can use to enhance your language), but you will learn the basics of public speaking.

FIGURE 11.2

Giving a speech is as easy as counting to three.

THE THREE BASIC ELEMENTS OF A SPEECH
1. Content
2. Structure
3. Delivery

If you have already had some training and experience in public speaking, this beginning section can function as a quick "refresher" of your public speaking knowledge. If, however, you have had little or no training in public speaking, you should find the following five public speaking "trios" very useful. We have placed the basics of a speech in groups of three because these trios are fairly easy to remember. When you get anxious about presenting a speech in your small group communication class, you can remind yourself that "giving a speech is as easy as counting to three." Let's get counting.

The first public speaking trio to be aware of is the three basic elements of a speech: 1) content, 2) structure, and 3) delivery. In order to give a speech, you must have something to talk about (content), you must organize your thoughts (structure), and you must present your thoughts in spoken words (delivery). Let us take a closer look at each of these basic elements of a speech.

Content: Content is the foundation—the substance of a speech. In order to prepare a speech, you need to develop your speech content—the information, ideas, and opinions that you want to share with your audience. There are two sources for the information and ideas that you develop in a speech—your mind and other people's minds. You can develop the content of a speech by drawing upon your own life experience and your own thoughts, or you can supplement your own thoughts and experiences with the knowledge and opinions of other people. Your small group can help you develop the content of a speech, and you can gather research that will give you information and ideas that you can incorporate into your speech. In the next section of this chapter, we will give you some advice on gathering and using research in a speech.

Structure: In addition to content, a speech also needs structure. From the perspective of an audience, a speaker with lots of content but little or no structure is merely "babbling." As a public speaker, you need to organize and arrange your thoughts so your audience can easily receive them and relate them together. There are certain audience expectations that you need to fulfill as a speaker, and one of these expectations is that your speech will be structured in a way that will make your content comprehensible. Content (even good content) is incoherent without clear structure.

In the next section of this chapter, after giving some tips on how to gather and use research in a speech, we will briefly explain how to outline a speech. A good speech outline (especially a fully-developed, logically-structured preparation outline) will help to ensure that your speech has content and structure. However, a speech preparation outline only gets you 2/3 of the way there—it ensures that your speech has content and structure, but you still have to stand and deliver your speech.

FIGURE 11.3

Like a three-legged stool, a successful speech needs good content, good structure, and good delivery.

Delivery: Delivery is the third basic element of a speech. Like a three-legged stool that needs all three legs, a successful speech needs all three basic elements of a speech—good content, good structure, and good delivery. A speech can look good on paper, but when you stand to deliver a speech, you need words to come out of your mouth, and you need to deliver these words effectively. In addition to your spoken words (your verbal communication), your speech delivery also involves your posture, your facial expressions, your eye contact, and your hand gestures (your nonverbal communication). To deliver an effective speech, you must use good verbal and nonverbal communication.

THE THREE BASIC PARTS OF A SPEECH
1. Introduction
2. Body
3. Conclusion

When you outline a speech, remember that "giving a speech is as easy as counting to three." The three main parts of a speech that you need to outline (and the three main parts of a speech that you need to deliver) are 1) the speech **introduction**, 2) the speech **body**, and 3) the speech **conclusion**.

The ancient Greek philosopher Plato asserted that the three main parts of a speech are like the parts of an animal body: just as an animal has a head, a body, and a tail, so a speech has an introduction, a body, and a conclusion. When you construct a speech, make sure you do not create a monstrosity. Just as you would not want to create an animal with no head, you do not want to give a speech without an introduction. An animal without a tail would be a sorry sight, and so is a speech without a conclusion.

Imagine an animal with a very long head and a very long tail but almost no body in the middle—it would be weird, right? Some speakers create a "weird" speech when they have a long speech introduction and a long speech conclusion but they have very little substance in the speech body. If you have a chance to evaluate speech outlines in your small group, help your small group members construct well-balanced speeches by pointing out when the different parts of a speech are underdeveloped or overdeveloped. The bulk of a speech should be located in the speech body. For example, a five-minute speech that would fill a three-page preparation outline might have a half page introduction and a half page conclusion with a two-page speech body in between.

FIGURE 11.4
An "introduction" head

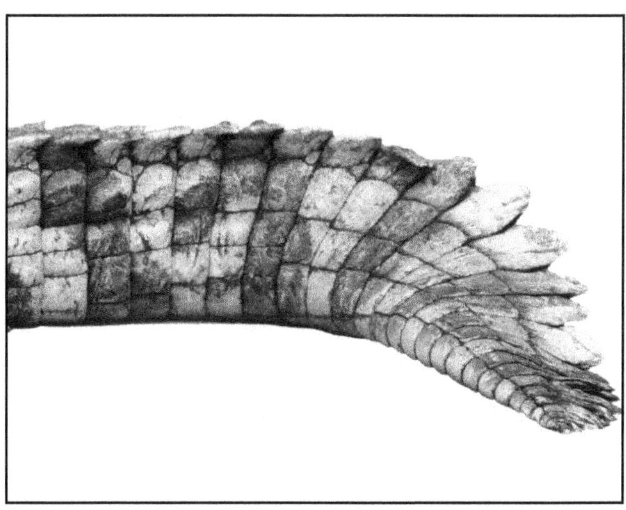

FIGURE 11.5
A "conclusion" tail

THE FIVE BASIC TASKS OF A SPEECH INTRODUCTION
1. Gain attention
2. Provide listener relevance link
3. Establish speaker credibility
4. State your purpose
5. Preview your main ideas

When you are developing the introduction for a speech, remember that "giving a speech is as easy as counting to five:" make sure you 1) gain the attention of your audience, 2) provide listener relevance link, 3) establish speaker credibility, 4) state your purpose, and 5) preview the main ideas of your speech body. In order for your audience to be ready to listen to your speech body, they must be focused on your speech topic, they must understand why you are speaking about this topic, and they must know how you are going to talk about this topic. Your attention getter focuses your audience on your speech topic, the listener relevance link tells the audience why the topic is important, your speaker credibility describes why you should be believable, your purpose explains the main point you want to make about this topic, and your speech preview reveals the main supporting ideas you will develop in the body of your speech. Let's take a closer look at each basic introductory task.

Gain attention: In the first few seconds of your speech, you need to focus your audience's attention on your speech. Even if there is no physical noise in the room you are speaking in, there are all sorts of "psychological noises" distracting the members of your audience. When you first stand up to speak, they may be thinking about the last speech they just heard, or about the fight they had that morning with a family member, or about where they are going to eat their next meal. You need to focus their attention on you and your speech with an attention getter.

Your attention getter should be provocative, appropriate, and relevant. By "provocative," we mean interesting. The last thing you want is a boring attention getter. Instead, aim for the "eyebrow raise." You will know your attention getter is provocative (and effective) if the audience members raise their eyebrows when they hear it. You can begin with a brief story or joke, a quotation, a startling fact or statistic, a provocative question, or a reference to a recent or historical event.

However, make sure your attention getter is not too provocative—it should not be so shocking that your audience will have difficulty listening to the rest of your speech. For example, you could begin a speech by stripping naked while shouting profanity—this attention getter would be provocative, but not appropriate. Your attention getter should be in good taste.

FIGURE 11.6

An effective attention getter will raise eyebrows.

Most importantly, your attention getter should be relevant—it should lead into your speech topic. No matter how interesting a story is or how funny a joke may be, if it does not relate to your speech topic, it will just be a distraction in the long run. Remember, your goal is not just to focus your audience's attention—it is to focus your audience's attention on your speech topic. You should be able to smoothly introduce or transition into your speech topic at the end of your attention getter.*

Listener Relevance Link: After you catch the attention of the audience, you need to tell your audience why your topic is important. In other words, why do they want to spend the next several minutes learning about this topic.

Speaker Credibility: You caught their attention and demonstrated the importance of the topic, now it's time to answer the question as to why we should listen to you. Credibility may be established verbally by identifying your credentials or background with the topic. It may also be established by nonverbal communication such as your clothing and physical appearance. Finally, if you are prepared, you will create an impression of confidence and ultimately, credibility.

***State your purpose:** A thesis is more than a topic. A topic is an idea, whereas a thesis is an assertion. A topic is general, whereas a purpose is specific. A topic is *what* you are talking about, whereas a purpose is *why* you want to talk about your topic. To make sure that your speech has more than just a general topic, you can complete a sentence like the following: "I want to talk about ____________ because I want my audience to realize ____________." The first blank in this sentence is your topic (what you want to talk about), and the second blank is your purpose (why you want to talk about it).

A purpose focuses your speech. There are three purposes in public speaking: to inform, to persuade, and to entertain. If you only introduce a general topic area in your speech introduction, you can wander all over the place in your speech body. However, if you have a specific purpose you want to support, then all the main points in your speech body should relate to this purpose, and any points that do not relate to your purpose should be eliminated from your speech. Before you construct your speech body, you should know the main point you are trying to make (you should develop a speech purpose); before your audience hears your speech body, they should know the main point you are trying to make (you should clearly state your speech purpose).

Preview your main ideas: The transition into your speech body is the speech preview. At the end of your introduction, you do not need to preview everything you are going to talk about in your speech body, but you do need to preview the main ideas you are going to cover. If you have put effort into structuring your speech body, then you want to make this structure clear to your audience. If you have five main points in your speech body (signified by five Roman numerals in your outline), then you want to clearly preview these five main points.

Think of your speech preview as a "road map" to the speech body—you want to give an accurate map of your speech body. You could not follow someone's driving directions if you were using a road map that omitted several roads; similarly, your audience will not be able to follow your thoughts if your speech preview omits important main points that you are going to make. An accurate speech preview will make the structure of your speech body obvious, and it will help your audience follow along as you develop your thoughts.

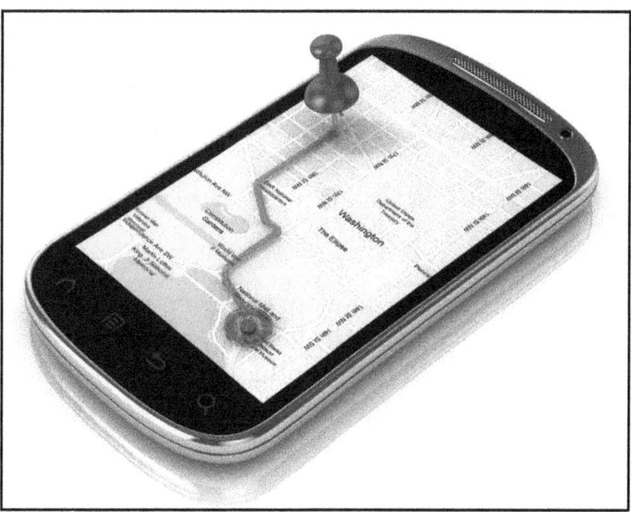

FIGURE 11.7
Think of your speech preview as a road map that helps your audience follow along as you give your speech.

The body of the speech should contain 2–5 main points. There are over thirty different ways to structure a speech body, including chronological order, spatial order, topical order, compare/contrast, divide/classify, cause/effect, pro/con, inductive argument by example, deductive chain of reasoning, and Monroe's motivated sequence. You can organize the ideas in a speech body by level of importance, or by level of acceptance, or by level of complexity. You can place your most important ideas first, or you can place your best ideas last (emphatic order), or you can sandwich your weakest ideas or arguments in between your strongest points.

THE THREE BASIC TASKS OF A SPEECH BODY
1. Make approximately three main points
2. Fully develop your main points
3. Provide clear transitions from point to point

In this basic speech primer, we are going to keep it simple and suggest this rule of thumb: *in the body of your speech, make approximately three points.* If you make approximately three points, and if you fully develop these points, you will be on your way to developing a solid speech body.

The second basic task of a speech body is to *fully develop your main points.* Once you introduce a main point, you need to fully explain and support this point with evidence and reasoning. You can give specific examples which support your point, you can quote or paraphrase research sources, or you can provide arguments that back up your point.

FIGURE 11.8
Clear transition sentences help a speech flow smoothly from point to point.

Of course, sometimes you may only have two main points to make in a speech; if this is the case, be aware that you will need to provide lots of supporting evidence or reasoning for these two main points, and even if you fully develop these points, your speech body may still be a bit underdeveloped. Sometimes you may need to make more than three main points, but be aware that if you have many more points to make, you will have to develop each point very briefly, or if you fully develop all of these points, you will have to give a much longer speech. For a five-minute speech, stick to the rule of thumb, and make approximately three main points.

The third basic task of a speech body is to *provide clear transitions from point to point.* Do not be afraid to number and label your points. Provide "signposts" which let your audience know where you are at in your speech body—"first," "second," "third." As you introduce your main points, present them *as* main points: "The first main point I would like to make is . . . ", "My final main point is . . . ." You can also provide clear transition sentences which move the audience smoothly from one point to the next. "Now that we have considered my first main point, let's move on to my second point, which is . . . ."

When you are developing the conclusion of a speech, remember that "giving a speech is as easy as counting to three." As you conclude, 1) restate your purpose in a memorable way, 2) summarize the main ideas of the speech body, and 3) provide closure by tieing your conclusion to your attention-getter. Think of your conclusion as a backwards introduction, and you should be able to remember these three tasks. In your introduction, you need to preview your main ideas; in your conclusion you need to review your main ideas. In your introduction, you need to state your purpose; in your conclusion, you need to restate your purpose. In your introduction, you begin with an attention getter; in your conclusion, you end with a "closer." Let's take a close look at each basic conclusion task.

THREE BASIC TASKS OF A SPEECH CONCLUSION
1. Restate the purpose in a memorable way
2. Summarize the main ideas of the speech body
3. Provide closure—tie into the attention-getter

Restate the purpose in a memorable way: Oral discourse is necessarily more repetitive than written discourse. When people listen to a live speech, there is no way for them to "rewind the tape" and listen to the speech again, so public speakers must repeat their important ideas. Since your thesis is the main point of your speech, the reason for giving your speech, it deserves to be stated once at the beginning of your speech and once at the end of your speech. Note, however, that you should repeat your thesis *in a memorable way.* Make your restated thesis memorable. Repetition does not have to be boring. At the beginning of your speech, your thesis should be clear. At the end of your speech, your thesis should be poetic and powerful.

FIGURE 11.9

A speech review can help your audience appreciate and remember what they have learned from your speech.

Summarize the main ideas of the speech body: We will say it again—oral discourse is necessarily more repetitive than written discourse. Just as you restate the thesis of a speech in your speech conclusion, you also need to review the main ideas that you have covered in the body of a speech. For public speaking, you need to tell your audience what you are going to tell them (preview your main ideas in your introduction), tell them (develop your main ideas in your speech body), and tell them what you told them (review your main ideas in your conclusion).

Your speech preview is more important than your speech review because it sets up your speech body and clarifies the structure of the speech that is about to unfold. For this reason, the preview of your ideas may be a little more detailed than the review. However, although your review may be a bit briefer than your preview, it should not be omitted. If you want your main ideas to stick in the minds of your audience members, you need to repeat them once, twice, three times—the third time is often the charm. Remember, repetition does not have to be boring. Just as you want to restate your thesis in a memorable way, you want to review the main ideas of your speech body in an interesting manner. Do not plod through your review as if it was an onerous duty—present it as if the ideas you covered are important and worth reviewing.

Provide closure: You know that you have not closed a speech effectively when you say your final words and there is a long, awkward pause . . . and then your audience finally begins to weakly applaud. At the end of your speech, you want to use an effective closer that clearly signals that your speech has ended. However, a generic closer like, "That's it; I'm done now," or, "Thank you for listening to my speech; I hope you learned something" does not provide a memorable ending.

You should associate closers (used in speech conclusions) with attention getters (used in speech introductions) because almost every strategy that can be used to gain attention at the beginning of a speech can be used to provide closure at the end of a speech. You can close a speech with a story, a joke, a quotation, a startling fact or statement, or a reference to a recent or historical event. Just as you want to use a provocative, "eyebrow-raising" attention getter at the beginning of your speech, you want to use a memorable closer that calls forth enthusiastic audience applause at the end of your speech.

In some speeches, especially persuasive speeches, speakers sometimes need to accomplish another task in their speech conclusion—they need to give a "call to action" which asks the audience to respond to their speech in some specific way. Your closer for a speech, even if it is not a persuasive speech, could be a call to action of some kind. For example, if you are giving an informative speech, you can close by asking your audience to use their newly-gained knowledge to improve their lives or the lives of others.

One other closing strategy that is often very effective is called the "wrap-around closer." When you use a "wrap-around closer," you end your speech by referring back to your original attention getter. You do not repeat your attention getter exactly, but you reference your attention getter in order to "wrap-around" to where your speech began. This strategy gives your speech a sense of completeness, and it can lead to a very satisfying close.

FIGURE 11.10

Five Crucial Public Speaking Skills

In addition to knowing the basic parts and tasks of a speech, there are some essential skills you need to develop in order to become an effective public speaker. In this section, you will learn 1) how to gather and use research, 2) how to outline a speech, 3) how to deliver a speech using brief note cards, 4) how to make and use visual aids, and 5) how to manage your public speaking anxiety. If you develop these five crucial skills, you should be able to make solid oral presentations in your small group communication course, and you will have the skills you need to represent yourself and your small group in public settings.

HOW TO GATHER AND USE RESEARCH

One of the advantages of working in a small group is that you can share the workload with the other members of your small group. If you had to research a subject for a small group project all by yourself, it might take several hours to find a few quality sources; however, if each member of your small group researches the subject individually and you then all pool your research together, you can quickly amass a lot of information for a group research project. For example, if you have six members in your small group, and if you each find five pieces of research for a group project, when you compile this research together, your small group will have around *thirty* pieces of research at hand.

There are many different sources you can access to gather your research. If you go online, you can find personal web pages, governmental and organizational web pages, online dictionaries and encyclopedias, and electronic libraries that will give you access to electronic versions of books, magazines, and professional journals. However, do not overlook your college or local library. Traditional libraries have large reference sections with specialized dictionaries, encyclopedias, and almanacs that you cannot find online. Documentary movies and radio and television broadcasts can also be a useful source of information.

FIGURE 11.11

Working together, your small group should be able to quickly gather a lot of information.

You can also conduct your own surveys or interviews to gather research information. If you conduct an informal survey, you need to make the informal nature of the survey clear to your listening audience if you end up using the survey information in an oral presentation. If you conduct an interview, make sure you record the date of the interview and the background or credentials of the person interviewed.

Whatever information or evidence you collect, you will need to decide if you will quote directly from a source or if you will paraphrase a source. If you quote a source directly, you should place the other person's words in quotation marks, and you should quote your source faithfully and accurately. If you paraphrase a source, you need to put the other person's ideas into your own words. Changing one or two words of a sentence or paragraph is not a valid paraphrase.

When the members of a small group all pitch in to gather research, it is not difficult to quickly amass a large amount of information—the trick is to keep track of all this research and information. We recommend that your small group ask each member to copy any research material that they think the group, or any member of the group, might need to use. For example, if you run across a good web article related to a topic your group needs to research, you should print out the entire web article to share with your group, or print out the section of the article that you think is useful. Your small group can place the copied evidence in a binder that all group members can access.

Since you will have to credit your research sources in your oral presentations, make sure you keep track of the sources of any information you copy. When you copy a web article or a section of a web article, copy or write down the web address and the date you accessed the website. Similarly, when you copy out a few pages of a book, make sure that you write down the title, author, publisher, and publication date of the book. When you copy a section of a magazine or newspaper article, write down the title and the date or issue number of the magazine or newspaper. If you lose track of this source information, you will not be able to use the information you have copied, no matter how useful that information may be. *Whenever you use someone else's words or ideas in an oral presentation, you must give credit to the original source.*

Using someone else's words or ideas without giving them credit is called **plagiarism**. Plagiarism is a serious academic offense, and it can result in an "F" grade for an assignment or dismissal from a course or an academic institution. Many college students are aware that they should not plagiarize when writing essays for their college courses, but they are not aware that the same burden of crediting sources rests upon public speakers. Whether you are writing *or* speaking, you must credit your sources; otherwise, you are guilty of intellectual theft. Some students also think that if they paraphrase a source, they no longer have to credit this source; however, plagiarism is using someone else's words *or ideas* without giving them credit—paraphrasing does not free you from the burden of crediting a source.

Using the journalist's five questions can help you keep track of your research source information. When compiling information or evidence to be used by your small group, remember these five questions, and be able to answer them: Who? What? When? Where? and, Why? More specifically, **Who** is the person or organization that you are quoting or paraphrasing? **What** did they write or say? **When** was this information published, and/or when did you access this information? **Where** was this information found? **Why** should we believe this information? (What makes it credible or trustworthy?)

FIGURE 11.12

When giving an oral source citation, "[illegible]" is the most important question to answer.

If you can answer the journalist's five questions, you will be able to give a good **oral source citation**. An oral source citation is a sentence that you speak in your speech that informs the audience about the source you are quoting or paraphrasing. Since an oral source citation is a sentence that you speak, there is no formal or standard form of an oral source citation. Depending on your speaking style, you can be very formal or very informal when crediting your sources in a speech, but the rule of thumb to follow is this: *when orally citing a source, give your audience enough information that they could find and check out the source themselves if they so desired.*

The most important question to answer when giving an oral source citation is the "where" question: where did you find your information, and where does your audience need to look to find this information for themselves? Telling your audience *who* said something is insufficient. For example, if you quote Dr. Sarah Jones in your speech and you say, "Dr. Sarah Jones says . . . ," you also need to tell your audience *where* her words can be found. Are her words found in a magazine article? Are they found on a webpage? Were they spoken in an interview you conducted? Unless your listening audience knows *where* to look, they cannot check this source out for themselves.

If you keep track of your sources as you gather your research, you will be able to share useful, usable information with your small group members, and you all will be able to use this research in your speeches because you will be able to provide the necessary oral source citations. Examples of types of supporting material are found in Chapter 12.

OUTLINING A SPEECH

When giving a speech for a small group presentation, it is very unlikely that you will be asked or required to read your speech word-for-word from a manuscript. Manuscript delivery is appropriate for very formal occasions, but for most public speaking situations, it would be inappropriate and ineffective to read your speech from a manuscript.

In the United States, most public speakers are expected to speak **extemporaneously**. Instead of reading their speeches, public speakers usually outline their speeches in detail, but then they shrink their detailed preparation outlines down into a brief delivery outline (which is often placed on a few note cards). The extemporaneous method allows speakers to prepare and practice their speeches ahead of time, but since they speak using only "key word" note cards, they avoid reading their speeches, and they speak in a much more natural, much more audience-friendly style.

The beginning point for extemporaneous delivery is a detailed, logically-structured preparation outline. A detailed preparation helps you accomplish several different things.

- First, it helps you develop and organize your ideas. All your ideas are labeled with numbers and letters, and these numbers and letters indicate your main points and your subpoints.
- Second, it helps you work out the sentences you wish to speak in your speech, including your important transition sentences and your verbal source citations.
- Third, it helps you remember the ideas in your speech. The numbers and letters you use to label your ideas act as memory prompts.
- Fourth, it helps ensure that the parts of your speech are balanced and that you are managing your time wisely. When you see your speech introduction, body, and conclusion on paper, you can estimate how long each section of your speech will take, and you can see if any sections are underdeveloped or overdeveloped.
- Fifth, and most important, a detailed preparation outline lets you improve your speech *before* you deliver it—you can share this outline with small group members and others so that they can give you feedback about the structure and content of your speech.

Hopefully, the five reasons given above have sold you on the benefits of constructing a detailed preparation outline for your speech. There is some effort that goes into constructing a detailed preparation outline, but this effort will pay off. If you outline your speech ahead of time, you will have a well-developed, well-balanced, clearly-structured, fully-thought-out speech. Here are seven outlining guidelines that will help you construct a logically-structured preparation outline that will be easy to analyze and evaluate.

FIGURE 11.13

1. Label the three main parts of your speech "Introduction," "Body," and "Conclusion." You do not want your evaluators to have difficulty locating these three main parts of your speech when they look at your outline.
2. Use capital letters (A, B, C) to label your first-level subpoints, Arabic numbers (1, 2, 3) to label your second-level subpoints, and lower-case letters (a, b, c) to label your third-level subpoints. This outlining system is used throughout the United States, so anyone reading your outline should be able to quickly grasp your main points and subpoints if you use this standard numbering and lettering system.
3. Subdivide and use subpoints whenever you have two or more things you want to say. For example, if the first main idea in your speech body (labeled Roman numeral I) has two supporting points, these two subpoints should be labeled with the capital letters A and B. If your B subpoint has three supporting subpoints, they should be labeled with the Arabic numbers 1, 2, and 3.

FIGURE 11.14

Do not use too many numbers and letters in your outline. You do not necessarily need a number or letter for every single sentence in your outline. Numbers and letters are used to label and clearly mark your ideas, and sometimes a single idea may be developed in two or three sentences. If you have gone through half the alphabet in order to label a subsection of an outline, you are probably adding too many label markers. On the other hand, do not use too few numbers and letters in your outline. If you visually scan an outline and see a "paragraphy" section, this section probably needs to be further subdivided. Remember, if you have two or more things you need to say, subdivide and use subpoints.

4. Indent to make your main points and subpoints stand out. Your Roman numerals should be located at the far left margin of your paper, your capital letters should be indented about five or so spaces to the right, then your Arabic numerals are indented another five or so spaces, etc. These indentations make your main points and subpoints stand out from one another. In addition to the number and letter markers, the white spaces created by the outline indentations provide further visual cues to distinguish your main points and your subpoints.
5. For a fully developed speech preparation outline, use complete sentences throughout. During your delivery, the sentences on your preparation outline may not come out of your mouth exactly the way you have them on paper, but writing sentences in your preparation outline lets you practice expressing your ideas in specific words. A complete-sentence outline is also the best way to fully develop your ideas, and it allows your small group members (and other people looking at your outline) to give you useful feedback.

   Make sure you include transition sentences in your speech outline. After each Roman numeral in your speech body, you should have a transition sentence introducing each main point you want to make. Smooth transitions can turn a good speech into a great speech, and one way to get smooth transitions is to practice your transition sentences on paper until they can come out of your mouth easily during a speech.

6. Include oral source citations in your speech outline. If you use any sources in your speech—if you use anyone else's words or ideas—you need to credit your sources. Remember, oral source citations are sentences that you speak during a speech, so these sentences should be placed in your speech outline where appropriate.

Oral source citations are different than written source citations. Written source citations (the citations that appear in parentheses in books and essays) usually are placed at the end of a quotation or paraphrase. However, in a speech, your oral source citations should usually be spoken *before* you quote or paraphrase a source. Introducing your source before your information or evidence allows you to build up the credibility of your source, and it lets you prepare your audience for the information they are about to hear.

To help you visualize the structure of a speech preparation outline, we have provided an abstract outline for a simple, fairly brief, extemporaneous speech below. You can use this abstract outline as a template for your own extemporaneous speeches. However, you may need to add or subtract numbers or letters to your outline if you have more or less to say. For example, if you add a section to your introduction to establish your credibility, your introduction would need four Roman numerals. If you only had two main points to make in your speech body, your speech body would only need two Roman numerals. Make adjustments as necessary.*

ORGANIZATIONAL STRUCTURE OF AN EFFECTIVE SPEECH SAMPLE OUTLINE

I. Introduction

A. **Attention-getter**—Examples include: Quotation, Startling Statistic, Rhetorical Question, Humorous Anecdote.

B. **Listener Relevance Link**—Some authors refer to this step as Topic Significance. You need to let the audience know why they should bother to listen to your presentation. Why is your topic important to them?

C. **Speaker Credibility**—This is about you. Why are you a believable person to speak on your subject? This can be done either verbally or in a nonverbal manner. Verbally—You would indicate your qualifications to speak on the subject. Nonverbal—Can be accomplished in a couple of ways. First, if you were speaking in person, your clothing establishes credibility. Second, by appearing confident, you establish credibility. The best way to appear confident is to be prepared.

D. **Purpose Statement**—Indicate to your audience what the purpose of the presentation is. In public speaking, there are only three types of purposes—to inform, to persuade, and to entertain.

E. **Preview of Organizational Structure**—Preview the areas that will be addressed in the body of your speech.

II. Body of the Speech—You should have 2–5 main points. There are many ways to organize the body of your speech—topic, spatial, chronological, cause/effect, disadvantages/advantages, problem-causing solution, etc. Each point should be developed with verbal and/or visual supporting material.

A. Point 1

B. Point 2

C. Point 3

D. Point 4

E. Point 5

III. Conclusion

A. **Restate Purpose**—Remind your audience as to the purpose of the speech.

B. **Summarize Main Points**—Briefly summarize the main points from the body of the speech.

C. **Tie-in the Attention-Getter**—Make reference to the opening statement to wrap up the speech.

*MAKING AND USING "KEY WORD" NOTE CARDS

Your delivery outline is an abbreviated version of your detailed preparation outline. To aid in memory recall, it should have the exact same logical structure as your preparation outline. Every Roman numeral, capital letter, Arabic number, and lowercase letter that appears in your preparation outline should appear in your delivery outline. Each letter and number in your delivery outline should trigger your memory and help you recall the detailed information contained in the corresponding section of your preparation outline.

The major difference between your detailed preparation outline and your abbreviated delivery outline is what follows the numbers and letters in the outline—whereas a fully developed preparation outline has complete sentences following the numbers and letters in the outline, a delivery outline only has key words or short phrases after each number and letter. This difference is crucial. DO NOT WRITE OUT COMPLETE SENTENCES IN YOUR ABBREVIATED DELIVERY OUTLINE. In your delivery outline, you only want to trigger your memory with key words or phrases so you can speak extemporaneously about the ideas being addressed.

There is one exception to this general rule regarding key words and phrases in a delivery outline—if you are directly quoting someone else's words in your speech, then you may include a quotation in complete sentences. Make sure you place quotation marks around the direct quotation, and make sure you introduce the quotation with an oral source citation so your audience knows that you are reading someone else's words at this point in your speech.

If you type up your delivery outline on a standard eight-and-a-half-inch by eleven-inch piece of paper, use an easy-to-read font, and use only one side of the paper. The advantage of using a piece of paper for your delivery outline is that the outline is easy to see and read, and there is only one piece of paper to keep track of on the podium. However, if a podium is not available, it can be fairly awkward to hold a large piece of paper in your hands, especially if your hands are shaking.

FIGURE 11.15

Complete sentences are not allowed in a "key word" delivery outline.

Note cards work well for almost any extemporaneous speaking situation, so we will give you instructions on how to prepare "key word" note cards. Write legibly on three-by-five inch or four-by-six inch cards. Use only one side of each note card. Leave plenty of white space on your cards. Remember, you are only writing down key words and phrases on your note cards, and you want these words and phrases to stand out.

When delivering your speech, you only have a few seconds to scan your note cards, so you want easy-to-read cards. Do not use bullet points on your note cards. Stick with the same numbers and letters that you used in your preparation outline, and indent these numbers and letters on your note cards to help you locate your main ideas and supporting points quickly.

You should only need a few note cards for a speech. We recommend using one note card for each major section or idea of your speech. For example, if you are giving a speech with three main points, you could use five note cards, one note card for your speech introduction, one note card for each of your main points, and one note card for your speech conclusion. The advantage of placing each major section of your speech on a separate note card is that you can literally hold the different parts or chunks of your speech in your hand, and you can feel when it is time to move on to your next point or speech section.

Do not scribble out your delivery note cards right before your speech. You need to give yourself time to practice delivering your speech using your note cards. Extemporaneous speeches are prepared *and practiced* ahead of time. Do not spend too much time working over your detailed preparation outline and then rush to throw together some delivery note cards at the last minute. Once your preparation outline is decent, transfer your ideas over to your delivery note cards, and practice delivering these ideas extemporaneously from your note cards until your ideas flow smoothly with just a glance at your "key word" memory prompts.

Do not be surprised if you struggle with your delivery the first time you practice with your note cards. You may have too much written on your note cards, or you may not have enough written, or you may find that you can't read your own handwriting, so you may have to revise and rewrite your note cards. However, even if your note cards are legible, and even if they have just the right amount of words, you may need a few run-throughs to fully internalize your speech and to smooth out your delivery. You may have to practice delivering a five-minute speech a half-dozen times, but this is only a half-hour investment. If you have spent hours researching and outlining a speech, then you should not hesitate to spend a half hour perfecting its delivery.

FIGURE 11.16

As we end this section on making and using "key word" note cards, we will emphasize once more what you do ***not*** want to put on these note cards: DO NOT PLACE COMPLETE SENTENCES ON YOUR NOTE CARDS. You may be worried about forgetting your ideas, and you may tell yourself that you will not read these sentences, but if you get nervous while delivering your speech, that is exactly what you might end up doing—you might end up burying your head in your note cards and reading your speech word-for-word. Do not even give yourself the opportunity to make this mistake. If your note cards only have key words or phrases, you will be able to establish good eye contact with your audience, and you will have to *speak* (not read!) to them.

HOW TO MAKE AND USE VISUAL AIDS

In order to gain and maintain the attention of modern audiences, public speakers need to know how to make and use visual aids. Historians talk about a cultural shift that occurred in the ancient world. Oral cultures (cultures that privileged and valued the spoken word) became literate cultures (cultures that privileged and valued the written word). In our modern age, with the advent of electronic media, another major cultural shift is occurring—literate cultures are becoming audio-visual cultures.

FIGURE 11.17

Many modern audiences expect and need visual stimulation.

After watching thousands of hours of television shows, movies, and video clips, modern audiences are conditioned for aural and visual stimulation. You may have some important words to speak to your audience, but if you do not supplement these spoken words with effective visual aids, these words may never reach their mark. Your words need to be reinforced with visual aids.

There are several purposes that visual aids fulfill. First, well-prepared, professional-looking visual aids enhance your credibility as a speaker. Visual aids may take some time and effort to prepare, but when you use them in a speech, you can gain the good will and respect of your audience very quickly. When they see that you are putting time and effort into communicating your ideas both verbally and visually, they will make an effort to pay attention and to listen to what you have to say.

Second, visual aids gain and maintain the attention of your audience. In addition to your verbal attention getter, you can generate interest in your speech with a visual attention getter. A startling picture or arresting image can quickly rivet the attention of your audience.

Third, visual aids can help you to emphasize a point. For example, you can emphasize your verbal thesis with a "thesis reinforcer" visual aid. If you are asserting that your speech will help your audience members work together more effectively in small group teams, you can hold up or show a picture of a happy, smiling small group when you state this "selling point" thesis.

Fourth, visual aids can reveal your speech structure. When it is time to preview the main points in your speech body, you can point to a "preview chart" and verbalize the main points displayed there. Similarly, a "review chart" can help you quickly review your main points at the end of your speech. In addition, throughout your speech body, you can display images and captions that help you introduce each of your main points.

Fifth, visual aids can aid in memory. When you present important facts and figures that you actually want your audience to remember, reinforce these facts and figures with visual charts, graphs, and images. If you want your audience to remember an oral source citation for a crucial source in your speech, display a visual aid that also contains the source information.

Sixth, visual aids can clarify ideas. If "a picture is worth a thousand words," then a few well-chosen images can help you to quickly explain a difficult concept. When you are struggling to express a concept or idea in words, think about adding a visual aid at this point in your speech to aid in understanding.

Seventh, visual aids add authenticity. They make what you are talking about seem real to your audience. If you think your audience might question whether someone or something actually exists, showing a picture of the person or thing can go a long way in erasing their doubts.

Now that you know the purposes of visual aids, you should have no problem creating many visual aids to illustrate and support the ideas in a speech. You can reinforce your introductory tasks with an attention-getting visual aid, a "thesis reinforcer" visual, and a preview chart. In the body of your speech, you can use visual aids to introduce your main points, aid in memory, clarify ideas, and add authenticity. You can reinforce your concluding tasks with a visual aid to emphasize your restated thesis, a review chart to visualize once more the main points you covered, and a visual "closer" to end your speech effectively. If you incorporate many visual aids into your speech, you may never even need to look at your "key word" delivery note cards!

There is much to learn about the design and use of visual aids. In this simple visual aid primer, we will give you several lists to keep in mind. We will list for you 1) types of visual aids, 2) visual aid media, 3) guidelines for making visual aids, and 4) guidelines for using visual aids. We do not have space to fully expand on the information in these lists, but they should point you in the right direction, and you can ask your instructor to further explain any principle or thing with which you are unfamiliar.

PURPOSES OF VISUAL AIDS
1. Enhance speaker credibility
2. Gain and maintain attention
3. Emphasize a point
4. Reveal speech structure
5. Aid in memory
6. Clarify an idea
7. Add authenticity

TYPES OF VISUAL AIDS
1. Three-dimensional objects or props
2. Pictures or drawings
3. Charts or graphs
4. Video clips
5. Maps
6. Textual graphics (words)
7. People

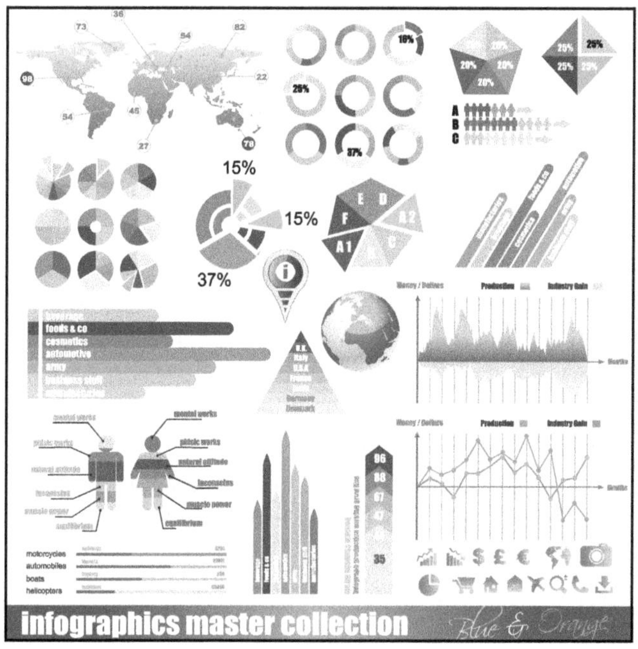

FIGURE 11.18

Charts and graphs clarify facts and figures.

FIGURE 11.19

Pictures gain and maintain attention

FIGURE 11.20

In addition to types of visual aids, you need to think about the visual aid media you will use to display your visual aids. For example, if you want to show a picture to your audience, what method or device will you use to display or project this picture? Should you place it in front of a document camera? Should you mount it on a posterboard? Should you import it into a PowerPoint presentation? You must make good choices about how to display your visual aids. When you are choosing the visual aid media to use, consider the needs of your audience, the purpose of your speech, the size of the room in which you will speak, and your familiarity with the presentation equipment.

VISUAL AID MEDIA
1. Chalk or marker board
2. Computer screen
3. Document camera
4. Flip chart
5. Handout
6. Overhead transparency
7. Poster board
8. Video projector

TEN GUIDELINES FOR MAKING VISUAL AIDS
1. **Make professional-looking visual aids.** Visual aids only enhance your credibility as a speaker when they look professional. If your visual aids look sloppy and amateurish, they will detract from your speech presentation.
2. **Make a sufficient amount of visual aids.** If you want to use visual aids to help you gain and maintain attention, emphasize points, reveal your speech structure, aid in memory, clarify ideas, and add authenticity, you will need quite a few. You need enough visual aids to enhance all the different ideas and parts of your speech.
3. **Make different types of visual aids.** Audiences lose interest when they see the same type of visual over and over. Use a combination of pictures, drawings, charts, graphs, and textual graphics.
4. **Keep your visual aids simple.** Your audience must be able to grasp the meaning or point of your visual aid very quickly. Do not use complex drawings or very detailed pictures that your audience would want to analyze and appreciate at length.
5. **Make them large enough to be seen.** Use large images, and use large words. The audience members in the very back of the room should be able to easily see and understand your visual aids.
6. **Do not use multiple images on one visual aid.** Your audience will not know what image they should look at, and from a distance multiple images can blur together or look too "busy." Give your audience one main image on which to focus.
7. **Do not use too many words.** Usually you should have only one or two words on a visual aid, and almost never more than five. An audience cannot listen to your speech and read a lot of words at the same time. Do not undermine your "key word" note cards by placing complete sentences on your visual aids.
8. **Use an easy-to-read font for your textual graphics.** Do not use a hard-to-read computer font with very thin, very thick, or very ornate letters. Use a simple, block-style font that your audience can easily read.
9. **Use a high-contrast font color for your textual graphics.** Do not use a light-colored font on a light background or a dark-colored font on a dark background—the lack of contrast will make the words disappear. Use a light-colored font on a dark background, or a dark-colored font on a light background.
10. **Combine an evocative image with a few words.** Most of your visual aids should contain one evocative image enhanced with just a few words. The words should help your audience quickly understand the purpose or point of the image.

TEN GUIDELINES FOR USING VISUAL AIDS
1. **Plan out how you will display your visual aids.** In addition to choosing your visual aid media, think through how you will use that media. For example, if you use a poster board, will you hold the poster board, will you place it on an easel, or will you pin it to a wall?
2. **Practice using your visual aids.** Practice delivering your speech using your note cards and your visual aids. You need to plot out and practice how you will manipulate these materials.
3. **Test out and prepare any presentation technology ahead of time.** Make sure all the equipment is working. You do not want to be wrestling with audio-video equipment or a computer in front of your audience when it is time for your speech to begin.
4. **Have a back-up plan.** When using technology, remember Murphy's Law—if something can go wrong, it will go wrong. If you are giving an important speech, have alternate methods for displaying your visual aids in case of equipment failure.
5. **Position your visual aids where they are easy to reach.** Place your poster boards in a stack. Hang your flip chart on a wall. Adjust the computer keyboard so you can easily press the space bar to advance your PowerPoint slides.
6. **Display your visual aids only when you want your audience to focus on them.** The visual aids should enhance, not distract from, your verbal message. This guideline explains why you should not pass a picture around or give your audience an outline handout during your speech.
7. **Do not stand in front of or hide behind your visual aids.** You are the star of the speech, so your audience must be able to see you. Your visual aids are designed to enhance your verbal message, so your audience must be able to see your visual aids.
8. **Face the audience, not your visual aids.** You need to maintain eye contact, and you need to be able to monitor your audience at all times. The audience needs to see your face, not the back of your head.
9. **Refer to and verbalize your visual aids.** Your visual aids become a part of your speech when you point them out and verbalize them. If you never refer to them, they are basically invisible. However, when you verbalize them, the combination of "showing and telling" helps your audience understand and remember your points.
10. **Put away all of your visual aids after your speech is finished.** Exit from the PowerPoint program. Remove your flash drive from the computer. Erase the marker board. Take down your poster boards. Be respectful of the speakers that follow you.

FIGURE 11.21

FIGURE 11.22

HOW TO MANAGE YOUR PUBLIC SPEAKING ANXIETY

Social scientists have identified several different forms of communication apprehension. Some people get anxious in one-on-one interpersonal communication situations. Some people get anxious about communicating in small groups. However, so many people are anxious about public speaking that communication scholars and public speaking instructors have given it an acronym: PSA (public speaking anxiety). This section will help you to manage your public speaking anxiety by describing the common symptoms of PSA, listing the common causes of PSA, and giving you some tips on how to reduce your PSA before, during, and after your speech.

The Symptoms of Public Speaking Anxiety

It can be very disconcerting when your body does things that you are not expecting it to do. You may be caught off guard when you stand up to speak in public and experience some of the following symptoms of public speaking anxiety. Your heart may beat more quickly and more loudly. You may flush red and break out in a sweat. Your mouth may suddenly become very dry, or you may suddenly have the urge to urinate. Your hands may shake, and your arms and legs may tremble. You may feel nauseous or queasy. You may find yourself speaking very quickly or using lots of filler words like "uh," "um," or "ya know." Your mind may also go totally blank.

All of the symptoms listed above are quite normal. When you think that you are in a dangerous situation, your body is biologically programmed for the "fight or flight" response. Extra adrenalin is released into your system so that you can stand and face the danger (the fight response) or flee to safety (the flight response).

The flood of adrenalin resulting from the fight or flight response is responsible for almost all the common symptoms of public speaking anxiety. The sudden release of adrenalin causes your heart rate to increase, which pumps more blood through your body, which causes you to flush and turn red, which causes you to sweat profusely, etc. The extra energy created by the adrenalin in your system has to dissipate somehow, so your body shakes and twitches as this extra energy is discharged.

Knowing about the fight or flight response helps you understand why your body responds the way it does in a perceived "danger" situation. You are not defective, weird, or abnormal if you experience anxiety symptoms produced by the fight or flight response. However, we still need to address why public speaking would ever be perceived as a "danger" situation. In the next section, we present some of the causes of public speaking anxiety.

The Causes of Public Speaking Anxiety

Good doctors know that they must do more than just treat the symptoms of an illness. In order to provide an effective cure for a disease, physicians must identify the causes of the disease; then they can develop a long-term cure that attacks these root causes. Similarly, if you can identify the causes of your public speaking anxiety, you may be able to greatly reduce (or even eliminate) many of your symptoms of PSA by addressing these causes. We present now some common causes of public speaking anxiety.

Fear of the unknown. We fear the unknown, and often when speaking in public one "unknown" we have to deal with is the audience. We often do not personally know many of the people sitting in the audience, so we do not know how these audience members will react to our public speaking efforts. Another "unknown" faced by public speakers is an unknown outcome—we do not know how the speech will go. Recognizing this uncertainty leads us into our next cause of PSA.

FIGURE 11.23
When the cause of a problem is identified, the problem can be treated.

Performance anxiety. There is no denying that a formal public speech is a performance. The speaker is "on stage" and the audience members are spectators. After the speech concludes, the audience members usually show their appreciation for the speech performance by applauding. Performance anxiety is one reason why a moderate level of PSA is appropriate and even necessary; a speaker without any PSA is probably going to give a speech that is "flat."

Unrealistic expectations. Some speakers have unrealistic expectations about giving a perfect, flawless performance. Speakers who give themselves no room for error put themselves under tremendous pressure. Their perfectionism leads to a sense of "failing" if anything in their speech is less than perfect. Some speakers have unrealistic expectations about a fantastic audience response. They do not realize that a public speech is a communication transaction between the speaker and the audience and that sometimes audience members do not fulfill their responsibilities. It is unrealistic to think that everyone in the audience will give you a standing ovation, or laugh at all your jokes, or even give you their undivided attention.

Fear of being harshly criticized. Because public speaking is a performance, there is an evaluation component. Public performers are sometimes rewarded with hearty applause, but sometimes their efforts are met by jeers and shouts of "Boo!" Even if people have never received harsh criticism for their public speaking efforts, they may imagine that such criticism awaits. They fear that their audience will be bored, or unimpressed, or hostile. They are afraid that their best efforts will be met by yawns, or frowns, or outright ridicule.

Negative self-talk. Often the negative criticism we fear from our audience actually originates in ourselves. We can often be our own worst critic. Our intrapersonal communication or internal dialogue is called "self-talk," and our self-talk can be positive or negative. Very negative self-talk during a speech can make a person "freeze up," and it can make you "awfulize" both your speech performance and the constructive criticism offered by your instructor and peers. You may tell yourself, "I did a terrible job," and "the audience hated my speech."

Fear of the symptoms of speech anxiety. Surprisingly, many people are not actually afraid of giving a speech—they are afraid of being afraid. They are afraid that they will experience the symptoms of public speaking anxiety. Usually this fear is based on a prior public speaking experience when some strong symptoms of PSA were activated. If the experience of these past symptoms is viewed and remembered as a "traumatic" event, any onset of similar symptoms of PSA can trigger anxiety in the present. Unfortunately, people who are afraid of the symptoms of PSA can get caught in a vicious cycle of fear. Their anxiety about experiencing the symptoms of PSA brings about the onset of these symptoms. When they realize the symptoms of PSA are occurring, their anxiety increases, which makes the symptoms increase, etc.

Now that you know some of the symptoms and causes of PSA, we will give you three tips to reduce your public speaking anxiety before, during and after your speech:

THREE WAYS TO REDUCE PSA BEFORE YOUR SPEECH
1. **Envision success.** Positive self-talk can help you create a positive self-fulfilling prophecy. Envision the public speech you want to give in order to improve your odds of actually giving such a speech. If you are mired in inaccurate, negative thoughts about public speaking, retrain your brain and break out of these unhealthy thought patterns.
2. **Thoroughly prepare and practice your speech.** Preparing a detailed preparation outline for extemporaneous speaking will give you confidence because you know that you have fully developed and clearly arranged the ideas in your speech. Practicing delivering your speech with your note cards and visual aids will reduce your "performance anxiety" because you have some sense of how your speech performance will go.
3. **Prepare yourself and your speaking environment.** Get a good night's sleep. Eat a nutritious breakfast. Arrive early and check out the room set-up for your speech. Test all the equipment you will be using. Prepare yourself mentally by reviewing your speech outline and note cards. Prepare yourself physically with relaxation and warm-up exercises.

FIGURE 11.24

Positive imagery can help to create a competent, confident speaker.

THREE WAYS TO REDUCE PSA DURING YOUR SPEECH

1. **Expect and accept some symptoms of speech anxiety.** First, anticipate the common symptoms of speech anxiety that you will most likely experience. Second, *give yourself permission* to experience these symptoms. If you give yourself permission to experience these symptoms, then there is nothing to fear when your face flushes, or your heart beats rapidly, or your hands shake. You need to accept the fact that you will usually experience some symptoms of speech anxiety when you speak in public, and you need to learn to manage these symptoms effectively.
2. **Act confident to become confident.** Even if you do not feel confident, you can act confident. As a speaker, you have the responsibility to put your audience at ease and prepare them to listen to your speech, so it is fitting and proper that you present yourself as a competent, confident speaker. However, as you hold your head up proudly, project your voice firmly, and look your audience members squarely in the eye when you speak, these physical actions can actually help you to become confident.
3. **Focus on your message.** If you focus on being evaluated, you may experience "performance anxiety" and you may fear negative criticism that could arise. Do not think of your speech as a time to be evaluated, but as a time to share your message with your audience. Focusing on your message also gives you a reasonable, attainable speech goal. If you get your message across to your audience, then you can consider your speech a success.

FIGURE 11.25

THREE WAYS TO REDUCE PSA AFTER YOUR SPEECH

1. **Give yourself credit for what you did well.** Recognize what you did well in both the preparation and presentation of your speech. Recognizing your strengths as a speaker will boost your self-esteem and give you confidence that you are able to face future speech situations.
2. **Receive verbal and written criticism graciously.** If verbal or written feedback to your speech is offered, do not get into an argument with the evaluators. Do not get defensive. Politely thank the evaluators for their feedback, and dismiss any feedback that you think is way off base. Strive to gain an accurate perception of both the strengths and weaknesses of your speech.
3. **Reward yourself for your efforts and your performance.** Positive reinforcement works. After you have recognized what you accomplished, reward yourself. Have a post-speech celebration with some friends or family members. Describe and rehearse what went well, and you will create good memories that can be associated with your speech.

FIGURE 11.26

You can celebrate your speaking success with your small group.

Types of Small Group Presentations

We will end this chapter by describing five types of small group presentations that involve public speaking. You may have to speak in public as: 1) a small group spokesperson, 2) part of a small group "tag team" presentation, 3) a participant in a panel presentation, 4) a participant in a symposium, or 5) a participant in a forum. We will briefly describe each public speaking situation, and we will give you speaking tips for each situation.

FIVE PUBLIC SPEAKING SITUATIONS INVOLVING SMALL GROUPS
1. Acting as a small group spokesperson
2. A "tag team" small group presentation
3. A small group panel discussion
4. A small group symposium
5. A small group forum

ACTING AS A SMALL GROUP SPOKESPERSON

Once a small group has had a discussion or made a decision, this discussion or decision may need to be reported to people outside the small group. Often, a small group will elect or appoint one group member to act as their small group spokesperson. This spokesperson has the responsibility of representing and speaking for the small group as a whole in public.

Sometimes a spokesperson will share the results of a small group discussion very informally. For example, after your group in your small group communication class has had an in-class discussion, your instructor may ask one group member to share the results of this discussion with the entire class. This group member does not have time to prepare a speech outline, so he or she will have to speak "off the cuff" using "impromptu" delivery.

Sometimes a spokesperson will share the results of a small group decision-making or problem-solving process in a very formal manner. For example, a committee chair may have to present a formal oral report at a large company gathering to share the results of a committee decision or project. This formal speech should be fully outlined and then supplemented with key word note cards and visual aids for effective extemporaneous delivery.

Tips for acting as a small group spokesperson: If you need to act as spokesperson for a small group, keep these tips in mind. First, determine whether an informal or formal speech is needed, and prepare accordingly. You do not want to represent your small group with a few "off the cuff" remarks if others are expecting you to have a fully prepared and practiced speech. Second, make sure you refer to and acknowledge your small group appropriately at the beginning of your public remarks. You want to make it clear that you are speaking as the representative for your small group. Third, use the pronoun "we" often when reporting your group discussion and decisions. Do not, however, present your personal opinion as if it was the opinion of your entire group—do not say "we think" when it is really just your thought or opinion. You can also note if your group discussion involved dissenting opinions, or if a group decision was reached unanimously or by majority vote.

FIGURE 11.27

A "TAG TEAM" SMALL GROUP PRESENTATION

In a "tag team" small group presentation, each member of a small group speaks for a very brief time and then "tags" the next member to continue the group presentation. A tag team presentation gets all the group members involved, and it allows the group to present a united public front. In a tag team presentation, the first group member usually handles the introductory duties; the remaining members each develop one main point, and the final speaker handles the conclusion duties.

Tips for a "tag team" small group presentation: A tag team presentation is only appropriate when each member will speak for approximately one minute. A six-member group would take about six minutes for a tag team presentation. If the small group has a much shorter presentation, then appointing a spokesperson to speak for the group would be more appropriate. If the group has a much longer presentation, then each member needs to give an independent speech with its own introduction, body, and conclusion.

FIGURE 11.28

Every group member speaks briefly in a tag team presentation.

Smooth transitions are important for a tag team presentation. Each speaker needs to smoothly set up and introduce the speaker that is to follow. The next speaker in line should be able to begin his or her point without an introduction. Think of the tag team presentation as one cohesive speech that is presented by several different people. If effective transitions are used, each point should dovetail into the next section of the speech.

If you are a member of a tag team presentation, remember that every member of your group is "on stage" the entire time of the presentation. You are speaking as a cohesive unit, so you should all maintain speaking poise throughout the presentation. Do not "zone out" or whisper to other group members before or after your part of the tag team presentation. Keep the audience attention focused on the member who is speaking.

A SMALL GROUP PANEL DISCUSSION

A panel discussion is the most frequently used format for a public small group discussion. A panel discussion is a structured discussion that takes place in front of an audience. A moderator introduces the panelists to the audience and asks a series of questions that the panelists are expected to answer. The purpose of a panel presentation is usually to inform the audience about a topic or problem or to get the audience to think about a controversial issue.

Tips for organizing and moderating a panel discussion: A panel usually consists of three to seven panelists. Panelists should be seated at a long table facing the audience. Name cards can be placed in front of each panelist to help the audience identify the participants. Panelists should know ahead of time what is to be discussed in order to prepare thoughtful answers. Panelists should be given instructions to offer brief answers about thirty to sixty seconds long. The moderator should begin the panel discussion by welcoming the audience, introducing the topic to be discussed, and introducing the panelists. The moderator can address questions to specific panelists, or the moderator can pose a question to the entire panel. The moderator should guide the discussion and make sure that all panelists participate, and then conclude the panel discussion with some final comments. A panel discussion usually lasts thirty to sixty minutes.

FIGURE 11.29

Tips for panel participants: Dress appropriately for a public appearance. Prepare thoughtful answers to the panel questions, but do not plan your group discussion ahead of time. You can use "key word" notes to help you remember facts and figures, but you should not read your response from a prepared text. You are participating in a "live" public discussion, so your answers should be extemporaneous. As you answer questions, you have several options: 1) you can agree with a previous answer and provide additional evidence or support for that answer, 2) you can disagree with a previous answer, and explain why you disagree, or 3) you can give a different answer that has not yet been voiced.

A SMALL GROUP SYMPOSIUM

A symposium usually consists of a series of speeches on a related topic. Symposium speakers are asked to cover a different area or to present a different viewpoint on the central symposium topic. Unlike panelists in a panel discussion that give short answers to a series of questions, symposium speakers usually present fully-developed extemporaneous speeches, often with visual aids. A symposium may last from thirty minutes to sixty minutes, and symposium speeches may be anywhere between five minutes and ten minutes long.

Tips for organizers and moderators of small group symposia: Make sure that each speaker knows exactly what part of the topic he or she is supposed to cover. You do not want symposium speeches that are covering the same ground. You can begin the symposium by welcoming the audience, briefly introducing each symposium speaker, and announcing the order of the symposium speeches. Make sure that the speakers know their time limits, and intervene if a speaker is addressing a topic that is assigned to another symposium speaker.

Tips for symposium speakers: Take your speaking task seriously—an audience is assembling to hear what you have to say on an important or controversial topic. Research and organize your speech well. If you are speaking extemporaneously, prepare a detailed preparation outline, and then shrink this outline down into an abbreviated "key word" delivery outline. Prepare readable, usable "key word" note cards and professional-looking visual aids. Practice delivering your symposium speech using your note cards and visual aids. If you prepare and practice your symposium speech ahead of time, you should be able to make an excellent contribution to the symposium.*

A SMALL GROUP FORUM DISCUSSION

A forum discussion usually occurs after a panel discussion or a symposium, but it can also occur after an individual speech. A forum discussion lets the audience get involved and share their opinions and feedback. At the end of a panel discussion or a symposium, the moderator announces that audience members will have a chance to express their viewpoints or ask follow-up questions. A specific time is then set aside for the audience members to ask questions or make comments.

Tips for organizing and moderating a forum discussion: To get good audience participation, announce clear rules for the forum comments and questions. You can ask audience members to form a line to take their turn at a podium, or you can ask audience members to submit questions or comments that you will read to the panelists or symposium participants. You can ask audience members to keep their comments or questions brief (no more than thirty seconds), and you can limit them to one comment or question. Set a time limit for the forum, and announce when time is almost up. Accept questions or comments until the time limit has been reached. Allow the final speaker to conclude his or her comments, and then thank the audience members for their participation.

FIGURE 11.30

A forum allows audience members to make comments and ask questions.

Tips for forum participants: If you are a panelist or symposium speaker, be prepared for audience members to challenge you or to disagree with your opinion. Do not get too defensive—allow audience members to disagree with your point of view. If you are asked a direct question, try to answer it the best you can. However, if you do not know the answer to a question, it is okay to admit that you do not have an answer at that moment.

Summary

After reading this chapter, you are equipped with the knowledge you need to speak in public and to make effective small group presentations. You know the basic elements of a speech, the basic parts of a speech, and the basic tasks of a speech introduction, body, and conclusion. You know how to gather and use research. You know how to develop a detailed speech preparation outline. You know how to make and use "key word" note cards and visual aids. You know how to manage your public speaking anxiety. Finally, you know the different types of public presentations you might have to make as a small group member, including acting as a spokesperson, being part in a tag team presentation, and participating in a small group panel discussion, symposium, or forum discussion.

Glossary

Attention getter: One of the basic elements of a speech introduction. Public speakers must begin their speeches by gaining the attention of the audience.

Body: One of the three main parts of a speech. Speakers develop their main ideas in the body of their speech.

Closer: The last element of a speech conclusion. Public speakers must end their speeches by providing closure and letting their audience know that the speech has fully concluded.

Conclusion: One of the three main parts of a speech. The speech conclusion follows the speech body, and in the conclusion a speaker typically restates the thesis, reviews the main points of the speech body, and provides closure.

Content: One of the three basic elements of a speech. In order to give a speech, a speaker must have something to say—this is the speech content.

Delivery: One of the three basic elements of a speech. After developing and arranging the content of a speech, a speaker must deliver a speech orally.

Forum discussion: A type of small group presentation, usually following a panel discussion or a symposium. A forum discussion allows audience members to make comments or ask questions.

Introduction: One of the three main parts of a speech. In the speech introduction, a speaker typically gains attention, states a thesis, and previews the main ideas in the speech body.

Oral source citation: A sentence spoken in a speech that tells an audience where they can find the information or evidence being used in a speech. Oral source citations usually come before the evidence or information is presented to the audience in order to build up the credibility of the source.

Panel discussion: A type of small group presentation. Panel participants are asked a series of questions and give brief answers in front of a live audience.

Plagiarism: Using someone else's words or ideas without giving them credit. Public speakers use oral source citations in their speeches to avoid plagiarism.

Preview: One of the basic tasks of a speech introduction. A speech preview reveals the structure of the speech body by briefly referring to the main ideas to be covered in the speech.

Public speaking anxiety: The most common form of communication apprehension—the fear of presenting a speech in public.

Review: A basic task of a speech conclusion. In a speech conclusion, a speaker typically reviews the main ideas that were covered in the body of the speech.

Restated thesis: A basic element of a speech conclusion. In a speech conclusion, a speaker typically restates his or her thesis in a memorable way.

Spokesperson: A person who speaks for a group or organization. Small groups will sometimes appoint a group member to act as a spokesperson to represent and speak for the small group in public.

Structure: One of the three basic elements of a speech. A speaker must organize the ideas in a speech so that they are understandable to the audience.

Symposium: A type of small group presentation consisting of several independent speeches related to a central topic or theme.

Tag team presentation: A type of small group presentation. Small group members orally present the different sections of one cohesive speech. Each member presents a part of the speech and then introduces the next speaker, until the final speaker concludes the speech.

Textual graphics: The most common type of visual aid. Textual graphics are words.

Thesis: A basic element of a speech introduction. In the speech introduction, the speaker typically states the main point they want to make about the speech topic—this is called the speech thesis.

Visual aids: Images, objects, or printed words that are shown to an audience in order to reinforce the oral message of a public speech.

Wrap-around closer: A particular type of closing device that can be used at the end of a speech. The speaker "wraps around" to the beginning of the speech and refers back to the attention getter in order to give the speech a sense of completeness.

Works Cited or Consulted

Thorson-Hevle, Andrea, Staller, Mark, & Korcok, Michael. (2014). *Contemporary public speaking: How to craft and deliver a powerful speech.* Dubuque, Iowa: Kendall Hunt. (*A public speaking textbook written by Bakersfield College Communication instructors.*)

Chapter 12:

Using Technology Effectively in Small Groups

Chapter Objectives

- Appreciate the prevalence of virtual communication.
- Identify several types of virtual communication.
- Compare the drawbacks and advantages of virtual meetings.
- Learn new ways to organize small groups.
- Learn new ways to conduct a small group meeting.

Technology and Small Groups

Technology has infiltrated the very core of our society. It is no surprise then that our communication in small groups will be established through technological means. Small group communication meetings are already full of their own difficulties and benefits, and adding technology to that situation serves to increase the chances of difficulties, but also may increase the advantages as well. Given that our culture is determined to keep technology as an ever-present fixture in our lives, we need to understand its implications, advantages, disadvantages, and usability.

The focus of this chapter is unlike the others. Here we are simply trying to establish and engrave the idea that technology has a place in small group communication, and it is necessary that you understand how it functions, how to use it, and the differences and similarities among the different types. If you have never used any form of technology to have a meeting with a group before, don't fear. This chapter is not written for the established longtime user of multiple forms of technology during small group meetings. It is beneficial to those individuals, but it is priceless to those of you who have little to no experience with these forms of communication. Herein you will find a discussion of the types of technology you may need to use in the future, the benefits and costs of each type of technology, and some practical tips for how to use it for your next small group need.

FIGURE 12.1

Technology is everywhere. Learning how to properly manage and interact in the technology world is an essential skill we will need.

Virtual Meetings

In order to understand this chapter we should establish some terms concretely. The first concept we need to understand is "virtual groups." A **virtual group** is any small group whose members interact with each other through electronic technologies. It used to be that virtual groups were 100% electronic groups. Today we most often see a hybrid group where a small group meets in person sometimes and electronically other times. You may belong to a virtual group if your family (a small group) uses technology to have family meetings online because one or more members are not available to have meetings in person. If you have such meetings using technology like your computer's webcam, your IPad's FaceTime or your phone's Skype, you may have had what is called a virtual meeting. **Virtual meetings** are gatherings of people from different locations using technology to facilitate the meeting. Virtual meetings have been a great advantage to our society, especially in recent years. Because of virtual meetings, we are able to conduct interviews with the questioner and interviewer in different places or even states or countries. We are able to take statements during court trials from people in facilities they are not allowed to leave from. We are able see loved ones in the military no matter where they are.

FIGURE 12.2

A virtual meeting permits us to connect with people all over the globe.

Some basic advantages of virtual groups are:

1. Finding a meeting place that works for everyone is not an issue as it often is for face-to-face groups.
2. Wasted time is with unproductive moments is reduced in comparison to face-to-face meetings.
3. Provide a clear and accurate record of events. While some groups assign a "secretary" or note taker, it is still not as reliable as having an actual recorded meeting. Many of the technologies we will discuss in this chapter allow you to take audio and visual records of your meetings. Many of the platforms even archive them for you or allow you to email them to others.
4. An ability to have greater control over what people see. Specifically with voice-only or teleconferencing, the noticeability of physical difference diminishes. The disadvantages that may come from people seeing your ethnicity, disability, attire, or even religious indicators decreases, and thus, the chances of being oppressed or judged for those reasons.
5. Engaging in conflict becomes easier. Sometimes it is easier to be honest or critical when you don't have a fear of being punched in the face. More often, we don't really have a fear of being hit as much as we just have more distance between us, which makes us feel safer and more secure.
6. If meetings are text only meetings, which means members communicate only through the written form like email, then some people will have a reduction in anxiety as a result. Many people who experience anxiety say that looking people in the eye is one of the harder things for them; they also note that it's stressful when everyone is looking at them. Text-only virtual meetings alleviate those anxieties.

Potential disadvantages of virtual communication:

1. Disruptions—virtual communication is vulnerable to a multitude of disruptions, such as, easily lost connections, poor quality, loss of audio or visual at the last moment, poor internet connections, bad cords, wrong cords, incompatible programs and computers, etc.
2. Limited communication signals—virtual communication diminishes the amount of communication signals you receive and thus use to interpret meaning. For instance, it is harder to tell what emotion someone is feeling when you can only see their face on a screen (missing body language), their body and face but not make eye contact (missing displays of respect and intent), or nothing but the written word, and thus, you can't read any of their facial, tonal, or body language cues to help understand the message correctly.
3. Inexperienced and frustrated group members—virtual communication can cause problems with members who lack experience. Some people have a very limited experience with technology, and that makes them feel insecure and frustrated at times. When members feel insecure or frustrated they are often less efficient group members.
4. Uncontrollable and unforeseen technical failures—virtual communication is known to cause delays or even stop working without notice. Technology can fail you, and the more you rely on it, the more critical it is when it fails.

There are two different forms of technologies we need to discuss in order to move forward; asynchronous and synchronous communication. Asynchronous media communication is any communication that allows members to communicate anytime and anywhere, such as texting, Facebooking, or emailing. Synchronous media communication allows for simultaneous communication between group members. You use synchronous communication when you video chat with your loved ones or have a phone call with three or more people. To give you an idea of how much Americans use their asynchronous and synchronous communication consider the following statistics:

1. According to a study reported on CNN (2013), "Cell owners between the ages of 18 and 24 exchange an average of 109.5 messages on a normal day—more than 3,200 texts per month."
2. According to the same study, "55% of people who send or receive more than 51 texts per day report preferring them to phone calls." [1]
3. "With over 500 million users, Facebook is now used by 1 in every 13 people on earth, with over 250 million of them (over 50%) who log in every day. The average user still has about 130 friends"[2]
4. About 20% of Americans use video chatting, conferencing, or calling.[3]

In short, virtual meetings have changed the way we function in our social lives and work lives, as well as altered our very societal functioning. Virtual meetings permit the exchange of information in many forms. In this section, we will focus on identifying the various types of virtual meetings, discuss their advantages and drawbacks, and provide some helpful, practical tips to help you during your next virtual group meeting.

---

[1] http://www.cnn.com/2011/09/22/tech/mobile/americans-prefer-text-messages/
[2] http://www.digitalbuzzblog.com/facebook-statistics-stats-facts-2011/
[3] According to the PEW Research Center 2013 http://pewinternet.org/Reports/2010/Video-chat.aspx

VIDEO CONFERENCING

One of the more common forms of virtual meetings is video conferencing, which is a conference that permits members to see each other via a computer (or computer-like device) in real time while in different locations. Connections can be made with any person anywhere in the world as long as they have a computer, computer web camera, and a high-speed internet connection. If you haven't already, you will likely be interviewed for a job using video conferencing. Video conferencing is available in various price ranges; some are expensive and others free. And there is a vast amount of midline price options to choose from. Make sure you understand and are experienced with the software you will use for your meetings. There is nothing worse then thinking "I got this" because you know how to use one brand of video conferencing and then find that this new one is "NOTHING" like the one you are accustomed to using. There is a learning point in all of the technology areas, even when you are excellent at communicating in the virtual world; there will always be something you have not used before, and that will inevitably throw you a curveball in a moment you really don't have the time or patience for.

Advantages of Video Conferencing:

1. Decreases travel costs
   - Decreases operational costs by 50%
   - Decreases or eliminates long distance calling costs
   - Decreases flight, bus, cab, and hotel costs
2. Uses contemporary technology.
3. Brings different groups together that have the same goals.
4. Works on bad weather days when roads are closed.
5. Allows people who are sick or have a physical disability to continue participation when they otherwise wouldn't have been able to.
6. Supports green initiatives.
7. Fixed-pricing on software makes it highly cost effective.

Disadvantages of Video Conferencing:

1. Non-verbal communication-non-verbal signals and displays are harder to see through the medium and thus more mistakes with interpreting communication may occur.
2. Body language is harder to see and thus feedback can be made more difficult.
3. Technical problems-can slow the meeting, disrupt the momentum, frustrate, or even cancel a meeting.
4. Using tangible visual aids, handouts, and portfolios becomes more difficult and awkward to use.

There are several video conferencing platforms available. We will cover the most popular, highest rated for usability, and most widely used in business and small group meetings.

Skype: The great thing about Skype is that if you want to have a meeting where all people involved are in two different locations, you can use the platform for free. It is also very simple to use. You can download the program quickly and easily. Even the most inexperienced users can use Skype without much issue. The drawbacks to Skype are: 1) poor image quality, when compared with more professional and expensive platforms; 2) long lag time between sending and receiving of information; 3) the video is not always reliable.

How to Make the Most of Your Virtual Meeting:

FIGURE 12.3

1. In advance of the meeting test the devices, software, cables, cords, lighting, and temperature of the space being used.
2. Have a backup plan if this meeting fails for any reason related to technology. Have PDF's and Word documents emailed to members in advance of the meeting.
3. Create rules for structure and expectations in advance.
4. Craft an agenda in advance and distribute it via email before the meeting starts.
5. Encourage participation from all members just as you would a face-to-face meeting.
6. Elect someone to control or monitor the communications—this person will help let everyone know when it is time to talk and when to move on, etc.
7. To keep your meeting on schedule use a timer.
8. Keep the meetings focused and on task.
9. Keep the meeting short and let people know at the start about how long the meeting will be.
10. Cover the most important items first.

VIDEO CALLS

Video calls are meeting technologies that permit the reception and transmission of video signals between users in different locations using their cell phone devices. Video call or video chat services as they are sometimes called, include services like Google Talk, iChat, and Skype. In a recent study from the Pew Research Centers Internet and American Life Project, it was determined that 23% of internet users and 7% of cell phone users have participated in video calls (Pew Internet.org, 2013).

TELECONFERENCE

The difference between a videoconference and teleconference is that teleconference uses phone lines to connect members and only allows participants to hear each other; it does not allow them to see each other. This is most often accomplished using cellular phones and devices that allow multiple people to connect simultaneously regardless of their location. Many businesses use teleconferencing to connect anywhere from 3–100 people or more. Landline phones and cell phones can be used for these calls or you can use a conferencing technology. A conferencing technology is a device that allows the person or persons calling in to be heard through a speaker. This device also permits muting, call waiting, and all the other capabilities of telephones.

The benefits of teleconferencing are:

1. You can connect a large amount of people but not have to see them all.
2. You can wear unprofessional attire and still come off as professional.
3. You don't have to worry that people won't know how to use the phone like you do with Internet and computer devices.

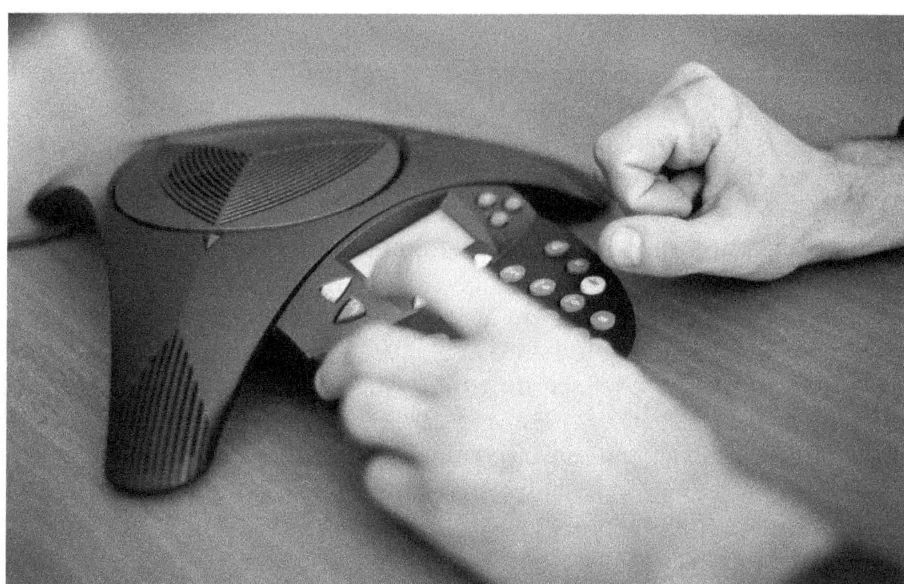

FIGURE 12.4

New and fun communication devices are available. These new tools make conference calls painless and more efficient than ever before.

How to Make the Most of Your Teleconference

1. Have all callers identify themselves and say hello at the start of the call. Introductions allow hearers to associate a name with a voice that may help them later on.
2. In advance of the meeting, establish an agreed upon way to determine whose turn it is to speak and who needs to stop speaking—go over the rules after introductions.
3. Decrease potential for background noise around you. When there are multiple callers and they all have background noises the call can quickly become hard to hear and frustrating.
4. Discuss the time it will start and what is considered too late to join the meeting.
5. Discuss how tardy attendees will join the call—will they introduce themselves, be caught up-to-speed, or be asked to be quiet and catch up silently?
6. Keep calls focused. Do not let chitchat and stories take you off task.
7. Keep the call organized.
8. Keep the call short.

FIGURE 12.5

TEXT-ONLY VIRTUAL COMMUNICATION

You probably have the most experience with text-only virtual communication. Text-only virtual communication means the communication does not have video or audio communication it only has the written word. Emailing and texting are the most used forms of text-only communication. Emailing has become such a part of our lives that we can hardly imagine how we functioned without it. Many of you have probably never lived in a world where emailing didn't exist.

Emailing can be a wonderful tool to use for small group communication. Emails are used to create messages and send them to other group members. Because it is an asynchronous form of communication, members can read the message at their own will. If you write the email at 2 A.M. (as I often do) your members don't have to be up at 2 A.M. to receive the message. Emails will sit in the inbox (like a mailbox) until the person or persons you sent it to open it. This is really nice for small group communication, because it is so very hard to match schedules. Today everyone works, has a family, has group or community involvements, has kids, or dogs. The point is, everyone is busy and trying to establish times to meet which makes exchanging information difficult. Emailing allows you to send your contribution in when you have the time and it allows others to look at it when they have the time. Emailing is also wonderful for those who need more time to create their responses than others tend to. For some, face-to-face or other synchronous forms of communication can be stressful. If you need to have time to reflect and craft your responses, then emailing is going to work wonderfully for you. If you are not one who needs a lot of time emailing, it can still benefit you because you can respond as quickly as you like or take the time you didn't realize you needed.

Another perk of emailing or texting is that you can avoid long conversations if you need to. Generally, texts and emails are more to the point and quicker than phone conversations. On the phone, you might feel obligated to have a conversation that you didn't feel any obligation to have through texting or emailing. For instance, if you have to call a member for a quick answer to a simple question, you might feel like you should ask how they are doing which may lead to another conversation of some length. Texting and emailing alleviate some of the social rules we have when communicating verbally.

There are some drawbacks to emailing though. Because emailing and texting are text-only forms of communication, they leave out much of the communication we commonly use to understand what people are saying and with what emotion they are feeling. Many fights have been started over emails that were poorly communicated or poorly interpreted. Another downside to email is actually also one of its advantages. Because you can send the email at any time and people can respond at any time, it can be a slower way to get things accomplished in the long run. Time-sensitive information may not always get read in time with email. To its credit, recent emailing companies have now created applications you can download to your smartphones that will let you know the moment you get an email. But, for those of us who receive over a hundred emails a day, these alerts can be more annoying than helpful. The big downside to email is that most people who know how to use email don't know the rules of emailing. After reading this chapter, you will now be one of the uneducated emailers out there. These are some of the most important emailing tips:

1. Use easy to read fonts like Arial or New Times Roman.
2. Do not forget an email never goes away and can always be given to others without your consent or knowledge.
3. Establish a relevant subject line—the receiver should know right away what your email is about from your subject line.
4. Make the subject line searchable—this means if your receiver wants to find that specific email, words in the subject will help them discern the right email from the wrong email.
5. Keep the email short—be concise and clear, leave out all unnecessary information.
6. Provide context at the beginning of your email—refresh the receiver's mind as to who you are.
7. Use bullets and numbering when possible—avoid paragraphs, as most things can be numbered or distinguished with bullet points.
8. Bold important concepts and words—bolding grabs the reader's attention, so use it sparingly or the effect will be lost.
9. Do not use email as a means of avoiding person-to-person conflict. When emotions are involved face-to-face communication is usually best.
10. In an immediate response is needed, be sure to type the deadline in the subject line and in the body of the email.
11. Do not beat around the bush—be to the point in asking your questions.
12. If the email is long, place a clear action request in the first paragraph—do not wait until the end to tell the recipient what you are asking for.

13. CC people that you want your recipient to know also saw this email, but who are not required to respond to it.
14. BCC people that you want to see the email but do not want your "To" recipient to know saw it.
15. Create a "signature" that contains not only your name, but also details about your position, mailing address or phone number if it's necessary for these people to know that information.
16. Do not go off topic—tangents are awful in emails.
17. Only use "Reply All" when everyone really needs to see your response.
18. Do not send an email if you are angry, write it and come back to it when you have calmed down.
19. Do not expect a fast response. Unless you specifically indicate it is urgent and provide a deadline, it is rude to send a follow-up email before at least two days have passed.
20. Keep the language, grammar, and punctuation formal unless you have an established close relationship where informal rules apply all around.
21. Never use capital letters unless you want the person to think you are yelling at them.
22. Do not send people chain letters, links to discounted places, or even warnings about viruses—it's just more clutter for their box and you probably just compromised their email security.
23. Avoid sarcasm and recognize that people will always interpret messages based on their assumptions, past experiences, and presumptions about you, and this is not always a good thing.
24. Avoid the emotion icon indicators—these little faces, while cute, can be misread as sarcasm, disrespect, or unprofessional.
25. Use "Ms." instead of "Mrs." or "Miss" as those distinctions only serve to comment on whether a woman is married or not and is fundamentally unimportant. We don't have different terms for married men. Using "Ms." is inclusive language and will save you time investigating unimportant information.

Tips to Improve Your Text-Only Communication

1. Keep your ideas clear and concise.
2. Use concrete not vague words.
3. When you have multiple things to discuss, consider numbering them.
4. When you are resending a communication that had multiple things discussed number them if they did not.
5. If you are answering questions, copy the questions and place your response under it in a different font and color.
6. Do not use emotional words that may be misunderstood.
7. Refrain from sarcasm.

Online Collaboration Tools

There are many online collaboration tools available to you. Each tool has its perks and limitations. **Online collaboration tools** are various platforms, applications, or programs that aid your online small group communication. Some tools allow you to send out electronic invites to your meeting, permit you to keep track of those who attend, create calendars that work with your established calendars, use whiteboards, multiple screens, and even take control of other people's computers. There is an endless list of things these amazing tools are capable of. The trick is knowing which one works for your needs, your group, and your audience. The list in the coming section will provide you with information on some collaboration tools you may find useful now or in the future.

There are several free online tools that can help make your group work easier and more convenient. Consider using the tool ***Dropbox***. This tool allows you to share files with your group members in a way that doesn't require file uploading. You simply make a file for your group, send an invite to your members to give them access, and then add items to the file as you like which will immediately become visible to your group. Dropbox is great because you can use it on your computers and smart devices such as, Mac, Windows, Android, iOS, and even Blackberry.

Slack is unique in that you can use many different software tools inside it. Tools that manage office type items, development items, and more. You can have conversations with your group and it will be archived and organized in ways that make it easy to search through for key words latter on. You can also use multiple channels for the communication. This tool is really great, but is a bit more complicated and involved than some of the others on the list. This tool is best used in large groups and companies.

Skype is a tool many people know about and use, but often forget they can use in the small group context. Skype isn't perfect, but it really is a great tool for video chatting with your group members. You can use it from many devices and schedule calls in advance. You have an account that is password protected and you control who can see you and when.

© Stuart Jenner, 2013. Used under license from Shutterstock, Inc.

FIGURE 12.6

Perhaps the most widely used and most accessible of the free online collaboration tools, is ***Google Groups***. *Google Groups* requires you to have a ***Gmail*** account, which is free. Google Groups allows you to send email to your members, share all kinds of content with them (docs, slides, contacts, videos, etc), invite members to meetings, and even share calendars.

Once you are a *Google* member (have a *Gmail* account) you can use all of the *Google* products and this comes in handy when doing a group project. For instance, you can see all the versions of a document your team has been working on, you can convert files into various other formats, you can even translate language. A nice feature of *Google Groups* is your discussions will be archived so you can search through them latter, you can work on a document or slide at the exact same time your other members are working on it, and you can see exactly what they are doing in real time. This is a truly innovative tool and it works well.

Online Collaboration Tools	
Adobe Acrobat Connect Pro	• Downloadable program • Allow others to see your screen in real-time • Control the degree of interference allowed • Track changes and progress • Edit recordings • Pay per use, monthly, or annually
Go To Meeting	• Shareable screen • Ability to send email messages to confirm ability for members to attend meeting • Ability to have multiple presenters • Messaging in chat form available • Ability to record meeting • Ability to create attendance reports • Costs about $50 a month
Arkadin	• Sharable screen • Share files with group • No download required • Create a workspace that all members can contribute and edit • Can integrate logo and branding communication • Free to try—after that, you must contact the company for costs
Dimdim	• Share screen with others • Share control of screen with others • Ability to have multiple presenters • Able to send private messages • Costs about $10 a month
Live Meeting (Microsoft Office)	• Share entire screen or part of screen with others • File sharing and storage • Messaging in chat form available • Text slides, web-based slides, whiteboards, and annotation available • Costs about $4 a month per user
Beam Your Screen	• Share your screen with others • You can control participants' ability to control screen • Record meetings • Create reports on meetings • Create usage reports • Share files • Free trial then $30 a month or more depending on subscription length and number of users
Spreed	• Sharable screen • Remote controllable desktop • Whiteboard available and interactive • Messaging in chat form • Ability to record and save meetings • Free for three members, about $20 per session for more members
Yugma	• Sharable desktop • Free teleconferencing built in • Ability to record meetings • Ability to share control with other participants • Ability to message in chat form • Free for 0–20 members, about $15 for more members
ScheduleOnce	• Create meeting invites and calendars • Teleconferencing and video conferencing available • Works with your current calendar • Manage schedules for others • Coordinate room use and members to attend • Free 14 day trial and $0–49 depending on type of subscription chosen
Google Groups	• Invite members • Share content • Work at the same time with members in multiple locations on the same one document • Share calendars • Record communications (meetings) • Free with a free Gmail account

FIGURE 12.7

Technology Based Facilitation and Presentation Tools

Perhaps the most important idea speakers need to learn about presentation aids is that the aid should first and foremost serve to help the audience better understand and be emotionally moved by your ideas. An effective presentation aid will appeal to the pathos through a vivid use of images that reinforce, exemplify, and/or organize the speakers ideas. The secondary role of the presentation aid is to help the speaker stay organized and on topic. Using note cards or an outline when also using a technology aid tends to reflect poorly on the speaker. The technology aid will inherently help the speaker stay focused and trigger the memory. Note cards are distracting for the audience and often become a burden for the speaker. Use technology to enhance your speech; do not use it if you are not prepared enough to give the speech without it. The phrase "technology-based facilitation and presentation tools" refers to any technology presentation aid you might use to give your presentation. PowerPoint, Prezi, and KeyNote are the most commonly used.

When speakers use presentation aid technologies, it can be easy to forget you're talking to your audience as opposed to teaching them. Remember to carry on your presentation in a professional yet conversational approach and tone. If you have more than four people in the audience, consider using a projector instead of a regular computer screen, laptop, or small TV and be sure to test it well before your presentation.

You may use technology based presentation aids in your group meetings and/or when performing in front of an audience. The rules are similar for both of these purposes, but there are some differences you should be aware of.

First, your group meetings are more informal than your group presentations. Given this, you can use large laptop screens to show members your ideas. You can also send each member a copy of your document or slides so that while you are explaining it, they can follow along.

This is a nice option because it gives you and your team the ability to have meetings in-person and in a variety of spaces. You are not locked down to a conference center, a smart room, or a formal presentation area, which can help the climate of the group meeting, and allow for more creativity, self-disclosures, and openness in general.

In contrast, when you give a group presentation to an audience you will want to communicate a degree of professionalism and energy that is usually better established by using a projector, large TV screen, a SmartBoard, or other such technology. While it is possible that your audience could all have laptops and smart devices and thus view your docs and slides on their own devices; in a professional presentation, it is important you have control over what is being looked at and when. Additionally, if you are presenting using one main technology screen and everyone is looking at that screen, then that is the only technology you need to worry about breaking down. If you have a meeting where everyone

FIGURE 12.8

is using their own devices, you have a greater chance of someone's device failing, disconnecting, or being incompatible with the file you sent. You do not want to spend time during your presentation troubleshooting every issue that may arise when people use their own devices. Chances of interruptions in your presentation need to be minimized, so if you can provide a presentation with only one technology and you control that one technology, do it.

Second, your group meetings may be less formal in terms of attire than your group presentations. This may not always be the case; you need to make this assessment of course. But, generally, you can assume a presentation of any kind should be done in professional, credible attire. If your meetings are held only over the phone and no one can actually see you, this is a moot issue. If, however, you are presenting in-person or using video conferencing it is very important you dress and groom for the seriousness of your topic, occasion, and expectations.

Other than these two main differences, there are a lot of similarities between the group meetings and the group presentations in terms of using technology. You first want to consider your audience. Considering your audience is a communication concept that asserts the importance of presenters assessing their audience in an effort to better reach them. I'm sure you can see the importance of considering the audience you will have when you make your presentation, but your own members should be considered as well, because you will need to reach, teach, motivate, or persuade them a time or two as well.

One of the first things you want to think about is the age of your audience. The age of the audience is very important in terms of what technology choices you make because different generations have different experiences, expectations, and abilities regarding technology. If your audience is between the ages of 18–30, the quality of your visual presentation aids needs to increase significantly. This age range not only uses technology more than any other group, but they are good at it. This fact makes it imperative that your technology-based presentation be competent and well rehearsed.

FIGURE 12.9

Use your technology to help you conduct research to gather information to analyze your potential audiences.

Similarly, if you have an audience that is less likely to have experience with technology, consider the way you use technology and make it simple and helpful. You do not want to use technology that is complicated or overwhelming for your audience. When your technology becomes a distraction it is not worth it. For instance, if you were giving a presentation and asked your audience to give you feedback for a poll you are conducting, you might give them a paper with a QR code on it. You tell your audience to scan it with their smart device and answer the few questions. Some audiences would love this and know exactly what you are asking of them. Other audiences will not only be confused about what a smartphone is, but how a little square will help them answer polling questions.

Perhaps you have a great amount of experience with technology and can use it with ease and confidence, why then should you care about audience analysis? You should care because if you have members in your group that are inexperienced or lack confidence with technology, then you also need to adjust. Be willing to help your group understand and learn how to use different technologies. Don't limit what you use just because one person in the group hasn't used it before—teach them! Polls show that the older a person is the less they know how to use different types of technology based presentation tools, but that doesn't mean you should assume the 50-year-old in your group is totally incompetent when it comes to technology. Always ask your group for their experiences and be willing to help when help is needed. You should also be willing to be honest if you are the member with the least amount of experience with technology.

Establishing early on the degree to which members of your group and your audience are comfortable with technology is important. Use group member feedback as a guide to increase the competence of some members and decrease expectations of others. In the end, the most important thing is to establish what technology will work best for your project and ensure your group is trained, prepared, and confident while using it.

USING SOFTWARE-BASED PRESENTATION TOOLS

Software-based technologies are simply programs that we use to accompany and enhance our presentations. ***PowerPoint*** is the most well known form of software-based technologies used for presenting during formal and informal speeches. *PowerPoint* refers to a software program created by Microsoft that allows a user to create multiple slides that are projected onto a screen. The slides can have images, text, embedded links to the Internet, video, audio, and more. *PowerPoint* can be an ideal tool in keeping your audience on track and interested. However, as wonderful as it can be, it is still the most frequently misused and poorly utilized presentation aid. You will want to use this type of presentation aid when you feel it will more effectively explain your idea, demonstrate your points, enhance your points, create an emotional impact, and when you know the rules and guidelines for how to craft and use it appropriately. This software is available online or to be purchased on CD's. It comes by itself or with the entire Office Suite (Excel, Word, etc). This can be expensive, but more and more educational sites are providing the tool at a huge discount or totally free. At Bakersfield College in California students can download it for free onto up to five devices!

Another dynamic software-based presentation tool is ***Prezi***. *Prezi* is available for purchase online from 5-20 dollars a month. You need to always have internet access in order to create and play the *Prezi*. Technically you can purchase it as a downloadable software, but it pricey than *PowerPoint*. *Prezi* has some really beautiful template options that can be more unique and visually appealing than *PowerPoint*. However, unlike *PowerPoint* it is much harder to control the size of text. In fact, you have no control over the font size and look on the templates provided. This can be problematic because it is essential that public speakers have visually appealing slides that are clear and easy for the audience to see. If we can't alter the size of the font re run the risk of ou audience not getting the information Although the visual elements are really nice the small font sizes can prove to be distracting and problematic. What is really great though about *Prezi* is it has a zoom feature. This works much like your camera, as you click the slide is zoomed in on. This can be a nice feature or it can get irritating with too much in and out going on.

Keynote is the other common presentation tool. *Keynote* is quite similar to *PowerPoint* and is only available on Apple products. *Keynote* is considered a higher end version of *PowerPoint* in many ways, as it offers templates that are polished and more professional looking. *Keynote* is known for its seamless transitioning, easy incorporation of video, crisp and vivid options, and ease of use on *IPads*, *IPhones*, and Apple computers. *Keynote* can also export to other tools, like ***YouTube*** and ***QuickTime*** easily. Unfortunately, *Keynote* does not have a perfect record for being 100% compatible with non-Apple products. Some features won't communicate from one device to another. In the next section I will walk you through various steps and tips you should consider when using a software-based technology.

FIGURE 12.10

VISUAL GUIDELINES FOR SOFTWARE-BASED PRESENTATION AIDS

When creating a presentation using PowerPoint, Prezi, or otherwise, you should approach it with visual style in mind. The first design principle is repetition. Speakers need to consistently remind their audience of key ideas. Slides should be used for previewing the main points of your speech, transitioning into each main point, and reviewing main points, but it can also be used to create an impact, make a connection, provide further examination, exemplification, and create a vivid display of information.

Repetition

Repetition is also important in technology presentations like PowerPoint and Prezi. Repetition refers to the restatement of a concept multiple times at different points in time. You should have a preview slide and a review slide in most informative and persuasive speeches. If you are taking a class, clarify the requirements with your professor, but the general rule is to have a preview and review slide at minimum. These slides give the audience a map of where you are going and what they have covered and results in a clearer understanding. The other slides should be impactful and consider the purpose of your speech, the specific audience, and the given occasion.

Consistency

You should strive for consistency in your slide themes, background, and overall look. This does not mean that every slide must be exactly the same color and have the exact same types of images. What I mean when I say, "keep it consistent," is that your presentation should seem cohesive. You should have a color scheme that you keep throughout the presentation. You should have the same font style and size used for main headings on each slide and the sub-headers should be the same font style and size as well. You might have a header that is Calibri Black font size 72 and a sub-header that is Calibri light blue size 50, while your regular text for quotations might be a 42 Calibri in dark blue. In this presentation you will want the background color to always be the same unless you want to get the audiences attention that you are moving onto a new idea, in which case you may have a main point slide that has a different color background, but be sure to use that same color background on all your main point slides throughout the presentation or it will appear messy and as if a child put it together. Remember, just because a kid can do a software-based technology aid doesn't mean they can do it well. The difference is you know the rules and follow them.

Proximity and Alignment

Having good "proximity and alignment" is just a fancy way of saying you need to make sure your items are centered on your page or placed in alignment with other items on your slide so that your slide looks planned and professional. Slides that are misaligned look sloppy and thrown together last minute. A well-aligned slide will look crisp and reflect well on the speaker. You can indicate what is most important and what is a sub point, for instance, simply by placing things in a different way. When using PowerPoint or a similar software, use gridlines to help you keep things aligned. Remember, you do not have to center everything, but you do need to make sure things are aligned and look nice. Studies show that the human eye likes one image on a slide and words on the right or left of it. These words should be aligned to look as clean and simple as possible.

FIGURE 12.11

Proximity refers to how close items on the slide are to one another and what that communicates. Things that are close together tell the audience they are related in some way. When we put things farther apart, we are generating an idea of dissimilarity. Take for instance a title slide. On a title slide you will have the tile of your presentation, who authored it, and perhaps an image that represents the idea. If you put all this information together without a space, it becomes hard to discern the title, who is the author, and what is important. The title of the presentation should be the largest, and if there is a semicolon used and the title continues, simply make that part smaller and put it in underneath the title. Your name as the author should be significantly smaller, you are not the important concept the audience needs to remember; your message is.

Your name should not only be smaller, but also much farther away from the title. The spacing indicates to the audience what is most important—the title of the presentation and thus the topic. The image should be rather small on a title slide and should not steal the show, but still be present and visible.

High Quality Images

Images must be relevant to your subject and have a clear purpose in adding something to the presentation. The images should be easily seen and understood. This means the audience member in the back should easily see the image and understand its importance or function. If your audience has to strain to see or take time to think about what a given image means to the speech, then you have failed to use your aid well and hindered your speech in the process.

FIGURE 12.12

Edit Nonessentials

This means you need to examine your presentation and assess what elements are not essential and do not have a clear purpose that helps your intent. Any visual clutter needs to go. Visual clutter is any information in the form of words or images that overwhelm a slide or have little purpose. The slides should be clean and easy to understand, not messy and full. Animation effects are usually ineffective and tend to be more distracting than helpful. If you animate a slide show with a noise or an image that moves, be certain it is necessary and helps you explain your point or increase your appeal to the emotions. Otherwise, transitions on slides with loud noises that occur over and over get annoying and seem juvenile.

PowerPoint slides should not have full sentences. Full sentences are reserved for the speaker. There is one small exception, and exceptions should rarely be used. A direct quote can be a full sentence. However, if you use a quote, it must be more powerfully captured on a PowerPoint slide than if it were verbally spoken—it must be more impactful, meaningful, and effectively delivered in that way. If the quote is only present to act as a fancy note card for the speaker, it is not acceptable. Statistics and quotes can become ineffective and useless if read straight off a boring PowerPoint slide. It's important to find visually appealing ways to display statistics and quotes. Instead of putting quotation marks around numbers, find a visual way to demonstrate the numbers by icons or graphs. Quotations should have their own slide and not have to compete with other content unless the image on the page with it is reinforcing or exemplifying the quote in a way that significantly increases the impact of the quote. Just remember, a great speaker can deliver a powerful quote far better than symbols on a slide.

Creativity

Your presentation needs to have cohesiveness, but that doesn't mean you can't put a little pizazz in there. A speaker is an artist and words and images are your tools with which you create a captivating work of art. That art can be informative, persuasive, or any number of other intents, but in its sum any speech is a form of art. It's up to the speaker to paint the canvas the way they want the audience to see it. So, amidst all these rules I just gave you, remember to also consider the artistic and creative approach to making a presentation. Creativity and imagination are incredibly powerful tools. Try to think outside the box and discover alternative ways to explain, examine, or persuade while using your presentation aid.

What do the most memorable speeches of all time have in common? They all had passion; the speakers all meant what they said to the core of who they were. Their words had power because it was authentic or emotion evoking. Allow your passion and creativity to shine through during your presentation through the images and technologies you use. Don't shy away from creative and stimulating images and/or approaches.

The Five to Eight Rule

There should only be about five to eight words per slide. The rule in the past was called "the rule of six" which argued there should never be more than six lines on a given slide. There should never be more than six words on a given line. There should never be more than six words in the header. We have found that when presenters are given the option to use more words, they will, and often to the detriment of the audience and themselves. Given this, the standard is now a limit of five to words per slide and no more than 5–8 lines of words. I can thank my friend and fellow professor Helen Acosta at Bakersfield College for making me aware of the rule change in 2012. Please note your citation does not count in the five to eight word count but your header does!

Keeping your slide to five to eight words on a given slide makes the slide impactful and also forces you to pick only the best and most relevant ideas. This also keeps the speaker from continually glancing or reading from the slides and using the slides as a fancy note card, which I like to call a baby blanket. You are fundamentally Linus from *Charlie Brown* when you read word-for-word from your PowerPoint slides. As Lucy might say, "Grow up, put down the baby blanket, and start presenting like a big kid!"

Checklist for Your Group Software Presentations

1. The presentation is visually interesting.
2. The presentation elaborates, extends, or exemplifies points as opposed to distracting from them.
3. The presentation never has more than eight words on a slide unless it is a quote.
4. All quotes are cited appropriately. For example: "Most students and professors violate the basic guidelines" (Thorson, 2016). The citation should generally be centered below the quote, a smaller font size than the quote, and be in a less contrasting font color, this way the audience easily and quickly knows what the important information is.
5. All images are cited appropriately. For example, directly centered under the image should be the website the image was taken from and the year it was retrieved. If the image is a personal photo, the photographers last name and the year the photo was taken should be cited. The citation on images should not have high contrast and can be very small, but still should be seen. A size 18 font is common.
6. Every member has a copy of the slides and speech that should be presented. This will save the day if someone can't make it to the presentation and they had an important part of the presentation.
7. Ensure your presentation works on the computer you will be using the day of your speech.
8. Have at least two slide advancing wireless remotes, otherwise known as clickers, in case they are not compatible with the computers available.
9. Have cords to connect your own laptop in case something goes wrong with the room computer.
10. Have a timing device and a way to alert members in a non-distracting way that they are going over time. See the list of timer apps below.
11. Double check that all images are visible. Sometimes images will translate as question marks or not show up at all. Store a copy of all images on a flash drive so that you can reload them if you need to.
12. Bring handouts and electronic copies of your handouts just in case.
13. Make sure all members know who is speaking, and when and what they should be doing when they are not speaking; should they be seated, stand to the side, click the slides, pass out papers, etc.
14. Practice your speech with the technology several times. This means using a clicker or clicking manually. If this is not seamless, it hurts your credibility.
15. Have multiple storage devices that have the presentation saved on them and email members the presentation in advance as well.

Timer Apps

Metronome
Presentation Timer Pro
Countdown Timer
Prompster
SpeakerClock

POWERPOINT RULES

Don't Do This:	Why and How
Don't use the presentation as a note card	• You should know your information so well that you wouldn't need a slide to help you along the way. • The audience will be irritated with your lack of preparation and lose interest in the speech. • If all of the important information is in the slides, why are you there? • Practice and know your speech instead of relying on your aids. • Do use the "notes" section on PowerPoint slide. This section is where you can type out what you intend to say during that part of your speech. If for some reason you go blank or need help that information will be there for you. Make sure to select the option that allows you to see the slide and the notes, but only allows the audience to see the slide.
Don't use full sentences	• There is only one exception to the rule of "never use full sentences in a PowerPoint;" you may use a full sentence when that sentence is a direct quote. • If you use a direct quote, the quote needs to be relevant, memorable, and incredibly necessary.
Don't use bullet points	• Most of the time bullets are not necessary. • If you are demonstrating a list of things, then it is okay, otherwise avoid placing bullets on everything. And remember, if you don't have a number two subpoint, you can't provide a bullet for number one subpoint. • Ask yourself if there is a more visually stimulating way to get points across without typing them in bullets. • Consider one word for each idea and a picture for example.
Don't allow clutter	• Noise can come from unnecessary graphics or images that compete with what you are really trying to communicate. • Less is more. Long quotes are overwhelming. If you need a quote, type only the most necessary and impactful part of the quote on the slide. • Citation information should be in a smaller font as to not take attention away from the impactful image or quote.
Don't use multiple images per slide	• You should have one image on a slide. The only exception is if you must show a comparison between two things. • More than this and your audience will be over stimulated.
Don't use backgrounds, themes, or templates that don't consider your needs and the needs of the audience	• Your background should not compete with your information. • Your general scheme should be clear and consistent and provide something that enhances the presentation, not take away from it. • Don't use background with images unless the image is very translucent and won't be visible when you have an image added to a slide
Don't use distracting fonts	• Use fonts that can be easily read from far away. • Resist the temptation to have the beautiful script and calligraphy, they just can't be seen from far away.
Don't use small fonts	• The standard rule is to never use less than 28pt font—this is when using a large projection screen. • If you are using a screen that is 30–60 inches (like a TV screen) you should never use less than 36 point font • Citations can be smaller than the standard recommended font size but should still be visible. 20 point font is usually a nice size for citations under an image or after a quotation.
Don't use hard to see text	• Always shoot for high contrast between the color of your font and the background color. • Do not use neon colors they are stressful on the eye • Avoid fonts that have tags and cursive letters • Avoid using the shadow tool

Don't use fuzzy, small, odd, or watermarked images	• You may need to stretch an image to make it big enough on the slide; doing so can make the image odd and unclear. • Make sure you double check all images and be sure they can be easily seen from far away. • Never use small, disproportional, or fuzzy images. • Never use watermarked images. They scream to the audience: "Thief!"
Cite your sources and images	• Quotes and statistics must be cited. • Use the appropriate style of citing (APA, MLA, or otherwise). The communication discipline standardly uses APA, which means your in-text citations should include the authors last name and the year at minimum. "It would look like this" (Hines, 2016). • Images should be cited with the web address and the year you retrieved the image • The citation for an image should be displayed directly under the image and in a substantially smaller font than the font you are normally using. • Quotes and other direct information should be cited with the authors last name, year it was published, and the page number the information is found on. Although your oral citation doesn't require the page number, rules dictate that when we have a written direct quote (even if on a slide), the page number should also be cited. You can check with your professor or company to see if they will bend this rule. • If your quote is from an online source that doesn't have a page number you will need to write the paragraph number the information is located in. An example of an APA quoted text from a source with page numbers: "The cat was black" (Thorson, 2013, p. 128). • An example of APA quoted text from online source without pages: "The cat was black" (Thorson, 2013, para. 12).
Don't use multiple ideas per slide	• Each slide should have one clear idea being presented. • More than one and the audience can become overwhelmed and lost and your slide will appear messy. • Break up the ideas onto separate slides and use impactful images.
Don't rely on text	• Limit words to five to eight per slide beyond source citations. • Ask yourself if all those words and lines are really helping your audience understand. If not, delete and reshape the slide so that it has as few words as possible but gets the point across. • You can usually paraphrase information. If you absolutely need a direct quote then use only the important and impactful part of the quote, you can fill in the rest of it with your speaking.

FIGURE 12.13

ORGANIZE YOUR GROUP WITH TECHNOLOGY

There are many ways to organize your group meetings. Previous chapters discussed the use of agendas, rules, and norms to help you organize. You can use technology to help your organizing efforts. Using the table discussed previously, you can pick a tool that has the ability to create invites, set schedules, and produce reports. Consider using a tool like *GoToMeeting*.

With ***GoToMeeting***, you can set up a meeting with all the people in your group by sending out invites they respond to. You will get attendance lists back to your email account and calendar so you can be alerted before the meeting and be reminded of the meeting in the future. The great thing about the different tools listed in the previous table is not only do they provide the benefits of videoconferencing or teleconferencing, but some of them can help you with scheduling, alerts, and reports.

If you don't need to use an online video or teleconferencing tool, technology tools may still be a wise choice. Consider using these tools to schedule meetings, organize tasks, keep records, and more. Use the table to help you get an idea of what is available and how it might suit your small group needs.

Tips for Delivering with Technology

Some people believe that anyone can give a good speech especially if given technology. This couldn't be further from the truth. Feeling comfortable speaking in front of people and using presentation technology doesn't mean you are a good speaker and certainly doesn't mean your technology will be effective. Public speaking is a skill that must practiced and speaking with technology is an additional skill set. Don't make the mistake of assuming because you have spoken with technology before it will be easy each time thereafter. As you can see, there are a great many guidelines and rules that come with giving a speech with technology. I'm sure there are many rules you have never been taught before now and perhaps you didn't think there were any rules. Public speaking is a skill and an area in the communication discipline that is very different from other forms of communication. As such, we have particular expectations.

Giving a great speech is hard, giving a great speech with technology is even harder, but the rewards can be immense. A technology like *PowerPoint*, *Keynote*, or *Prezi* offers a substantial benefit to both the speaker and the audience. Technology can help the speaker keep track of time, appeal to different types of learners, make the presentation more interesting, emphasize points, and provide examples that people can more easily understand. You should only use software based presentation technology, like *PowerPoint*, if you need to reinforce your point, provide examples, emphasize a concept or organize and simplify complex ideas. If you're using the software to accomplish these goals then you have started on the right path. But, this alone will not ensure a good speech. I've compiled a list of tips and tricks. I've learned, been taught, or researched through the years to help you on your next amazing speech!

1. Practice. Practice. Practice. You must practice with your technology in order to have a chance at being good at using it. Don't just assume things will work well on presentation day. Practice over and over so you get the feel for the technology and a sense of what may go wrong and how to fix it. If you have practiced a 5-10 minute speech less than 30 times it's simply not enough.
2. Use a clicker. Being strapped to the computer clicking the arrow button takes away from your presentation and makes you look unprofessional and juvenile. A clicker will allow you to freely walk and stand in front of the audience. When an audience can see the entire body of the speaker they are more likely to understand the message and they are more likely to maintain their attention to the topic.
3. Have a back up set of batteries just in case your clicker batteries run out.
4. Have a back up clicker in case your clicker stops working for some other disappointing reason or isn't compatible with the computer you present with.
5. Remember you do not need to gesture towards the computer when clicking from slide to slide. Unprepared and under practiced speakers tend to point and click instead of clicking while gesturing in a natural way.

6. Plan well in advance who will be speaking in what order. You should know which members will use technology and when they will speak. Planning this in advance will help everyone feel more comfortable and look polished and practiced to your evaluator.
7. Save your files in multiple forms in case the computer you have to use isn't compatible with the version you made it on.
8. Save a copy of your presentation as a PDF. My colleague Helen Acosta informed me of this brilliant tip and since then it has saved at least six of my students. If for any reason the software isn't working or your file is damaged, a PDF version can still function in much the same way!
9. Save your presentation on a portable device like a flash drive and also email yourself the presentation. Making sure you have your file saved in two places that you can access is important on presentation day and any other day.
10. Practice and time yourself. It is essential that speakers stay within the time limits they are given. The only way to ensure that you stay on time is to practice and time each time. Average your times and then you have a better idea of what will happen on presentation day.
11. Decide if non-speaking members will stand or sit when others are speaking. Some groups present in chunks, which means each person speaks for a large amount of time and then another member speaks. If this is the case for your group, plan in advance where non-speaking members will be during the speakers presentation. Members standing around next to or behind a speaker can be distracting, especially if they appear bored or anxious. Think about what your audience is seeing and whether your group is cluttering the message, distracting from the message, or adding to it.
12. Don't be tempted by teleprompter apps. Teleprompter apps claim to help speakers, but really they just create one more barrier in the process. The apps are usually used like note cards, which are also ineffective and should be avoided.
13. Get rid of the note cards! A good presentation with technology will not require note cards. If you still need note cards then you need to practice more. A special occasion speech can have note cards, a planned and practiced speech with slides should not. It reflects a lack of preparation and is too much like a fifth grade book report.
14. Practice standing up and verbally. Practicing in your head or seated is not advantageous unless that is the way in which you will be presenting the material on presentation day.
15. Video tape yourself presenting during your practice sessions to give you an accurate look at how you are standing in relation to the screen, how your use your body and gestures, how your tones and volume, rate, and pitch and enunciation are doing and so much more.

FIGURE 12.14

Making sure your group is organized is important. Use whatever tools you can to make your group effective. Mind mapping is a wonderful tool.

16. Practice without your notes. Not having your notes on presentation day but practicing with your notes every time is setting yourself up for a failure.
17. Remember to look at the audience not the screen. Presenters often look at the screen unnecessarily and for prolonged periods of time. Often this is a nervous response, but sometimes speakers just simply forget that we don't have to look at the screen all the time. It's okay to glance at the slides occasionally, but don't draw attention to it.
18. Use your technology to inspire your speaking. This means, remember to craft your presentation in a way that will help your appeal to pathos not hinder it.
19. Don't let the slides do your job. Just because the slide has a great example or demonstrates your point in a great way, doesn't mean you are off the hook. The audience is there to see you and you must deliver the message. Keep the focus on you and your points and don't let the presentation upstage you.
20. Remember that your gestures and facial expression and other body language are 80% of the message, so be sure you are using them. Speakers who use their facial expressions and body to reinforce their words and enhance their meaning move audiences. There is immense power in the expressions our body can make-don't forget that just because you are using a set of great slides.

Summary

This chapter has provided you with information about technology you may encounter while working or presenting in small groups. We established the differences between face-to-face and virtual groups. You now have an understanding of the various types of virtual meetings and the advantages and disadvantages of the many types. This chapter also established several rules and guidelines you should follow. Our world is becoming more reliant on communication everyday and there are no signs that it will slow down anytime soon. If you find yourself overwhelmed by the options presented in this chapter, do not be discouraged. Instead, use that feeling to spur you to investigate some of these options. If you haven't used a *Google Doc*, try it. If you have never video conferenced, give it a go. If you have never used a *GoToMeeting* or even ever heard of some of the options you read about give them a try. You will not learn to use these technologies simply by reading this chapter, you must experience it. Use this chapter as a guide and inspiration for your next group endeavor.

Tools to Help Organize Your Group	
Evernote	This technology can be downloaded from evernote.com. The advantages of this technology is it allows you and your group to: • Take and save notes • Create and save files, clips, and pics • Save all information and have it available and sync'd to all of your devices • Allows you to capture an image online and save it to discuss later • Work with your group sharing notes, pics, files, and more • Make itineraries, confirm meetings, scan items, manage trips (flight, land, and sea)
iMindMap	This tool is great for those of you who learn and organize best through visuals vs. just linear outlines. It's also a great tool to use in presentations to offer it a more visually appealing 4D effect. The advantages of this technology is it allows you to: • Create mind maps • Create visually unique communication • Create charts and graphs and flow charts in a unique way • Can be used in your presentations • Is sharable with others
Diigo	Diigo.com is a popular tool for organizing information in one place. This is an amazing technology that will help you in researching, organizing your research, and sharing your research with others. Some of its perks are: • Achieved webpages which alleviates weak link issues later on • Digital highlighters • Digital sticky notes • Highlighters and sticky notes are usable on most smartphones too • Ability to generate a personal library of links, pictures, web pages, and notes • Increased collaboration
SpiderScribe	SpiderScribe is a tool that is capable of organizing everything in one place. Some of its capabilities include: • Ability to mindmap • Researching topics • Capture and connect ideas, files, images, and more • Create public and private groups to share information with • Be accessed anywhere including the Cloud

Glossary

Asynchronous communication media: Any media that allows members to communicate anytime and anywhere, such as texting, Facebooking, or emailing.

Synchronous media communication: Allows for simultaneous communication between group members.

Online collaboration tools: Various platforms, applications, or programs that aid your online small group communication.

Software-based technologies: Programs that we use to accompany and enhance our presentations.

Teleconference: Uses phone lines to connect members and only allows participants to hear others; it does not allow them to see each other.

Text-only virtual communication: The communication does not have video or audio. It only has the written word.

Video calls: Meeting technologies that permit the reception and transmission of video signals between users in different locations using their cell phone devices.

Video conferencing: A conference that permits members to see each other via a computer (or computer-like device) in real time while in different locations.

Virtual group: Any small group whose members interact with each other through electronic technologies.

Virtual meetings: Gatherings of people from different locations using technology to facilitate the meeting.

Works Cited or Consulted

Thorson-Hevle, A., Staller, M., and Korcok, M. (2015). Contemporary public speaking; How to craft a powerful speech. *Kendall Hunt Publishing.* (*An incredibly well-rounded approach to public speaking with chapters on language and technology that are not seen in other public speaking textbooks. The authors have over 150 years combined experience in Public Speaking*).

http://www.presentationzen.com

https://www.gotomeeting.com

http://www.apple.com/ios/keynote

https://prezi.com

https://products.office.com/en-US/powerpoint

https://acrobat.adobe.com/us/en/acrobat/pricing/compare-versions.html

http://www.beamyourscreen.com

https://evernote.com

https://imindmap.com/

https://www.diigo.com/

https://www.spiderscribe.net

https://groups.google.com

www.scheduleonce.com

https://www.yugma.com/

https://www0.livemeeting.com/cc/usda/join

CPSIA information can be obtained
at www.ICGtesting.com
Printed in the USA
LVHW05s1036290618
582147LV00003B/17/P

9 781524 939236